Changing Gods in Medieval China, 1127–1276

VALERIE HANSEN

Changing Gods in Medieval China, 1127–1276

PRINCETON UNIVERSITY PRESS
PRINCETON, NEW JERSEY

Copyright © 1990 by Princeton University Press
Published by Princeton University Press,
41 William Street, Princeton, New Jersey 08540
In the United Kingdom: Princeton University Press,
Guildford, Surrey

Library of Congress Cataloging-in-Publication Data

Hansen, Valerie, 1958–
   Changing gods in medieval China, 1127–1276 / Valerie Hansen.
      p.   cm.
   Bibliography: p.
   Includes indexes.
   ISBN 0-691-05559-9 (alk. paper)
   1. Cults—China. 2. China—Religious life and customs. 3. China—History—Sung
dynasty, 960–1279. I. Title.
BL1802.H35 1989
299'.51'09021—dc19   88-26895
                                                                                  CIP

This book has been composed in Linotron Bembo

Printed in the United States of America
by Princeton University Press,
Princeton, New Jersey

Thanks to Dad, Bobbie, and Uncle Van for their unfailing generosity.

CONTENTS

List of Illustrations   viii
Preface   ix
Acknowledgments   xi

CHAPTER I   Introduction   3

CHAPTER II   Lay Choices   29

CHAPTER III Understanding the Gods   48

CHAPTER IV   The Granting of Titles   79

CHAPTER V   Popular Deities in Huzhou   105

CHAPTER VI   The Rise of Regional Cults   128

CHAPTER VII Conclusion   160

Appendix I: Comparison of *The Record of the Listener* and
              a Temple Inscription Recording the Same Miracle   167
Appendix II: Selected Translations from *The Record of the
              Listener*   171
Appendix III: Tables   176
Glossary   201
Bibliography   217
Index to Temple Inscriptions   243
Index   247

ILLUSTRATIONS

Figure 1. Titles Granted to Popular Deities Year by Year   80

Map 1. Huzhou Prefecture   106

Map 2. Regional Temples, 1100   134

Map 3. Regional Temples, 1150   135

Map 4. Regional Temples, 1200   136

Map 5. Regional Temples, 1250   137

Map 6. Regional Temples, 1275   138

PREFACE

The receptionist at the English-language school where I worked part-time in Taibei was unusual in several respects. For one, everyone called her Li Mama. Unlike most Taiwanese, she had learned perfect Mandarin and gleefully corrected the sloppy tones of the Americans who worked for her. Moreover, unlike most of the people I knew at that time, she was an active devotee of popular religion.

One day Li Mama told me she had gone to pray to a new god. I asked her why she had decided to pray to that particular deity, and she replied that the deity was *ling*.[1] As I had never heard the word before, Li Mama explained that a god was ling when he or she responded to requests. People in Taibei usually prayed when sick, or before taking the competitive college entrance examinations, or when hoping for a child. And if the deity cured them, or enabled them to get into a good university, or brought them a son, then that particular deity was ling. Li Mama had visited this new temple hoping that the god was ling, but if he was not, then she would go to another god. Her point was clear: people pray to gods to get things done, and they judge gods on the basis of their ability to perform miracles. At the time I had no way of knowing that ling (power or efficacy) was to become what I now see as the distinguishing characteristic of popular religion.

That conversation with Li Mama helped me to understand something that had puzzled me since my first visit to Taiwan. I had assumed Chinese people would categorize their own religious beliefs much as we did. Because we in the West view ourselves as Jewish, Catholic, or Protestant, all Chinese, I had reasoned, would similarly be Buddhist, Daoist, or Confucian. To my surprise, none of the people I met identified themselves as such. And, as far as I could tell, they all attended the same Buddhist, Daoist, and popular religious temples. Their behavior suddenly made sense to me. Like Li Mama, they were simply seeking a god who was ling.

Several years later, I was drawn to the study of the Song dynasty (960–1276), a period when medieval China underwent a commercial revolution. Yet, for all the work that has been done in the last twenty

1. Characters for all Chinese terms appear in the glossary.

years on Song society, economy, and government, no one has ever studied the popular religious pantheon in this period. I began by reading temple inscriptions. In recording the miracles of different deities, the authors of these inscriptions used one word over and over again: ling. Although this was the same word that Li Mama had used in talking to me, its meaning was not necessarily identical. What did the people of the twelfth and thirteenth centuries mean by efficacy? How did they measure a god's power?

Since then, I have explored these and other questions in the study of Chinese religion, ones that have taken me far beyond the issue of efficacy. Still, my original purpose of examining change from the perspective of the common people—the Li Mamas of their time—has not changed. If we are to make sense of Li Mama's religious practices, we cannot focus on doctrine alone. Throughout Chinese history, while learned monks and philosophers debated and reinterpreted the meaning of texts, both the illiterate majority and the literate elite looked to the gods for help with the problems they faced in daily life: illness, childbirth, famine, locusts, flooding, drought, and invasion. With first the Jurchens and then the Mongols hovering on the northern borders, and with the rapid economic growth of the commercial revolution, the Southern Song (1127–1276) was one of the most tumultuous periods in the Chinese past. This book, then, is a study both of the Chinese popular pantheon in the twelfth and thirteenth centuries and of the common people's understanding of the many changes taking place around them.

ACKNOWLEDGMENTS

I have many people to thank. Two eminent Song scholars guided my research: Chikusa Masaaki, a social historian of Buddhism at Kyoto University, and Robert Hartwell, an economic historian at the University of Pennsylvania. The differences in their research interests, their approaches, and even their personalities pushed me to be a broader, more flexible historian. Different as they were, they had some qualities in common: both welcomed me as a colleague from the first day they met me, both have an unparalleled command of the sources, and both gave unstintingly of their knowledge. Professor Hartwell recommended that I read temple inscriptions contained in epigraphical collections; Professor Chikusa urged me to go through Hong Mai's *The Record of the Listener* before doing any other research. In many ways, this book is the direct product of those suggestions.

Like all dissertations that become books, this project has gone through many stages. Arjun Appadurai discussed the theoretical underpinnings of my research design, and Susan Naquin read and gutted several drafts of my proposal. Nakasuna Akinori, Liu Xinru, Victor Mair, and Tonami Mamoru resolved many of the textual queries I had. Matsumoto Kōichi, Morita Kenji, Anna Seidel, Shiba Yoshinobu, and Sugiyama Masaaki all welcomed me into their intellectual community during the two years I was in Kyoto. Karen Kiest did a great job with the maps. Writing up and revising went smoothly only because Mary Jo Baldwin, Peter Bol, Judith Boltz, Tim Brook, Lothar von Falkenhausen, Dan Getz, Kate Gingrass, Thomas R. H. Havens, Neil Katkov, Kathleen Lentz, Anne McClaren, Dan Overmyer, Peter Sahlins, and Tom Selover read and commented on all or part of the manuscript. My editor, Margaret Case, has been consistently helpful, and the readers for Princeton University Press also made constructive suggestions. Individual chapters have been presented to the East Asian graduate students at Kyoto University, Sugiyama Masaaki's Yuan seminar in Kyoto, the First International Conference on Song Studies held in Hangzhou, the graduate seminar in Neo-Confucianism and the premodern China seminar at Columbia University, the Buddhist Studies forum at Harvard University, the religious studies department at Barnard College, and the history department at Yale University. I received valuable criticism on each occasion.

In the course of this project I have been funded by the American Council of Learned Societies, the Department of Education (Fulbright-Hays predoctoral support), Title VI monies for Foreign Languages and Area Studies, and the Mellon Foundation (dissertation grant in the humanities). The staffs of the library of the Institute for Humanistic Studies in Kyoto, the Bungakubu library at Kyoto University, the Tōyō Bunko in Tokyo, the Academia Sinica library in Nangang, Taiwan, the Zhejiang provincial library in Hangzhou, the Harvard-Yenching library in Cambridge, and the rare book rooms of the Beijing and Shanghai libraries have made the actual research possible.

Barend ter Haar of Leiden University deserves special thanks. Just before my final round of revisions, I discovered that he had done extensive research on popular deities, most of which he has yet to publish. Bound to me by neither institutional nor personal ties, he chose to assist me when it would have been natural for him to do otherwise. He checked my manuscript thoroughly, wrote copious comments in the margins, detected mistakes, and supplied valuable references. This is a much better book as a result.

I am most grateful to the people who, when I was facing a deadline, stopped whatever they were doing to help me. Bob Hymes and Ellen Neskar each heard and critiqued a different job talk the night before I gave it; their comments made it possible to tighten up the talks and the resulting chapters. Paul Smith answered countless phone calls with concision and clarity. David Ludden read through the first rough draft of my thesis immediately and offered far-reaching criticisms that shaped the final version. Cynthia Brokaw went through both the dissertation and the book manuscript, making invaluable suggestions each time. Elizabeth Kenney edited the whole manuscript just in time for me to incorporate her often brilliant changes into my final draft. Judith Zeitlin and Wu Hung made the last summer of revising considerably less frantic by supplying me with many dinners, companionship on the way to the swimming pool, and the title of this book.

These comments can only suggest the extent to which different people have helped me. Of course, I accept full responsibility for whatever errors remain.

Changing Gods in Medieval China, 1127–1276

CHAPTER I   Introduction

The 150 years between the Jurchen invasion of north China in 1127 and the Mongol conquest of south China in 1276 witnessed many changes. The majority of China's population settled in the south for the first time, a national market came into being, and local elites began to concentrate their activities in their home counties. Accordingly, the Southern Song (1127–1276) is widely viewed as the the final phase of China's medieval transformation, a process which had begun some six centuries earlier. Although little studied, religious change reflected— sometimes directly, sometimes indirectly—these other developments. Among the most important of many religious changes was the for- mation of the popular pantheon.

Temples dedicated to popular deities studded the medieval Chinese landscape. Contemporary writers pointed out that even the smallest villages contained more than one temple, while temples in the large cities numbered in the hundreds. The laity asked the gods to bring rain, to clear the skies, to drive out locusts, to expel bandits, to sup- press uprisings, to cure illnesses, to enable them to conceive, to pre- vent epidemics, and to help them pass the civil service examinations. If literate, they recorded the gods' miracles in response to their prayers. Many of these gods had been humans before their apotheoses. In pre- vious centuries, most local gods were not recognized by the central government; most were worshipped only within the confines of the communities where they had lived, died, or served as government of- ficials. At the end of the eleventh century the central government be- gan to award name plaques and official titles to deities who in earlier centuries would have gone unrecognized. In the commercial revolu- tion of the time, gods who had formerly controlled only natural forces acquired a command of market forces. And, unlike the gods of earlier periods, some came to be worshipped not just in their own commu- nities but across all of south China. This book is about those develop- ments and what they reveal about medieval Chinese society.

The 1127 loss of north China to a non-Han people, the Jurchen, forced the Song imperial government to abandon the capital in Kaifeng (Henan) and to flee to the south, where, in 1138, it established a tem-

porary residence for the emperor at Hangzhou (Zhejiang)[1] in the
Lower Yangzi valley.[2] The transfer of the Song capital from the north
to the south made official what had occurred two centuries earlier: the
southward shift of China's center of gravity. In 742, 60 percent of the
population had lived in the wheat and millet regions of the north, 40
percent in the rice-growing south; by 980, the proportions were re-
versed, with 38 percent in the north, 62 percent in the south (Hartwell
1978:5).[3] Because of underregistration, official population figures cannot be trusted completely, but a census in 1160 gave the population of
south China as 11,375,733 households, and in 1223, as 12,670,801
households, or somewhere between sixty and one hundred million
people (*Wenxian tongkao* 11:4b–5a).[4]

The period from 1127 to 1276 is called the Southern Song, because
the capital was located in and because the central government ruled
over the south. This book focuses on the changes of the Southern
Song—and not those spanning both the Tang (618–910) and Song
(960–1276) dynasties—for two reasons of method: the coverage of the
sources remains constant, and the geographical area is unchanged.
Many of the generalizations about the Tang-Song transition may in
fact reflect the vast differences in the source base at the beginning and
end of the period. In the seventh century, before the invention of
wood-block printing, all books had to be copied by hand. During the
ninth and tenth centuries books were printed on wood blocks for the
first time. At the end of the thirteenth century, the widespread use of
printing and less expensive paper lowered the cost of books considerably. Accordingly, many more books survive from the twelfth and

1. Place names will be given first as they were in the Song; their modern equivalents
will follow in parentheses. In cases where the name of the county or city has not
changed, I give only the modern province, as here.

2. The Lower Yangzi valley (Jiangnan) refers to the area south of the Yangzi river in
what are now the provinces of Jiangsu, Zhejiang, and Anhui.

3. I use modified social science footnotes throughout this book and use typeface to
distinguish between primary (in italics) and secondary (in plain type) sources. If the
citation is to a secondary work, as here, the reference will read: (author, date of publication: page number). Full publication information is contained in the secondary bibliography at the end of the book. The references to primary sources, all in classical
Chinese, read: (*title*, chapter or volume: page number). In the case of some texts that are
divided not into numerically ordered sections, but into named sections, the Chinese
name of the relevant section appears. Full publication information is contained in the
primary bibliography. I cite a few unpublished rubbings by library, name of collection,
and number.

4. Because the number of people in a household varied, all population estimates must
be tentative. I multiply the number of households by the commonly accepted factor of
five to arrive at these figures.

thirteenth centuries than from earlier periods. Alternatively, these generalizations about the Tang-Song transition reflect the vast differences between north China, where most people lived at the beginning of the period, and south China, where they lived at the end. We have almost no information about south China in the seventh century, because so few people of note lived there then; we have equally scant information about north China in the twelfth and thirteenth centuries, because it was under the rule of the non-Han Jurchen people. This study uses the plentiful sources from the twelfth and thirteenth centuries to analyze the popular religious changes taking place in the south. Of course, when necessary, it will touch on certain developments that predate the Southern Song, but only to provide background.

With the move to Hangzhou in 1127 came an influx of 20,000 high officials, tens of thousands of clerks, and 400,000 soldiers and their dependents (Shiba 1975a:19). Between 1170 and 1225, Hangzhou's population increased at a rate of .30 percent annually, reaching 391,300 households (containing perhaps two million people) in 1225 (Hartwell 1982:392–93).[5] It was probably the biggest city in the world at the time. Prior to the commercial development of the Song, government-regulated markets lay within city walls and were clearly distinguishable from the outlying villages. But in the Song, cities burst out of their walls, markets sprung up in villages, and city and countryside did not develop different cultural identities as they did in Europe (Shiba 1968:309–12). Because the distinction between urban areas and villages was a blurred, highly permeable one, it is impossible to estimate rates of urban versus rural population growth. We do know that medieval China contained four other major urbanized areas besides Hangzhou: Kaifeng (in Jin territory after 1127), Fuzhou and the big towns of northern Fujian, Nanchang and the cities near Lake Boyang (Jiangxi), and Chengdu and the surrounding area in Sichuan (Hartwell 1978:13).

In premodern China, where the imperial capital constituted the largest market for consumer goods, Hangzhou's transfer had an immediate and positive effect on the economy of the surrounding area. For the region of the Lower Yangzi transport costs to the capital fell after 1127 simply because Hangzhou was closer than Kaifeng had been. Those living nearby also benefited from government subsidies for grain transport to the capital (Hartwell 1982:386). Moreover, instead of the man- or horse-drawn carts that had dragged their loads overland to Kaifeng, boats plied their way along the many streams crisscrossing

5. This figure is for the prefecture of Hangzhou, as opposed to what we would call the city; it includes cultivators living in the rural area surrounding the capital.

the region of the Lower Yangzi valley to the new capital. Travelers also used man-made (sometimes said to be god-dug) canals: the Grand Canal ran north-south, and an east-west spur linked Huzhou (Zhejiang) with Suzhou (Jiangsu). No sharp technological breakthroughs occurred in the twelfth and thirteenth centuries, but techniques of ship construction steadily improved: most of the flat-bottomed, small boats used in the Lower Yangzi were propeled by punting, occasionally by oars. They were well-suited to the shallow rivulets of the area (Shiba 1968:64–70). Freight charges, calculated on the basis of distance, were surprisingly low.[6]

Two other changes, both predating the Southern Song, paved the way for the growth of markets in the twelfth and thirteenth centuries: an increase in the money supply and the introduction of double-cropped rice. During the Tang dynasty China had primarily a natural economy, supplemented by long-distance trade in luxury goods and salt. With the exception of the aristocratic stratum, most people lived in self-sufficient villages where they raised whatever grains they ate. But, between the eighth and eleventh centuries, the output of currency quadrupled while the population stayed almost constant (Hartwell 1978:3). By the eleventh century, paper money and other instruments of credit supplemented the bronze coins, gold, and silver already in use. Much of China's economy subsequently became monetized. In addition, new strains of Champa rice entered China in the eleventh century (Ho 1956). Because these seeds permitted two crops a year, they created a surplus, allowing regions to specialize in different crops. Some areas concentrated on rice production while others grew fruit and other agricultural commodities or engaged in the production of handicrafts. Further increasing rice production was the improvement of dam technology, which made it possible to reclaim low-land swampy areas as polder fields. While recent scholarship has called into question the rosy economic picture painted here, it is nonetheless clear that considerable economic growth occurred during this period.[7]

6. Shiba (1986:49–50) gives a figure of three cash a *dan* per *li* traveled, with a *dan* equaling 94.88 liters and a *li* 552.96 meters (Ogawa 1968:1224–25).

7. The work of several Japanese historians cautions against exaggerating the impact of the new seeds and polder technology in the Song. Although allowing double-cropping, the new strains of rice spoiled easily and tasted inferior to others; they were of such low quality that they could not be used to pay taxes in the Song (Shiba 1986:7; Watabe and Sakurai 1984). New technology facilitated the reclamation of much land, but the polder fields of the Lower Yangzi turned out to have had many defects as well: the flow of water was difficult to control, much of this land could not be irrigated efficiently, and these fields had to lie fallow every other year. Because of these difficulties, the output of the polder fields was often not taxed (Miyazawa 1985; Adachi 1985). It was not until the

Throughout the twelfth and thirteenth centuries, certain innovations in agricultural technology, deep-ploughing, dams, sluice gates, and treadle water pumps allowed gradual increases in rice production and made specialization within certain areas possible (Elvin 1973:113–30).

Hangzhou proved to be a market for the entire empire. In addition, the capital's residents bought fruit, meat, medicine, wine, and cloth shipped along the Grand Canal from the surrounding towns north and south of the Yangzi valley, medicine and cloth sent via the Yangzi River from Sichuan, and fruit, rice, and medicine brought by sea from Fujian and Guangdong (Quan 1972b:323; Shiba 1984b:60–61). This trade, stretching at times even across the Jin border, created a national market (Shiba 1968). Prices were not, however, uniform across China, and different currencies continued to be used in different places. Because trade routes did not reach up into the mountains, those living in remote villages were neither exposed to market networks nor able to buy goods from other places. While they remained firmly embedded in self-sufficient villages, the commercial revolution lifted others out of their village economies into an empirewide market. As consumers in different regions bought more and more goods produced in other parts of the empire, merchants traveled farther and farther from home. People began to hear of life in other parts of the empire and even had occasion to visit these other places in connection with trade.

The national market took shape at the same time a national curriculum for the civil service examinations did. The twelfth and thirteenth centuries witnessed an enormous increase in the number of people taking the exams in any given year: from 79,000 in the eleventh century to an estimated 400,000 in the thirteenth. Because the number of available posts did not change, a given individual's chances of passing the examinations plunged in some places to as low as 1 out of 333; in 1275, the legislated quota was 1 out of 200 (Chaffee 1985:35–36). Those who chose to defy the ever-increasing odds against success in the civil service examinations followed a standardized course of instruction and were drawn into the developing culture of the examinations. All candidates hoped to become officials, and the lucky few who actually took office served all over the empire in the course of their careers.

Yet other literati turned away from national politics to focus on local affairs. In the Northern Song (960–1127), a professional elite of approximately a hundred families had concentrated exclusively on national service, devoting their energies to employing all their sons in the

___

succeeding Ming (1368–1644) and Qing (1644–1911) dynasties that better-tasting double-cropped rice and more efficient polder technology were developed.

bureaucracy. Several mechanisms had given these families an enormous advantage over others; most important were preferential examinations held for those who, by virtue of their officeholding kin, were protected by the *yin* privilege.[8] Because these bureaucratic families could use the yin privilege to place not just their own relatives but even their in-laws in the bureaucracy, marriage played an important role in ensuring their continued success in securing government posts. Following the factional conflicts of the late eleventh century, when entire families were barred from taking the exams, these elites began to devote themselves to commerce and their own estates. As they did so, the scope of their marriage alliances constricted; gone were those unions that had extended across the empire (Hartwell 1982; Hymes 1986a, 1986b). The rise of organized lineages coincided with the shift away from national politics. No longer bent on careers in the bureaucracy, these elites found it more advantageous to marry locally, often within their own counties. They became the local gentry.

The oft-quoted advice of Yuan Cai (c. 1140–1190) suggests the extent to which these families diversified their activities in the Southern Song:

> If the sons of a gentleman (*shidaifu*) have no hereditary stipend to maintain and no permanent holdings to depend on, and they wish to be filial to their parents and to support children, then nothing is as good as being a scholar. For those whose talents are great, and who can obtain advanced degrees, the best course is to get an official post and become wealthy. Next best is to open one's gate as a teacher in order to receive a tutor's pay. For those who cannot obtain advanced degrees, the best course is to study correspondence so that one can write letters for others. Next best is to study punctuating and reading so that one can be a tutor to children.
>
> For those who cannot be a scholar, then medicine, Buddhism and Daoism, agriculture, trade, or crafts are all possible; all provide a living without bringing shame to one's ancestors. (*Yuanshi*

8. *Yin* literally means shadow; here it denotes the right of protection awarded to the kin of those who held office. Special civil service examinations were held for those with the yin privilege; the pass rate of 50 percent was much higher than that of the open examinations (Chaffee 1985:23). Song historians disagree about whether or not the exams were open, with some contending that only those who had been recommended by the locally powerful were permitted to sit for the exams (Hymes 1986a:43–48), and others arguing that anyone could (see Chaffee 1985:60, 223 n. 97 for a summary of the debate).

shifan 2:17b–18a; Ebrey 1984:267; Hymes 1987a:58; Shiba 1968:495)

Although government office offered the fastest and most prestigious route to wealth, the alternatives could be pursued locally and did not require residence in the capital. Most sons devoted themselves to commerce or to agriculture, while a selected few studied full time. For example, Lu Jiuxu managed the family apothecary while his brother, the famous Neo-Confucian Lu Jiuyuan, prepared for the civil service examinations (Hymes 1987a:16–17). The spread of genealogy writing and generational naming practices testify both to the anxiety of some of these families about sustaining their position in the flux of the twelfth and thirteenth centuries and to their awareness of the advantages of a larger family unit (Ebrey 1986:45–46). In short, the expansion of the civil service examinations brought some into the national arena for the first time, while the decision of many powerful families not to take the exams and the limitations of the transportation network kept others firmly ensconced in the local level.

This was an age, then, when elites chose between national service and local estates, when merchants traded locally, regionally, and nationally, and when small producers entered regional markets for the first time. Popular belief reflected these developments in devotees' lives: regional, even national, gods joined local ones by the end of the thirteenth century. At the beginning of the twelfth century, local pantheons consisted largely of formerly human gods, who came from or had visited the districts in which they were worshipped. Many had lived centuries earlier and had been aristocrats, generals, or emperors. They performed agricultural miracles, bringing rain, stopping floods, expelling locusts, or preventing blight. The elite families who turned away from national service and the villagers who remained unaffected by the commercial revolution continued to worship these local gods throughout the twelfth and thirteenth centuries.

They also incorporated low-born but still local gods into their pantheons. These were people whose lives were cut off in accidents or who died prematurely. Once they died, their tombs gave off auras or they appeared in dreams to tell their followers about their powers. Because the central government, besieged by non-Han peoples in the north and plagued by inadequate tax receipts, turned to the gods for help, it instituted more and more comprehensive policies to recognize the achievements of local gods. Previous dynasties had rewarded the accomplishments of a few gods by granting them titles, but, starting in the eleventh century, the Song took this practice to new heights. In their enthusiasm to identify powerful local gods, bureaucrats awarded many honors to these commoner deities.

In those areas drawn into the national market, gods appeared who could perform new types of miracles. They demonstrated sophisticated commercial talents in addition to the more usual control over the elements. Familiar with price variations among different markets, they advised their followers where to trade. One deity was even able to manipulate national demand as well as the government quota system to make an enormous profit. Those officials and merchants who credited their gods with commercial acuity also began to take their gods with them on their trips to the far corners of the empire. In 1100, people worshipped only gods from their home areas. But as the twelfth and thirteenth centuries progressed, they began to worship gods associated with other places, often the home towns of rich merchants or local officials. By 1275, temples to four formerly local deities stretched across all of south China. This change is not surprising. The expansion of the national market prompted contact among people of south China so that not just goods but also gods came to circulate, and the lower transport costs along southern waterways caused the geography of the heavens to contract at much the same time and in much the same way as that of the earth did.

Sources

Any assertion about change in medieval China must be tempered by an awareness of the limitations of the extant sources. Before the development of wood-block printing in the eighth century, all books had to be hand-copied, and the source base for this early period is restricted almost entirely to documents sponsored by the central government. By the eleventh century, the widespread use of wood-block printing and the availability of good, cheap paper made from mulberry bark lowered the cost of making a book so much that private publishing houses sprung up in all urban centers (Carter 1925; Shiba 1968:270; Tsien 1985:148–52; Twitchett 1981).[9] Although much more plentiful than those for earlier periods, the sources about the south in the twelfth and thirteenth centuries were still written almost exclusively from the point of view of the literate.

Even with the advent of printing, very few people had time to learn to read in medieval China. Years of study were required to attain mas-

9. In a rare documented comparison from the early eleventh century, an official reported that the cost of printing government pardons was one-tenth that of hand-copying them (*Xu zizhi tongjian changbian* 102:18b).

tery of the written language, classical Chinese, which had a different grammar and vocabulary from the dialects spoken at the time. Little positive evidence demonstrates that the common people read and wrote on a daily basis. Government officials put up placards announcing policy, but, as long as only one person in a village read them aloud, everyone could understand. Those who wrote manuals for magistrates made provisions for clerks and common people who could not sign their names (*Zuoyi zizhen* 1:4b, 7b; 5:28a). With very few exceptions, education was limited to men; the vast majority of women received no schooling at all. Even if peasants could read a few characters, they could not read classical Chinese, the language in which all books were written.

The extent of literacy—or illiteracy—remains an open question largely because no hard figures survive, and even anecdotal evidence is in short supply. Several indications suggest that the rate of literacy, although low, was probably increasing through the twelfth and thirteenth centuries, especially among certain segments of the population: city dwellers, merchants, and ambitious gentry. Because the distribution of books was greatest in the major urban centers of Fujian, the Lower Yangzi, Sichuan, and, above all, the capital of Hangzhou, people living in these places had the most exposure to the written word. The development of a commercial economy encouraged literacy among merchant groups, especially those involved in long-distance trade; they needed to be able to read and write, if only to keep accounts. If anywhere near 400,000 men took the exams in the thirteenth century (this estimate is high), many more must have received some schooling (Chaffee 1985:35). But, although certain groups were exposed to the written language, large pockets of illiteracy must have persisted, especially among those working the land.[10]

Literacy was greatest among government officials and the highest-level clergy. To pass the civil service examinations, the successful candidate had to demonstrate full mastery of the Confucian classics and commentaries on them, recognize passages on sight, and write essays in polished classical Chinese. Once appointed to office, district magistrates collected taxes, administered justice, and supervised local schools. Because they represented the emperor, who presided over the entire empire and who was viewed as the appointee of the gods, each

10. The first surveys of literacy from the New Territories, Hong Kong, in the twentieth century show that many people living in agricultural villages could not read. They delegated the job of reading and writing to a local specialist. Much as they hired someone to cure a sick child or to situate a grave, they paid someone to draft letters for them (Hayes 1985).

official was responsible as well for the spiritual well-being of his district. Those who took office conducted rituals in the spring and autumn and served as the clergy of the state cult (Lévi 1986; 1987). They were charged with ensuring that only officially sanctioned temples received government patronage, and they were obliged to petition the emperor about any new local gods. Finally, they were responsible for protecting their districts from disaster. It was in this capacity that officials visited temples to ask for rain or clear skies, for an end to epidemics or locust attacks, or for help in apprehending missing criminals.

Like these officials, Buddhist and Daoist clergy also studied for long years. Buddhist monks and nuns, living in monasteries and nunneries, were supposed to remain celibate, keep vegetarian diets, and otherwise live in accordance with Buddhist precepts, if they hoped to attain better rebirths and ultimately nirvana. They studied the Buddhist canon, which included apochryphal Chinese texts and original sutras translated mainly from Sanskrit and Central Asian languages. As in Buddhism, many different Daoist schools coexisted, but all shared the goal of attaining immortality, be it through outer alchemy (*waidan*) or through inner alchemy (*neidan*). Expensive inductions into secret lines of transmission characterized Daoist clerical training. As the candidate progressed further in his studies and reached successively higher levels, he received different registers and was given control over more and more deities who carried out his bidding.

The doctrinal content of Buddhism, Daoism, and Confucianism differed, but they all shared a conviction in the power of the written word. Their practitioners were supposed to be well-versed in the canon of texts recognized by their respective school. They may not have been as learned as is often assumed (see the next chapter for examples of semiliterate practitioners), but these religious specialists derived their capacity to perform rituals from a real—or purported— knowledge of the sacred word as it appeared in books. Confucian officials composed petitions to the emperor or prayers to the gods, Daoists wrote charms and registers, and Buddhists read notoriously difficult sutras aloud to cure the ill.

Buddhist, Daoist, and Confucian texts remained incomprehensible to those without long years of training. This training might well have been worth the time and effort, as it granted access to powerful technologies. As I will show, Confucian officials could beat recalcitrant gods, whom they viewed as their inferiors, in order to bring or end rain; Daoist practitioners could tap into the powers of the universe to purify local communities; and Buddhist monks could transfer merit by

reading aloud from sutras. Illiterate, semiliterate, or untrained lay people—the vast majority of China's population—had to go through
trained clergy to cure an illness, bring rain, or solve whatever problem
was at hand. Under no circumstances could the uninitiated attempt to
manipulate the forces of the universe by themselves.

Chinese popular religion differed from these textual religions in several important respects. One did not have to know how to read to pray
to the gods; nor did one have to be literate in order to grasp the principles that governed the gods' behavior. Paradoxically, the very absence of written materials in Song popular religion testifies to the participation of the illiterate. Importuning the deities was easy; the
supplicant did not pay money or go through an intercessor.[11] In some
temples, caretakers (*miaozhu*) or spirit mediums were available for
consultation and for aid in interpreting the god's response to prayers,
but anyone could always enter a popular temple and beseech the gods.
Because people could petition the gods directly, popular religion, unlike Buddhism, Daoism, and Confucianism, had no recognized clergy
and no established canon of texts.[12]
How were the basic tenets of popular religion transmitted? If there
were no sutras, how did people learn about the gods? Given the lack
of direct evidence, any answer must be tentative, but it seems that people talked to each other constantly about the miracles[13] of individual
gods. It was from these oral accounts that people learned the principles
by which the gods were thought to behave.[14] And it was on the basis
of these accounts that they decided to which god to pray. Were we able

11. It is possible that in the Song, as in contemporary Taiwan, devotees usually made
an offering of money or food, no matter how small or insignificant, but extant sources
cast no light on this problem (Wolf 1974:168).

12. See Charles H. Long's very helpful discussion in which he offers seven operative
definitions of popular religion. In the one most applicable to the Chinese context, he
defines popular religion as "the religion of the laity in a religious community in contrast
to that of the clergy. The clergy is the bearer of a learned tradition usually based upon
the prestige of literacy. . . . Another meaning of this kind of popular religion stems from
a society in which literacy is not confined to the clergy or to the elite. The laity may have
access to certain authoritative or quasi-authoritative texts without being in possession of
the power of normative interpretation and sanction of these texts" (1987:444).

13. The terms for miracle vary, but the most common term is *lingyan* (evidence of
efficacy, power). *Lingyi* (anomaly associated with power), *shenyi* (divine anomaly), or
simply *yi* (anomaly) also occur.

14. See Watson (1985) for a compelling discussion of how oral and written views of
Mazu (the Heavenly Consort) reflect the very different viewpoints of her male and female, elite and peasant, supporters in the nineteenth and twentieth centuries.

to visit China in the twelfth and thirteenth centuries, we could simply listen to the many conversations people had with one another about the gods. Obviously we cannot. How, then, are we to find out about popular religion in the Southern Song?

Fortunately, the literate had occasion to write down some of these conversations. In the Song, members of all social strata, high and low, supplicated deities in times of need. Everyone visited temples or consulted religious specialists when a family member fell ill. Peasants and officials beseeched the gods for rain or clear skies. The most educated consulted the gods before taking the civil service examinations; if contemporary observers can be trusted, they did so in droves. In their attempts to enlist the gods' assistance, officials, landlords, and merchants often backed the same cults as local cultivators did. Two types of documents, temple inscriptions (*miaoji*) and miscellaneous notes (*biji*), which contain more information about popular belief than standard sources, have provided much of the material for this study.[15] They both provide modified versions of miracle tales circulating at the time. Used judiciously, they make it possible to sketch the social context of popular religion in the twelfth and thirteenth centuries.

On certain occasions, often following the performance of a particularly marvelous miracle or the receipt of a title from the government, the followers, both literate and not, of a given deity joined together to sponsor the carving of a commemorative text onto a stele. Put up to impress people with the power of a god, steles were not necessarily designed to be read. The sheer magnitude of the stone (sometimes over two meters high and one and a half meters wide) amply conveyed both a deity's power and the extent of support for him. The texts carved on steles often include a biography of the deity before his or her apotheosis, a history of the deity's miracles, a list of titles received from the central government, and a physical description of the temple.[16]

As a rule, the inscriptions remain mute concerning the extent to which those commissioning a text told an author what to write. In cases where the author was a local scholar who was personally familiar with the deity in question, he probably drafted the text on his own. But when the author of the text lived at great distance, he must have

---

15. Because these sources concentrate on miracles, they contain little information about ancestor worship. Ancestors were thought to watch over the well-being of their descendents, but they did not usually perform miracles. For a masterful account of how ancestor worship changed in the medieval period, see Ebrey (1986). Chapters 4 and 5 detail instances where local lineages tried to transform their ancestors into gods.

16. For a more technical discussion of inscriptions in general, see Hansen (1987b). See the Index to Temple Inscriptions for all the inscriptions cited in this book.

received instructions, written or verbal, concerning what to include in his text. The local people would have had to tell him about the miracles the god performed in their district; they probably also told him what they knew of the god's pre-apotheosis biography.

One inscription dated 1099 from the Eternally Efficacious (Yong-ling) Temple in New Market township, Huzhou, contains an unusual admission: the author describes receiving a text that he subsequently revised. After recounting the deity's biography and listing his titles, Taishi Zhang states that even though there is no mention of the deity, a general named Zhu Si, in the historical records, the testimony of the elders guarantees the reliability of the account. Most uncharacteristically, he explains how he learned the information he has just related:

> One day a white-haired elderly man came by my gate and took an old record that he showed me, saying, "This is the lost real account of the earth god, General Zhu. The elders recount it; it is not false. I want it recorded. Because generations stretch far back, there are many whose biographies are not in the official histories. The old record states that he ended drought and repelled invaders. Does this not meet the qualifications for deities given in the sacrificial law as those who prevent disasters, forestall suffering, and die while serving their lords?"
>
> I read the record and *despised the unpolished style of the writing so I changed the wording* in order to write it on the wall. (*Tongzhi Huzhou* 53:9b, emphasis mine)

Although Taishi does not identify the elderly man, he clearly told him about General Zhu's miracles. This account suggests those commissioned to draft a text had the job of editing rough accounts into more flowing, elegant prose. In some cases the illiterate were able to make their voices heard, distorted as they might have been by the sound (or script) systems of literate spokesmen.

Given that most of the local people could not read the texts of the inscriptions, who was the intended audience? Very possibly, the deities themselves, hints one 1100 inscription from Licheng, Jinan (Shandong). During a drought the local magistrate, Ouyang Dachun, prayed at a dragon cave, and it subsequently rained. Ouyang

> selected a day to brave the scorching heat and to go eighty *li* with his clerks to thank the dragon on behalf of the people. Prior to this, the magistrate of Licheng, Ouyang Dachun, had dreamt of an imposing assemblage of flags and banners, armored guards

carrying shields and chariots. Someone said: "This is the Rapid Response Duke (Shunying hou)."

The dragon looked at Dachun and said, "I have received a title from the emperor as well as an order bestowing my rank. How is it that I do not get to see them?" (Beijing library, *Gedi* 1164, 1165, 4924)

On awakening, Ouyang Dachun told others of his dream, and indeed the deity had received a title twenty years previously, but the local people had not erected a commemorative stele. The magistrate then had the text of the original order carved on a stone, which was placed in the temple.

One 1107 inscription from Jiangsu explicitly identifies the intended audience. After describing the deity's gift of rain in response to the magistrate's prayer, the inscription concludes: "Thus, we have recorded this in stone to show future generations and, furthermore, to tell the deity" (*Jiangsu jinshi* 10:22b). Similarly, in 1225, when a group of local people in Nanjing donated money to carve a title-grant from 1132 in stone, they explained, "If this grant is lost and forgotten, not only will the deity's achievement not be known, but also obscured will be the nation's intent in honoring him so that he will bring good fortune to the people. Moreover our own sentiments will not be expressed" (*Jiangsu jinshi* 15:27b). If a god could not see his title, then he would not perform miracles. Because people of many different districts felt this way, they created a record independent of the standard bureaucratic sources that historians usually rely on.

Testimonials designed to impress their viewers with the power of the god in question, inscriptions put the best face on a given god's performance, attributing all miracles to him or her, but omitting any failures. The authors' intent is clear: to array all available evidence so that it proves the deity's power. Yet because the lists of miracles reveal the problems a given deity's devotees faced, they provide unparalleled insight into their day-to-day concerns. Inscriptions allow us to ascertain how devotees made their livings—whether they worked the land or had begun to trade at market. And biographies of the gods make it possible to determine their geographical origins, their pre-apotheosis ranks, and the dates of their deaths. By their very nature, inscriptions may have been biased, but, because they were derived from oral accounts circulating at the time, they allow glimpses into contemporary views of the gods.

Miscellaneous notes (*biji*) differ from temple inscriptions in that they consist of entries about the classics, official life, unusual places, strange tales, and the doings of gods. They are uneven, touching briefly on many different topics, treating none in depth. Yet they provide flashes of information appearing nowhere else (Franke 1961:116; Wilkinson 1973:173). If based on the report of a devotee, the entries about gods may, like temple inscriptions, be biased in favor of the gods. They may also have been altered to make them more entertaining, more memorable, or more strange. No one would include a tale in his miscellaneous notes unless it amused or piqued the curiosity of his readers.

Much longer than other collections of miscellaneous notes, the 207 extant (of originally 420) chapters of Hong Mai's *The Record of the Listener* (*Yijian zhi*), totaling over 1,800 pages in its modern edition, contain many more anecdotes about popular religion.[17] As this book draws heavily upon *The Record*, a careful examination of Hong Mai's prefaces, in which he describes his methods, refutes his critics, and hints at his purpose, seems in order.[18] Hong Mai was born into the prominent Hong family of Poyang, Jiangxi, in 1123, during his father's term of office as a low official in Jiaxing (where he encountered the ghost described in chapter 2).[19] Hong's father, Hong Hao, was sent as an emissary to the Jurchen-occupied north in 1129 and stayed there until 1143, steadfastly refusing to serve in the Jin government. His resistance made him a rallying figure for those who opposed compromise with the Jin; it also made him a threat to those, like Qin Gui (prime minister 1131–1132, 1138–1158), who advocated negotiating a peace. Hong's two brothers received advanced degrees (*jinshi*) in 1142; Hong Mai followed them in 1145. No small feat, they were henceforth known as the three Hongs. Hong Mai then entered the civil service, but his father's reputation cast a shadow on his career. Depending on which faction was in power, Hong was given less desirable posts in the

---

17. The length of *The Record of the Listener* and the different editions in use make citations cumbersome. I use the 1981 Zhonghua shuju edition punctuated and edited by He Zhuo throughout this study and cite first by section, then chapter, then number of anecdote within each chapter, giving the page number (or numbers) last. I have renumbered the Chinese divisions so that *jia* corresponds to 1, *yi* to 2, *bing* to 3, *ding* to 4, *zhijia* to 5, *zhiyi* to 6, *zhijing* to 7, *zhiding* to 8, *zhiwu* to 9, *zhigeng* to 10, *zhigui* to 11, *sanyi* to 12, *sanxin* to 13, *sanren* to 14, *bu* to 15, *zaibu* to 16, and *sanbu* to 17. There is, as yet, no accepted convention for citing from *The Record*, nor has the Peking edition enjoyed the wide use it deserves. See Chang Fu-jui's entry in the *Sung Bibliography* for a list of the original sections. Only about half of the collection is extant.

18. I am indebted to Judith Zeitlin for much help with and many conversations about the strange, the nature of fiction, and definitions of genres in Chinese literature. I cite the prefaces by section number and the page on which they appear in the 1981 edition.

19. For more about Hong's life, see Chang Fu-jui's biography of him in Franke 1976:469–78; Ōtsuka 1980; and Qian 1909.

provinces or appointed to prestigious posts in the capital. Following Qin Gui's death, he worked in the history office in Hangzhou and eventually attained the rank of Hanlin academician. He received no religious training and did not associate with clergy of any particular sect. He died in 1202.

During his career, and especially after his retirement, he collected tales to put into his collections of miscellaneous notes.[20] Hong Mai's interest in the strange and unusual resulted in high coverage of visions of deities in dreams and real life as well as of miracles they perform. Hong describes a world populated by common people (and officials as well) who go to religious specialists and temples; who dream of gods, dead friends, and relatives; who visit hell and come back; who effect miracle cures; and who frequent prostitutes and catch venereal disease. Because Hong is often talking about supernatural beings whose existence is open to question, unless one accepts that people did die, visit hell, and come back to life, or that deities really did appear in dreams and cause miracles, one cannot conclude these tales are, strictly speaking, true. *The Record of the Listener* was originally issued in forty-one (possibly more) installments from 1157 to 1202 and was published in separate editions in Fujian, Sichuan, Wuzhou (now Jinhua county, Zhejiang), and Hangzhou (*Yijian zhi* 2:185). Because, by the twelfth and thirteenth centuries, news of miracles traveled far, people knew of such events all over China. Hong's geographical range is correspondingly broad; he tells stories from the different circuits of the Southern Song, often about his native Jiangxi, sometimes from as far away as north China.

The title of *The Record of the Listener* (*Yijian zhi*, literally "Yi Jian's record")[21] provides an important clue regarding the book's nature. It contains a reference to the fourth-century B.C. philosopher Liezi:

> Among fish, there is one whose breadth is several thousand *li*.
> Its length can be surmised from that. Its name is *kun*. Among

20. Beginning *The Record of the Listener* in 1143 and *Notes from My Studio* (*Rongzhai suibi*) in 1163, Hong worked on two different sets of miscellaneous notes throughout the long years of his checkered career and especially following his retirement in 1190. Hong put strange stories into *The Record* and learned discussion and textual emendations in his *Notes from My Studio* (*Rongzhai suibi* 4:613). *Notes from My Studio* was directed at fellow officials and contains learned discussions of the classics, epigraphy, philology, and historical issues. When deities appear in *Notes from My Studio*, it is as objects of philological study; for example, Hong cites Han dynasty sources to explain names of the stove god and the god of the Yellow River (4:5:4:666–67; 4:5:14:676).

21. Although Yi Jian is a proper name, I render the title *Yijian zhi* as *The Record of the Listener* (or simply *The Record*).

birds, there is one called *peng*. Its wings are so broad they cover the clouds in the sky. The size of its body can be surmised from that. How have generations known that such creatures exist? The Great Yu traveled and saw them, Bo Yi recognized and named them, and Yi Jian heard of and recorded them. (*Liezi* 5:6a)

Unlike the Great Yu and Bo Yi, Yi Jian did not see these creatures with his own eyes. He only heard about them. Hong Mai assumes Yi Jian's role as he who listens and records; his compendium is not an eyewitness account, but a record of hearsay, some of it as unbelievable as the dimensions of the mythical *peng* and *kun*.

Unlike the authors of most other miscellaneous notes, Hong talked to people from all social strata.[22] In the preface to one installment, an unnamed Confucian interlocutor attacks Hong, saying: "[these tales] do not necessarily come from contemporary lords and gentry, but more often from poor people, errant monks, mountain travelers, Daoist practitioners, blind sorcerers, village women, low-ranking clerks, and foot soldiers." His remark enables us to identify Hong's informants; Hong spoke with many who did not belong to the literati. Hong counters the charges of the fictive critic, arguing that the informants of the great ancient historian Sima Qian (c. 100 B.C.) included doctors and artists in addition to officials (*Yijian zhi* 4:537). In his own compendium are many accounts relating the encounters of many different types of people—ranging from lowly cultivator to high official—with deities.

Hong Mai never provides a satisfying explanation for his enthusiatic, almost obsessive, collecting of tales. His stated goal was merely to entertain. In 1195, he explained: "Already old, I have no interest in serious reading and only like strange tales as I did when I was younger. Heaven has been kind to me: my ears are still good, and I can still enjoy the talk of guests" (*Yijian zhi* 6:795). The sheer length of the book belies his easy-going attitude.

Possibly, Hong had a more serious, unstated purpose, to challenge the increasingly dominant Neo-Confucian view of reality. Citing Han Yu (768–824), the Tang dynasty thinker who was a precursor of Neo-Confucianism, Hong provides the basic Neo-Confucian definition of a ghost as ethereal matter, without shape or sound—or, by implication, without real existence (*Han Yu wenji* 11:98). Pretending to accept this view, Hong Mai concedes that, if ghosts cannot be seen, heard, or

---

22. Herbert Franke comments, "It is equally clear that, written by and for scholars, they [miscellaneous notes] also reflect the ideology of the literate class with all their traditional concepts. Very seldom do we learn about the lower classes" (1961:116).

felt and hence do not exist, then none of his tales is about ghosts. But, by juxtaposing this point with his tales of ghostly encounters, he is, in fact, offering a powerful challenge to the Neo-Confucian view: even if philosophically appealing, Han Yu's definition does not apply to the phenomena of the real world. If ghosts are to be defined so narrowly, then how are the experiences Hong Mai describes to be classed? Aware of the Neo-Confucians' potential scorn for what he was doing, Hong cites the classical but iconoclastic thinker Mozi (470–391 B.C.) to justify the importance of recording even those events that fall outside the bounds of rational explanation (*Yijian zhi* 14:1467). Each time that Mozi's interlocutor says there are no such things as ghosts, Mozi repeats:

> From ancient times to now, for as long as people have lived, there have been those who have seen ghosts and deities and those who have heard the sounds of ghosts and deities, so how can one say there are no ghosts and deities? If no one had seen or heard them, then how could one say there were ghosts and deities? (*Mozi* 8:66)

Mozi's is a clear-cut approach to the evidence, and one clearly closer to Hong Mai's heart than Han Yu's.

Although about the strange, and often the supernatural, *The Record* is not Hong's fabrication. In several of the prefaces to the different sections, Hong stresses the measures he took to transcribe the tales accurately, saying *The Record* "contains things I have seen and heard with my eyes and ears. Each tale is clearly based on a source" (*Yijian zhi* 2:185).[23] Elsewhere he bemoans his failure to take down one tale and cites an instance of his informant's dying before he could hear his story (*Yijian zhi* 12:1303). In his longest statement about his working methods, dated 1196, Hong comments:

> Usually each time I hear a guest's tale, I write it down. If we are drinking and I do not have time, then the next morning I try to remember it and record it. Then I quickly show it to the person who told me the tale, in order to make sure that there are no differences in detail in the entire tale—and only then do I stop. Thus I do not lose what is told to me, and it is reliable and can be recounted. (*Yijian zhi* 10:1135)

23. Compare with Gan Bao's preface to the *Soushen ji*, a much earlier book in the *zhiguai* ("describing anomalies") tradition. "These things are not what has been heard or seen by one person's own ears and eyes. How could one dare say there are no inaccurate places?" (*Soushen ji*, preface:2; DeWoskin 1977:32).

Hong does realize that not all the stories he writes down are true. One man in Fujian tells him about a whale who swallowed a ship and its crew. When carpenters begin to saw their way out, the whale plunges into the ocean, killing himself and the men. Hong wryly inquires, "If the ship was completely submerged, who told the tale?" (*Bintui lu* 8:97).[24] He knows that his information is only as good as that of the people with whom he spoke. Although maintaining that he scrupulously records what he has been told, Hong Mai glosses over a major alteration: the tales he heard were in the vernacular, but he transcribes them into terse, classical Chinese. In doing so, he makes no attempt to capture the voice of the informant.

How reliable is *The Record* as a source about popular belief? It consists of thousands of short anecdotes, most one or two paragraphs long, which often give the date, place, and names of the people involved.[25] Although compiling strange tales, Hong uses the same format he would use in writing an official history. Several notes appearing within the body of the text of *The Record of the Listener* indicate factual errors in the stories.[26] Other notes reveal how careful Hong was: he records instances of his informants' asking to remain anonymous (3:16:13:504; 10:5:11:1261) and of information corresponding to an event recorded in the standard histories (2:10:6:267; 3:17:9:512; 15:1:7:1554). Of course, identification of informants in itself does not preclude the possibility that Hong made up both the stories and the names of his sources. Literary convention often dictated that an author give the name and birthplace of a source in order to add verisimilitude to a tale he himself had actually written.

Hong goes one step further than his predecessors, however: he always identifies an informant for each tale and, especially in later installments, credits others with collecting material filling entire chapters. The simple, sometimes monotonous, structure of the tales and their frequent repetition of the same themes testify persuasively to their origins as folktales. The lack of character development or literary

---

24. This work contains paraphrases of many lost prefaces to *The Record of the Listener*.

25. By identifying his informants, Hong Mai places himself squarely in the *zhiguai* tradition, which dates back to the Six Dynasties (A.D. 220–586). Literary scholars debate whether or not *zhiguai* tales constitute fiction. Kenneth DeWoskin (1977:39) comments that the authors of these books used historical techniques: "Note the frequent appeal to sources, the specificity about time and place. This not the writer as *fictor*."

26. Hong cites instances where purportedly successful exam candidates' names do not appear on the list of those who passed (*Yijian zhi* 8:6:6:1015–16; 11:2:10:1236–37), where a monastery named in a story is not located in a certain town (11:1:1:1222–23), and where he retells a story that he had originally incorrectly transcribed (10:4:4:1162–64; 11:6:9:1266–67).

embellishment further confirms Hong's claim that he merely transcribed what he heard. And the speed of compilation shows that *The Record* assumed an increasingly collaborative nature: a gap of five years divided the first and second installments, whereas only months separated the final installments. It is most unlikely that Hong Mai could have made up so many stories in such a short time. Much more likely, these are tales that people really told. Hong's prefaces strongly suggest that he was committed to transcribing faithfully the tales he heard (although in a different idiom from the spoken vernacular). Their truthfulness—or at least purported truthfulness—was a major source of their appeal. *The Record of the Listener* was the *Ripley's Believe It or Not* of the late twelfth century.

Furthermore, when it is possible to compare Hong Mai's tales with other accounts, his versions turn out to be remarkably accurate. In one case where Hong Mai and a temple inscription record the same incident,[27] Hong gives the following version, dated 1161:

> An old village woman of Huzhou suffered an aching arm for a long time with no respite. During the night she dreamt that a white-clothed woman came and said: "I am also like this. If you can cure my arm, I can cure yours."
>
> The old woman said: "Where do you live?"
>
> She replied: "I stay in the west corridor of Revering Peace Monastery."
>
> The woman then awoke. She went into town, to Revering Peace Monastery, and told what she had dreamt to monk Zhongdao of the Western Hall. He pondered and then said, "It must have been Guanyin [the Buddhist goddess of mercy]. Our hall has a white-robed image. Because of a gap in the thatch, her shoulder is hurt."
>
> He led her to the room to perform her obeisance, and indeed one arm was missing. The elderly woman then ordered workmen to repair it.
>
> When the image was complete, the woman's disease was cured. (*Yijian zhi* 1:10:15:88)

Liu Yizhi (1078–1160), a native of Gui'an county who became an official in the capital, wrote an inscription dated 1157 for a Guanyin hall attached to the same monastery. Here is his version:

> For a long time there was a statue of the bodhisattva Guanyin in between two pillars on the Western side of the monastery. Zhang of the prefecture had been sick for three years.

---

27. Full translations of these texts are given in appendix 1.

One night Zhang dreamt of a white-robed woman who said: "You cannot lift your arm. I also suffer from this. If you can heal my arm, I will also cure your shoulder and give you long life."

Zhang asked her where she lived, and she said, "I live in the west corridor of Heavenly Peace Monastery."

The next day Zhang was carried to the monastery to the statue of the bodhisattva, and it was just as Zhang had dreamt. Zhang looked at the statue with reverence and was moved to tears. Zhang examined the right arm of the bodhisattva and noticed it had been damaged by a piece of falling wood. Zhang ordered it repaired, and Zhang's illness was subsequently cured. (*Tiaoxi ji* 22:7b–8a; *Wuxing jinshi* 8:21a)

In the inscription, although Zhang's sex is not clear, the rest of the details match. Guanyin's speech is almost word-for-word the same in the two versions; the only differences are that she uses a different first-person pronoun (*wu* vs. *wo*) and a different word for heal (*yi* vs. *zheng*). The phrasing varies, but the word order and the meaning are identical. The variations may merely be differences between oral versions that were circulating during the twelfth century. Even though Liu Yizhi's inscription was intended as testimony to Guanyin's curing powers and Hong Mai's tale purportedly as a diversion for his audience, the two versions are surprisingly alike. The identical process of transmission accounts for the similarity between two very different types of sources. Both Hong Mai and Liu Yizhi heard the story about Guanyin in the vernacular and then transcribed it in classical Chinese. Certainly this one example is reassuring: Hong Mai proves himself to be a reliable informant. The enormous quantity of tales and the limited sources from the Song make it impossible to double-check all of Hong Mai's stories, but it is striking how often other sources back him up.

This book utilizes other sources in addition to inscriptions and *The Record*. The administrative law code of the Song, *The Collected Important Documents from the Song (Song huiyao)*, provides an official perspective on title-granting to the gods. Most entries in *The Important Documents* consist of an excerpt from a local official's petition to the emperor followed by the edict giving the emperor's assent. During the Song, one office in the capital kept records of all the edicts issued, divided them into topical categories, and compiled a new set for each emperor's reign. Government offices probably had a partial set, which bureaucrats could consult, of those edicts relevant to their functions. No complete set was ever published.[28] At the end of the Song, in 1270,

28. Li Xinchuan did publish an abridged version, but it circulated only within Sichuan (Chai 1982:23).

ten sets of edicts, one for each reign, existed. The most important section for the study of policy about popular deities consists of two chapters totaling over two hundred pages in the rites (*li*) section, which contains both government edicts concerning and lists of titles awarded to local deities (*Song huiyao, Li* 20:1–171; 21:1–64). There is no information about the last forty-five years of the dynasty.

Most Song sources tell only about an individual deity, as the protagonist of an anecdote, as the recipient of a title, or as the performer of miracles. Without the lists of gods appearing in local histories (*difang zhi, fangzhi,* also translated as gazetteer), it would be impossible to examine the changing composition of the pantheon. Copies of local histories circulated in the Song, and officials referred to the lists of temples they contained. An 1107 inscription from Liyang county, Jiangsu, reports that a district magistrate unsuccessfully prayed for rain at each of the nearby temples during a long drought. Upon consulting a local history, he learned about a temple twenty li to the northeast where the resident deity had always responded to entreaties. He prayed there, and rain followed (*Jiangsu jinshi* 10:22a). Hong Mai describes a similar use of the gazetteers in Xiazhou (now Yichang county, Hubei) in 1119–1125 in which an immortal responded to prayers with rain: "The local people revered the deity's grace and gave money to repair its temple, but they did not know if it was male or female, *so they checked several local histories* and asked the resident elders, but they did not know what course to pursue" (*Yijian zhi* 3:14:2:483, emphasis mine). So the local histories, like the elders, constituted a source of information about temples. The local histories, unlike the long-dead Song elders, can still be consulted.

In sum, this book draws on temple inscriptions and *The Record* to sketch the popular religious practices of the twelfth and thirteenth centuries. *The Important Documents* portrays the policy of the central government toward popular deities; local gazetteers make it possible both to examine the pantheon in one locality and to trace the rise of extra-local deities over all of southeast China. Collected papers (*wenji*) of different officials and other compilations of miscellaneous notes supplement these sources.

Students of Chinese religion may be surprised to find that neither the Buddhist nor Daoist canon is cited in the pages that follow. Let me explain why. This is a study of lay religion, and both canons are, by definition, written from the point of view of the learned clergy. Much of the scholarly literature about Chinese religion draws on these can-

ons; much of it, accordingly, concerns doctrinal changes. The canons
are the repositories for the learned traditions of these religions, and
they only rarely provide glimpses of the encounter between indige-
nous beliefs and the textual religions. Yet, at the same time that educated Buddhists translated sutras and Daoists debated doctrinal issues,
wandering, uneducated practitioners outside the capital did whatever
they could to win adherents.

Scholars working on both the Buddhist and Daoist canons have cau-
tioned of their limitations. Close imperial supervision of the Buddhists' translating and exegetical efforts was instituted in 402 and continued through later periods. Erik Zürcher characterizes the Buddhist
canon:

> A picture begins to emerge, and that picture is none too en-
> couraging for anybody who would like to get an impression of
> Chinese Buddhism in its totality; a tiny clerical establishment is
> working at imperial order in a handful of top-level official
> monasteries; they are charged with the production of texts,
> obviously as magical protection for state and dynasty; the pro-
> duction of those texts is to some extent regulated; their inclusion
> into the canon (apparently an imperial prerogative) certainly is.
> (1982b:164)

Michel Strickmann's comparison of the Buddhist and Daoist canons
further underlines their official nature:

> Evidence of official patronage for the two religions is found al-
> most from the start, and the accumulative and classificatory ef-
> forts of religious bibliographers were encouraged, sponsored, and
> doubtless "overseen" by the state. During the Tang, at least, we
> find it an established principle that writings identified as either
> Buddhist or Daoist should regularly be collected and placed in the
> appropriate canonical collections at the state's behest. An act of
> religious merit, or simply yet another indication of the state's dra-
> conian control of its subjects' spirits, the editorial process was fol-
> lowed by the copying (in time, printing) and distribution of the
> collections so established to a number of officially recognized cen-
> ters throughout the empire. (1977:59)

Versions of Daoist texts available in manuscript form (from the Dunhuang caves or in the stomachs of Ming statues) reveal that the texts
appearing in the Daoist canon, like their counterparts in the Buddhist
canon, underwent continuous editing. As early as the seventh century,
editors of the Daoist canon expurgated Buddhist terms from texts in

the Lingbao tradition and replaced them with Daoist equivalents (Bo-kenkamp 1983:468); as late as the fifteenth century, their successors abridged texts containing elements of Indian Buddhism (Franke 1972, 1977, 1984). Both the Buddhist and Daoist canons, in short, present their respective religious traditions as highly literate monks would have liked them to be—without elements of other rival religious traditions, without deviations from their own doctrinal traditions.

Read judiciously, of course, the Buddhist and Daoist canons will yield nuggets of information about the interaction between clerical and lay traditions. Yet, because so little is known about changes in lay religion in the twelfth and thirteenth centuries, I have decided to publish this study separately from a future study comparing clerical views of popular deities with those of their lay devotees. In an essay on Daoist hagiography in the Tang, Kristofer M. Schipper has written: "In its scriptural expression Tang Daoism drew a very clear line between local cults and saints and the 'pure' theology of the Tao. Cults to deified heroes were expressly forbidden. Moreover, as I have already noted, Taoist ritual in no way expresses concern with local cults. The pantheon is abstract, the prayers impersonal" (1985:831). My own preliminary work using Daoist sources indicates that his comments apply equally well to the Song. On being ordained, Daoist practitioners received a register specifying which spirit soldiers (*shenbing*) and generals (*shenjiang*) they may summon. *The Record of the Listener* gives many instances of Daoist adepts who called upon just those spirit soldiers and spirit generals to do cures and exorcisms. These spirit emissaries remained exclusively within the province of ordained Daoists. Lay people did not worship them. If popular gods turn up in these narratives, they do so only as something to be exorcised. When popular deities are mentioned at the end of the long lists of gods (reaching 3,600 in the Song) that constitute the Daoist pantheon, they are not referred to by name, but simply by class: for example, "gods of the mountains," not the god of a specific mountain. In the Daoist hierarchy, gods are thought to seek promotions, and lower gods remain subordinate to higher gods. Lay people did not accept these hierarchies; they prayed to gods who were efficacious, regardless of their purported rank.

This book, then, is a first step: an examination of local cults using secular sources, that is, materials not contained in the Buddhist and Daoist canons. Buddhist and Daoist practitioners and gods do appear in this study (see chapter 2). They appear here, not as their respective religious establishments would have them behave, but as lay people depict them. They go from place to place doing cures, summoning gods, and performing ceremonies—usually in the case of Buddhists, reading sutras, and in the case of Daoists, writing memorials to the heavens. The secular sources of the Song are so rich that they tell how those who did not belong to the clergy, those who had received neither Buddhist nor Daoist training, interacted with these specialists. The specialists, in turn, proved themselves familiar with the idioms of popular belief. They appealed to lay people to worship certain gods or to hire certain practitioners not for doctrinal reasons, but because they were more powerful, because they were more ling.

The primary aim of the individual chapters of this book is to analyze different aspects of popular religious change. Because lay people sought the help of the gods or religious specialists whenever they faced the unknown or the uncertain, popular religion cannot be separated out from the stuff of medieval life. Each chapter also touches on people, money, and the government and so provides a new vantage point for viewing the social, economic, and political changes of the Song. This book deliberately adopts the perspective of lay people. *The Record* and temple inscriptions make it possible to do so.

Chapter 2 tackles a long-standing problem for students of Chinese religion: What was the relationship among popular religion and the established religions of Buddhism, Daoism, and Confucianism? Popular religion was the religion of lay people, who, in the course of the twelfth and thirteenth centuries, had to choose among more and more gods in the popular pantheon and more and more religious practitioners. They made these choices on the basis of efficacy, or ling. Not concerned with ostensible religious affiliation, the laity hired the practitioner or worshipped the god they thought could cure the ill or bring rain.

Chapter 3 focuses on contemporary understanding of reciprocity and of the gods' desire for recognition. People used dreams, oracles, and spirit writing to consult the gods and drew on several interpretative mechanisms to account for the gods' responses. Interestingly, in an age of rapid economic development, the gods, like the men who worshipped them, diversified. No longer did they perform just the age-old miracles of bringing rain, expelling locusts, forestalling drought, and protecting their districts from rampaging troops. Some began to deal on the national grain market, to advise their followers on business deals, to manipulate the government's purchasing quotas, and, on occasion, even to bring their devotees a tenfold increase in profits. In short, by the thirteenth century, a few gods in the most commercialized areas exhibited a nice understanding of market dynamics.

Chapter 4 documents the government's changing policies toward popular deities, shows the increasing speed with which it granted titles to them, and suggests that the government's main purpose was to harness the power of the gods for the purposes of the state. The government's heightened level of activity in popular religion starting at the end of the eleventh century makes sense only in light of the widespread belief in reciprocity. Besieged on its northern border and short of funds, the central government looked to the gods for help. The only way to get that help, contemporary observers thought, was to grant the gods further recognition.

Chapters 5 and 6 explore the impact of the commercial revolution on the popular pantheon. Chapter 5, a case study of one prefecture, Huzhou, Zhejiang, argues that the commercial revolution had a very different impact on people, depending on how close to transportation routes they lived, and that, if read correctly, local pantheons illuminate those differences. People who lived in highland areas continued to worship traditional, local gods; those who lived in the more recently settled lowland areas prayed to newer gods of low birth. Chapter 6 focuses on the most startling change in this period: the appearance of regional deities who were worshipped beyond the base temples in their home counties all over southeast China. The increasing mobility of cultivators in areas along waterways resulted in their exposure to gods from other places, often to those of merchant groups. Both chapters draw heavily on surviving gazetteers.

In short, popular religious changes accompanied the broadening of the cultural and economic spheres of Chinese peasants in the twelfth and thirteenth centuries. Let us now turn to those changes.

CHAPTER II

Lay Choices

Whenever illness befell individuals or epidemics struck entire towns, whenever drought, locusts, or torrential rain hit agricultural communities, and whenever marauding troops or bandits threatened settlements, Chinese people who had no other means of tackling these problems looked to the gods for protection. An age of great commercial expansion and urbanization, the Song ushered in other new uncertainties; whenever farmers who were unfamiliar with market dynamics lacked accurate price information, they also prayed to the gods to assist them. Asking for help was relatively simple. One could pray directly to a god or hire an itinerant religious specialist to conduct a rite on one's behalf. Easy access and low cost meant that people of all social strata did both much of the time. But deciding whom to ask was not simple, nor was interpreting the ambiguous responses of the gods straightforward. Throughout the twelfth and thirteenth centuries, the number of gods and religious consultants increased, giving lay people an ever-widening, occasionally bewildering choice. This chapter draws on information from *The Record of the Listener* and other sources to depict the religious world as perceived by lay people.

Choosing among Gods

Let me begin my analysis of the popular pantheon with one of the few anecdotes Hong Mai tells about his own family.[1] His father, Hong Hao, served as a record keeper in Xiuzhou (now Jiaxing county, Zhejiang) sometime between 1119 and 1125. At that time, reports Hong, ghosts were often sighted at the government record office. One day Hong's nine-year-old brother saw a ghost, and then two days later a concubine, possessed by another ghost, fell to the ground. They tied her in bed with a leather belt, and then the ghost was able to speak, apparently because he had possessed the concubine. When Hong's father asks the ghost to identify himself, the ghost reluctantly explains that he is the spirit of a farmer, Stem Nine, who died two years earlier in a famine, and that the other ghost is his former neighbor.

1. A full translation appears in appendix 2.

Hong's father replies, "I worship Zhenwu² [a Daoist star divinity] because he is very efficacious, and I also have images of the Buddha, and of the earth and stove gods. How is it that you come here?" His implication is clear: these gods should be protecting his family from ghosts. The ghost helpfully explains why Hong Hao's precautions are useless:

> The Buddha is a benevolent deity who does not concern himself with such trivial matters; every night Zhenwu unbinds his hair, grasps his sword, and flies from the roof. I carefully avoid him, that's all. The earth god behind your house is not easily aroused. Only at the small temple in front of your house [to the stove god] am I reprimanded every time I'm seen. I just entered the kitchen, and His Lordship [the stove god] asked, "Where are you going?"
> I answered, "I'm just looking around."
> He upbraided me, "You're not allowed here."

Hong's father complains that, because the earth god has allowed the ghost to enter in spite of his regular offerings on the first and fifteenth day of the month, he will destroy the earth god's shrine to punish him. The ghost responds:

> Do you mean to say you don't understand? Even though he has money, how can he go without food? When I enter your house, if I get something, I must give him a share to keep him quiet, and that's why he has always permitted me to come. . . . Were I to proceed as you admonish and tell the earth god, he will be angry that I am so loquacious and will use a stick to drive me out.

Hong's father is surprised that the earth god, who serves as a divine policeman, has failed to prevent the ghosts from intruding. Stem Nine, in turn, is astonished that Hong's father, himself an official, has not grasped the basic principle of Chinese bureaucracy: graft. The runner's job, on earth or in the underworld, may have been to keep people away from the magistrate (or city god), but the time-honored way to obtain access was a bribe. Hong's father asks if the ghost has ever seen his ancestors at the family temple. The ghost allows that he has tried to get food from them at the monthly offerings, but one woman has always foiled his efforts. Just as Hong's father offers to give the ghost a fat goose, the ghost reports that the earth god expelled him and his

2. Because of a taboo character, the god Xuanwu was referred to as Zhenwu throughout the Song.

family, presumably for talking too much. He takes his leave (*Yijian zhi* 2:8:8:250).

Representatives of all elements of the Chinese supernatural world appear in this extraordinary tale: ancestors, ghosts, and gods associated with Buddhism (the Buddha), Daoism (Zhenwu), and popular traditions (the stove and earth gods). Earth and stove gods were among the most ancient deities in the popular pantheon. Their cults dated back to even before China was unified in 221 B.C., when villagers worshipped local earth gods, whose jurisdictions were limited to the immediate surroundings of wherever their temples were located. Devotees offered sacrifices to these gods before ploughing and after the harvest. The Buddha had been viewed as a popular deity ever since the arrival of Buddhism in China in the first and second centuries A.D. The cult to Zhenwu probably developed in the Five Dynasties (910–960) and Northern Song, when cults to other Daoist figures like the immortal Lü Dongbin also took off (Baldrian-Hussein 1986; Miyakawa 1973).

Nothing in Hong's tale suggests that his father categorized the gods according to the religious tradition with which they were originally associated. Because China's religious traditions were not mutually exclusive, lay people did not have to choose just one. Faced with a given problem, they looked to all the gods for help and simultaneously asked for protection from many gods from different traditions. Accordingly, Hong's father, an official, had images of the Buddha, Zhenwu, the earth god, and the stove deity in his house. He evaluates them according to their power, not their association with any particular tradition. In this tale, it is the lowest of gods, the stove god—not the distant Buddha, not the wandering Zhenwu, not the dozing earth god—who tries to protect the Hong household from the intrusive ghost.

At about the same time that Hong Hao encountered the ghost, an imperial emissary, Xu Jing, wrote a diary of his forty-two-day sea voyage to Korea, which details the different religious observances the crew performed. Three days into the voyage (on the nineteenth day of the third month, 1122) an official was sent ashore to erect a prayer platform where incense was offered to the King of the Eastern Sea (Donghai wang): "a divine being appeared who was shaped like a lizard (*xiyi*). It was actually the Dragon Lord of the Eastern Sea."[3] Xu's detached stance implies that he was not convinced of the apparition's divinity, although others may have been. The ships set sail on the twenty-fourth day and made further offerings of incense to the dragon

3. This temple received its first title at the request of another emissary to Korea in 1078 and received higher titles in the years that followed (*Yanyou siming* 15:22a).

(*Xuanhe fengshi* 34:186). On the twenty-fifth day they were caught in a thunderstorm and went ashore, where they climbed a mountain and made an offering to

> the god who rules over mountains and streams. There were many places for other gods to receive offerings at the same time. Each ship carved a small wooden model of a boat into which they placed Buddhist scriptures and dry rations. The names of the passengers were written down and placed in the wooden boats. Then they were cast into the sea. This was probably a way to exorcise disgusting things. (*Xuanhe fengshi* 34:187)

The last sentence suggests that Xu was not familiar with and did not approve of this type of observance, but it certainly sounds as if the sailors were performing a ritual they had done countless times before. It is not clear whether or not the boatmen would have agreed with Xu that they were making offerings to the imperially sanctioned god who ruled over mountains and streams. Xu may have tried to gloss over the overtly Buddhist nature of their observances for the sake of the Daoist emperor Huizong.

On the twenty-sixth day a strong wind from the northwest started to blow, impeding their journey northward. They sent a small boat to visit a shrine to Guanyin, the Buddhist goddess of mercy, to pray for a change in the wind:

> That night the monks and disciples burnt incense, recited sutras, and sang Buddhist hymns very devotedly. The three ranks of emissaries, officials, clerks, and soldiers all performed obeisance reverently. In the middle of the night the stars shone brightly. The wind-indicating flags moved. Everyone happily sprang to his feet. The wind had already shifted so that it came from the south.

The ships then delayed their departure for two more days because the wind kept changing, but at last, on the twenty-eighth, they set off in spite of the still shifting winds (*Xuanhe fengshi* 34:188).

In this instance as well the sailors on the ship seem to have visited the temple to Guanyin previously. Ocean-going vessels probably visited these different temples and performed these various rites as a matter of course, in much the same way that Hong Hao made different offerings to the gods in his home. None of these observances precluded the others. An ocean journey was a dangerous undertaking, and the passengers sought all the assistance they could, be it from the Dragon King of the Eastern Sea, the god who ruled over mountains and streams, or Guanyin. Their religious observances continued once the ship was under way. When they passed through shallow waters, in order to secure safe passage, they sacrificed a chicken to all those who had lost their lives there. And just before departing, they stopped at a dragon temple to pray for a safe trip back (*Xuanhe fengshi* 34:191; 39:210). Throughout his narrative, Xu adopts the same detached stance to list the religious observances of the crew that he used to describe the various customs of the Koreans. Both seem equally alien to him.

In the final entry summarizing their return voyage, Xu comments on the perils of travel at sea:

> I submit that the dangers of ocean voyages are great. One takes a boat as tiny as a leaf and floats it on an extremely vast dangerous sea. One can only cling to the good luck of one's ancestors, which should cause the gods of the waves to respond efficiently to save one. Otherwise, how can human strength suffice to get one home? (*Xuanhe fengshi* 39:211)

For the first time we hear Xu's own voice. Man, then, is so vulnerable when he is at sea that he can look only to the gods for help. The potential dangers fall into three categories: stupifying winds in which the boat loses its bearings, black winds in which nothing is visible, and tidal waves in which ships lose course or capsize. Xu resumes his narration of the journey home:

> The second boat arrived in the middle of the Yellow Sea. Three rudders snapped at the same time. I was right there. With the others in the boat I tore my hair and fervently prayed.
>
> Then an auspicious light appeared. It was the goddess of Yanyu island, Fuzhou, who had previously performed other miracles.[4] Thus, that day, even though the boat was in danger, we were able to replace the rudders. Once we had, the boat resumed its pitch and rocked in the water as it had before the accident. (*Xuanhe fengshi* 39:212)

Gone is Xu's detachment. Once he himself is in danger, he, like the sailors, begs the gods for help. And although he seems to have had doubts about the dragon sighting, praying to Guanyin, or making wooden models, he sounds totally convinced of the power of the goddess of Yanyu island, the Heavenly Consort, also known as Mazu (see

4. In fact Yanyu island was in Putian county, Xinghua prefecture, not in Fuzhou. The base temple to the goddess, the Heavenly Consort, was located there. Later sources favorable to her indicate that she received her first title in 1124 (ter Haar 1988:10; Li 1979:3).

chapter 5). His account encapsulates the perils of sea travel in the twelfth century. Faced with the many potential dangers, the men in their tiny leaf of a boat had no recourse but to seek divine protection. And seek divine protection they did—from every god whose temple lay along their course. Both Xu and Hong Mai's father lived at the same time, just before north China fell to the Jurchens, and both had very similar attitudes toward the gods of the pantheon. They held very different positions. For both, however, the hazards of life—be they in the course of an official's daily routine or on a perilous ocean voyage—were so great that they could not pray to just one god.

By the Song, popular pantheons, then, had come to include gods associated with the textual traditions of Buddhism, Daoism, and Confucianism. Almost all gods in local pantheons were thought to have been human beings prior to their apotheoses. With the exception of dragon temples, few cults to animals existed. When streams and mountains were worshipped, it was in an anthropomorphized form. Similarly, devotees prayed to the god of a given mountain or stream—not to the mountain or stream itself as they may have in earlier centuries.[5] When devotees did not know the identity of a god, they often referred to him (or her) by type: city god, earth god, or guardian of a monastery. Classing gods in this way facilitates the analysis of change in the medieval pantheon, but *The Record* and temple inscriptions suggest that lay people worshipped the different gods of the Chinese pantheon in exactly the same ways regardless of their origins.[6]

Figures like Guanyin (the Indian bodhisattva, Avalokitesvara) and Lü Dongbin (a Daoist immortal) who originated in the Buddhist and Daoist pantheons of China were present in popular pantheons all over China in the twelfth century (Baldrian-Hussein 1986; Stein 1986). One inscription written sometime after 1117 from a Guanyin hall in a monastery in Crow township (Wu *zhen*) in Wucheng county, Huzhou, gives a detailed picture of a monk's activities on behalf of Guanyin, the

---

5. See Wu (1987) for an example of a cult that underwent this shift. The white ape was depicted as an ape in the Han dynasty (207 B.C.–A.D. 220), but in the Tang he became a man with certain ape-like features.

6. By the second half of the twelfth century, the popular pantheon had already undergone significant change. Yet, because extant sources from the period preceding the development of wood-block printing are so much more limited in their coverage than those after it, it is almost impossible to know what local pantheons looked like in earlier centuries. No local histories, with their listings of the popular temples in a given place, are available before the eleventh century. Accordingly, early pantheons can be reconstructed—and only tentatively—on the basis of later local histories. See table 3 for such a reconstruction of the popular pantheon in Huzhou, Zhejiang, and an explanation of these different categories.

same goddess that Xu Jing and his crew visited. Monk Yang moved to a monastery when he was eleven, took the tonsure at eighteen, and was ordained at twenty. Then his teacher advised him to serve sentient beings:

> From that day on, he no longer accepted meals from believers nor did he bathe. He recited sutras morning and night without cease. He suddenly wanted to put up an image of Guanyin and to build a hall to house it. There was not enough capital. He was frustrated and would sigh loudly. Accordingly, he would poke his left eye with a needle and put a lighted stick of incense to it. Then he would put embers to his five fingers, seeking contributions. Those far and near who heard of or saw him competed to give money. (*Danyang ji* 9:2a–3a)

Once he had raised the money (by using techniques more often associated with spirit mediumship than with Buddhism) he went to a skilled carpenter in Hangzhou. Following long consultations, more self-mutilation by Yang, and several dreams, the carpenter produced a statue "radiant and majestic."

Without Monk Yang's efforts, there might not have been a statue of and possibly not even a cult to Guanyin, but by the early twelfth century she had established herself as a popular god in Crow township. "At the beginning of every year, the residents of the market town led the image to the different quarters of the town and had a big feast for seven days. Each time they encountered drought or flooding, they prayed, and rain or clear skies came immediately" (*Danyang ji* 9:2a). Because nothing in this passage bespeaks a knowledge of Buddhist doctrine, its account of parading the image around the town and praying to it could have been about any other deity. Initially drawn to the monastery by the self-torturing and publicity-seeking Monk Yang's activities, the people of Crow prayed to Guanyin to perform the same miracles as other deities.

In an 1157 inscription from another temple to Guanyin in Huzhou, Liu Yizhi recounts the events that culminated in the building of a new side hall and then records his objections to making a statue of Guanyin.[7] He argues that Guanyin has thirty-two[8] manifestations, and that through those manifestations she can go anywhere and do anything. But an image gives her a deceptive concreteness. He concludes by ac-

7. A full translation of the text appears in appendix 1.
8. The number of her manifestations is usually given as thirty-three, as it appears in the *Guanyin Sutra* (a separately printed chapter of the *Lotus Sutra*), but Guanyin has thirty-two manifestations in the *Surangama Sutra* (Tay 1976:163).

cusing the monk in charge of the temple of misleading the people by
putting up a statue. Monk Jujiu replies, "Not so. The goddess's manifestations are limitless. Because she has no one place of her own, but
is worshipped in the hearts of believers, she thus has a place. I see that
monks and lay people (*daosu*) go in front of the statue, gather their
robes and bow, burn incense and pray on their knees, and tell her of all
their illnesses and troubles and ask her for help" (*Tiaoxi ji* 22:9a).

Monk Jujiu seems to have persuaded Liu of his point: however undesirable an image of Guanyin might be from a doctrinal standpoint,
if the monastery is to attract followers, it cannot adhere to traditional
doctrine. It must offer potential followers a deity in terms familiar to
them. And those terms are not those of Buddhist theology but those
of popular religion. Monk Jujiu is aware of these realities in a way that
Liu Yizhi, a literatus, was not and that Yang, also a monk, was. After
all, Jujiu had to raise the money for the new hall. The two monks
embody an important trend: in their efforts to win popular support in
the Song, Buddhist monks increasingly used the discourse of popular
religion, by encouraging the worship of gods like Guanyin.

Even Confucius was worshipped as a popular deity, reports Hong
Mai. Sometime prior to 1160 a government official, Li Zhongyong,
retired to Fuliang county (Jiangxi) where he built a Confucian temple
and a school. Following his death in 1160, his descendants frittered
away the legacy, the temple fell into disrepair, and some of them even
came to squat on the land where the temple had been. Then in 1197,
one of the descendants fell terribly ill with a high fever, and neither
doctors nor prayers could cure him. Displaying the catholicism so typical of the Song, the sick man then summoned a Daoist to help. The
Daoist ordered a young boy to stand on a table, and the boy gazed into
the distance. A figure in official robes appeared with ten followers and
identified himself as Confucius[9] and the ten men as his disciples. In
response to the Daoist's query concerning the reason for his visit,
Confucius replies: "When I received Li's worship, he was extremely
diligent and pure. Since his death, his descendants have no longer been
attentive, and they have destroyed my temple and toppled my image.
In these past forty years, everything that once was here has disappeared
without the slightest trace. I am going to demonstrate my power in
order to warn them." Even though his temple lies in ruins, he has

9. He uses the title he had received from the Song government, Culture-Propagating
King (Wenxuan wang). See *Songshi* 105:2547–55 for a list of titles awarded to Confucius
and his disciples in the Song.

enough strength left to cause one of Li's descendants to fall ill. He then promises to bring good fortune to the Li family if they resume their former observances (*Yijian zhi* 12:10:15:1382–83).

In this tale the metamorphosis of Confucius into a popular deity is complete. He, like any other deity, wants his temple and image to be in good repair, because only then can he perform miracles. Hong Mai concludes a ten-chapter installment of *The Record* with this tale, saying: "I say temples are the place where gods are. Accordingly they are ruled by the god's spirit. As for this incident, its strangeness is especially obvious. It insults my Sage [Confucius] greatly. I put it at the end of this installment to warn those who are deceived." His placing it at a prominent place and his unusual editorializing reveal his awareness of the sensitive nature of the tale. One can imagine the scandalized reaction of Neo-Confucian scholars at the time; Zhu Xi (1130–1200), the formulator of the Neo-Confucian synthesis, objected to images and permitted the worship of only Confucius's ancestral tablet. He would have been aghast to hear that Confucius had appeared to a spirit medium. True to form, though, Hong Mai does not betray whether his comments are tongue-in-cheek or meant to be taken seriously. Can we hear him chuckling softly at the Neo-Confucians' discomfiture?

The few extant sources about popular religion before the twelfth and thirteenth centuries suggest that the only gods in local pantheons to attain government recognition were mountain gods or ancient heroes who had been high-ranking generals, if not emperors, before their deaths. Then, in the Song, a different type of deity started to win official recognition and commanded widespread popular support. Not necessarily of noble birth, men and women who died (often prematurely) in accidents, in battle, or from illness became the objects of worship. Often commoners, they had reputations limited to a local arena. Many Song writers, especially those critical of popular cults, decried these deities, arguing they did not fulfill the traditional requirements for divinity as given in the second-century B.C. Confucian classic, *The Book of Rites*: "Now according to the law of the sage kings, offerings should be made to him who has given the people law, to him who has died while serving his lord, to him who has worked to pacify the country, to him who has prevented disasters, and to him who has forestalled suffering" (*Liji, Jifa* 46:1590; Legge 1885:207–8, mod. auct.). This passage refers to the deities' acts before their apotheoses: the ancient kings and generals issued laws, died as martyrs, helped to subdue unrest within the country, and prevented suffering. *The Book of Rites* lists several gods who fulfill these standards: they include the legendary Yao, Shun, and the Yellow Emperor.

Yet, contrary to what conservative critics argued in the Song, this standard was so loose that followers of low-born gods argued it could be construed to comprise both classical heroes and divinities of more recent times. The last two phrases came to be interpreted as measures of a god's ability to perform miracles after death: could he or she prevent disasters and forestall suffering? The Song deities may or may not have died while serving their lords or their country, but they were all thought to be able to prevent calamities and suffering. Accordingly, this passage was frequently cited on their behalf.

Hong Mai provides a detailed account of the birth of such a deity and the government's almost immediate recognition.[10] In the 1130s, in Shunchang (now Nanbei county, Fujian), an army commander, Fan Wang, urged the local people not to take the headquarters of a local rebel, Yu Sheng, because their forces were not strong enough.[11] He and his son were killed, and his wife was dismembered when she resisted rape. Several months later, the insurgents were finally subdued: "The bricks where Commander Fan had been killed retained obscure outlines of his corpse, which were very faint. The people of the district gathered the bricks and joined together to build a shrine to him. They also painted his likeness on the wall of the temple to the god of walls and moats." In 1136 the vice-prefect petitioned the court about the deity, who was awarded a posthumous rank of *chengxin* gentleman. Permission was granted to build a temple to Fan.

Then the sheriff, who was directing the corvée laborers building the temple, dreamt that Commander Fan, clothed in the garb of a high official, came to visit him. Pointing to the southeast corner of the temple, the commander told him that the bandits had poked his eye out there and that he had so informed the local magistrate. On awakening, the sheriff checked the commander's story; everyone said his version of his own death was true, but no one had been aware that his eye had been gouged out. Upon investigation, it turned out that the district magistrate's wife had also dreamt that the commander came to visit her, and she confirmed the commander's story (*Yijian zhi* 1:20:9:182–83).

In the pages that follow will appear many variations on this tale.

10. A full translation of this account appears in appendix 2.

11. Fan Ruwei organized a rebellion in Fujian in 1131, Yu Sheng in this particular district (*Jianyan yilai xinian yaolu* 41:759, 761).

Certain aspects may vary, especially concerning the rhythm of the miracles or the timing of the grants of titles. But the salient characteristics will not. The importance of miracles or, depending on one's point of view, events defying straightforward explanation in a deity's career cannot be overstated. Without the mysterious apparition on the bricks, and without the dreams and the confirming detail that Commander Fan had indeed had his eye poked out, the cult of Commander Fan might have been stillborn. Once the miracles had begun, the local people, in a seemingly unorganized outpouring of support, built both a separate temple to Commander Fan and an altar in the temple of the god of moats and walls. Only then did local officials petition for a title. More miracles ensued.

At least in the early stages of the cult, neither large capital investments nor high literacy levels were necessary—just an eye for shadows on bricks—or, more to the point, an attuned sensitivity to the desires of the god. The cult began on a small plot of land and on the wall of the temple to the god of walls and moats. It is fair to assume, although direct evidence is sorely lacking on this point, that petitioning the central government to grant a title cost a fair amount of money.[12] And by that stage, one can infer a higher level of participation: the locally powerful told local officials about the new god and even paid for the award of his title. The use of corvée labor suggests that the government itself financed the construction of the temple. Throughout the Song, the central government, intensely concerned with recognizing powerful deities, kept a close watch over the rise of new deities and awarded them titles increasingly quickly. Fan Wang died in the early 1130s; in 1136 the government approved the prefect's petition to build a temple to him; and in 1158 the temple was granted a plaque (*Song huiyao, Li* 20:169b).

In many ways Commander Fan provides a textbook example of a popular deity. Time after time the sources tell of deities who got their start much as Commander Fan did, of people whose deaths were followed by strange occurrences. As in Commander Fan's case, the telltale signs of divinity often appeared in the immediate vicinity of the site where someone had died: a purple aura was given off, or it did not rain over the grave, or a well appeared where two girls had drowned (*Yijian zhi* 3:4:9:397; 1:12:9:182; *Jiading Chicheng* 31:15a). Temples were often built right on those locations, and, as long as the new gods proved powerful, local pantheons easily expanded to include them.

12. See chapter 4 for a discussion of the title-granting process.

Choosing among Gods and Practitioners

The above discussion has been slightly deceptive in suggesting that the only choice lay people had to make was among different deities. In fact, they had to choose not only among different gods, but also among different practitioners. Throughout the Southern Song, religious specialists—not just Buddhist monks and Daoist practitioners, but also geomancers, fortune-tellers, physiognomists, and healers—were moving from place to place, from marketplace to marketplace, offering their services to those in need.[13] They were summoned most often when someone was sick and asked to recite sutras, conduct ceremonies, or write charms to help alleviate suffering. On occasion they were also asked to do what gods did, to bring rain or to perform other miracles. When faced with a problem, the laity were free to consult any practitioner or god, regardless of affiliation.

Once again Hong Mai provides an example of the choices open to the laity.[14] After taking into custody more than ten innocent people who would be freed only upon the arrest of a local murderer,[15] a sheriff in Xincheng county, Hangzhou, entreated both heaven and the God of the Pine Stream (Songxi shen), saying:

> I would usually not dare to pray on my own behalf. Only if my parents were ill would I cut my thigh or cauterize my shoulder; there is no avenue that I would not exhaust in my selfishness. Barring this, even when my plight involved my wife or me, I have never dared to bother the gods. Now evil bandits have knifed two people, wounding one and killing the other, implicating those of the district and their kin. Concerned with the well-being and peace of the people within 100 *li* [55 kilometers], I ask that you above take notice.

Sheriff Chen stresses his reluctance to bother the deities in order to convey the desperation of the situation; as such, his denials are a rhetorical device. And in explaining what he would never dream of doing, he reveals what most people in the Song were doing frequently—namely, going to the gods with their own troubles, their spouse's, and their parents'.

13. By the Song, government officials performed Confucian rituals at regular intervals during the calendar year, and all candidates for office studied the Confucian classics, but no Confucian practitioners as such offered their services in the marketplace.

14. A full translation of this anecdote appears in appendix 2.

15. These arrests were standard practice under the provisions of the mutual responsibility system in force during the Song. Although innocent, these people belonged to the same mutual responsibility group as the murderer.

Following the murder of one of his subordinates who was looking for the murderer, Chen went to a Daoist monastery, where he consulted a spirit medium who could contact the Purple Maiden (Zigu), the most important spirit-writing god of the Song.[16] She wrote down the name of a county in Jiaxing (Zhejiang), where he sent troops. Ten days later he consulted her again, and she explained, "The original evil-doer has already been caught. But as my own strength is insufficient to deal with this matter for you, I could not avoid petitioning a higher god. Now, capturing the bandit is the accomplishment of the God of the Pine Stream, who has recently brought him to the border of Fuyang county [Hangzhou]." She also wrote the character *zi* (catalpa). After the soldiers brought the killer back, Chen freed the hostages and sent the man in a cangue to the prefectural office (*Yijian zhi* 15:12:15:1668). The resolution of the incident explains the meaning of the god's message: catalpa referred to East Catalpa gate in Jiaxing, where the criminal was apprehended. All gods were not equal in the Song pantheon; the Purple Maiden says that the God of the Pine Stream is more powerful than she, and he has presumably sent the spirit soldiers who guarded the fugitive until his arrest.

Sheriff Chen began by simultaneously addressing a local god and heaven. After a few days, when he still had heard nothing of the murderer and when one of his subordinates was killed, he did not go back to the temple of the God of the Pine Stream but instead tried spirit writing at a monastery. Throughout this narrative, Sheriff Chen displays an eclecticism completely typical of people seeking help in the Song. One can be sure that if the Purple Maiden had failed him, he would have approached even more gods and religious specialists.

Because, in sharp contrast to the eclectic laity, the clergy viewed different religious traditions as mutually exclusive technologies for tapping into the powers of the universe, they chose to limit themselves to ritual techniques associated with just one doctrinal tradition. A layman could consult any god or practitioner to his liking, but the clergyman could not. Both political and doctrinal developments contributed to a sharp increase in untrained, often illiterate, popular religious practitioners in the Southern Song, but no matter how untrained or how illiterate they were, they steadfastly identified with only one tradition.

Throughout the tenth and eleventh centuries, the central government had closely regulated Buddhist and Daoist monasteries by setting high standards for admission into the clergy. The primary way of ob-

16. See the next chapter for a discussion of spirit writing in the Song.

taining an ordination certificate (*dudie*) was to pass a series of difficult exams. On holidays, the emperor also bestowed certificates on a specified number of monks who had not taken the exams. Then, in Shenzong's reign (1068–1085), the government began to sell blank ordination certificates as a means of raising revenue, reducing the number granted by other means. By the Southern Song, after it had stopped holding these qualifying exams, knowledge of Buddhist sutras or Daoist texts was no longer the primary route to becoming an officially recognized Buddhist or Daoist. Practitioners who sought official recognition had to buy a certificate, the cost of which, formerly 130 *guan* (strings of cash), soared to anywhere between 800 and 1,000 *guan* in the Southern Song (Chikusa 1982a).[17]

Many Buddhists who could not afford these certificates became lay practitioners, sometimes wearing white clothes or taking the tonsure to distinguish themselves from the rest of the population (Chikusa 1982f:282–84). Hong Mai tells of an official in Taizhou (now Taixian, Jiangsu) who, in 1177, vowed to sponsor the ordination certificate of a monk if his wife recovered from a serious illness. She recovered, and they visited a monastery where five hundred uncertified monks gathered to draw lots. Since only one received the certificate, 499 did not (*Yijian zhi* 9:4:3:1079–80). A century earlier these monks could have taken a government-sponsored examination to receive their certificates; in 1177 they were dependent on a rich donor to buy one for them. Accordingly, they, and others interested in becoming monks, had much less incentive to master the many texts in the Buddhist canon.

At the same time that the government was limiting the number of ordination certificates, certain doctrinal changes were taking place in Buddhist theology that also encouraged the participation of less educated people. Both Pure Land and Chan Buddhism stressed sincerity of belief over knowledge of doctrine or wealth. Sutra recitation societies sprung up, especially in Ningbo and Hangzhou, where people gathered to recite Buddha's name a thousand times; the illiterate used grains, beads, and increasingly charts to record the number of repetitions (Takao 1939:61; 1975:108). Ignorance was no longer an obstacle to attaining salvation. Repetition of the Buddha's name would achieve the same results previously associated with long years of study.

Perhaps the most important change in Daoism between the Tang

17. A *guan* originally consisted of one thousand cash. It is usually translated as a string of cash; as the dynasty progressed, however, a string of cash came to contain sometimes as little as seven or eight hundred cash.

and the Song was the shift from the practice of outer alchemy (*waidan*) to that of inner alchemy (*neidan*). Inner alchemy, which drew on breathing techniques and other exercises to purify one's body, came to be linked with effectiveness of curing technique; Bai Yuchan (1194–1229) explained that one's success in healing hinged on the degree to which one had perfected oneself (Baldrian-Hussein 1984:15–16; Chen 1985:47). And no longer were these texts limited only to those who studied long years with recognized Daoist masters. Chen Nan (1171–1213) divided his inner alchemy teachings into three levels: the lowest was aimed, at least in theory, at the illiterate, although the use of writing belies his intent. Many of these new healing rites hinged on propagation of different *fa* ("methods," here rites to work cures and miracles), such as the thunder rites (*leifa*), in which practitioners tapped the power of thunder to summon soldier gods and to expel evil forces (Matsumoto 1979:45).

One possible reason for the sudden increase in the practice of these rites was an infusion of imperial support at the end of the Northern Song. Emperor Huizong (ruled 1100–1125) was a vigorous supporter of Daoism, giving Daoist names to Buddhist monasteries and monks, suppressing popular religious temples, and patronizing Daoism heavily.[18] In 1106 and 1116 Huizong actually issued edicts summoning successful Daoist practitioners to the capital so that they could demonstrate their powers to him. The extensive, if short-lived, imperial support at the beginning of the twelfth century resulted in the rapid dissemination of the rites, which Hong Mai witnessed later in the century.

Doctrinal changes and the suspension of government-administered examinations for Buddhist and Daoists combined to prompt the rise of uneducated practitioners. *The Record of the Listener* mentions several people who became Daoist practitioners following meetings with famous masters, dreams, or visions—but without formal training or purchase of an ordination certificate (Matsumoto 1979:46–47). One such Daoist was a man named Liu Daochang from Yuzhang (now Nanchang county, Jiangxi). Barely literate, he was a drunk and a good-for-nothing. Then one night he dreamt that an ordained Daoist (*daoshi*) gave him a book, telling him he could cure sick people with it.

18. Notably, although he was originally interested in the Daoism of the Maoshan and Celestial Masters schools, he came under the sway of two popular Daoist practitioners, Lin Lingsu and Wang Wenqing. Wang was the founder of the thunder rites practice. Matsumoto (1979:51–53) argues that one of the reasons underlying the Celestial Masters sect's success in the Song was that it supplemented higher Daoist practices with more popular miracle working.

He went home, put up an image of the Daoist divinity Zhenwu, and started to cure sick people and to perform purification ceremonies (*jiao*).[19] Hong describes his techniques, saying,

> The charms he wrote completely differed from the usual Daoist script. Whether for curing illness, or for blessing charm water, or for holding incense and burning ashes, or for saying an incantation over jujubes [a kind of date], all his charms were especially simple. . . . Today his methods are very popular. What was conveyed to him about the way has not been preserved. All we have are ten-odd charms that have been inscribed in stone. (*Yijian zhi* 4:2:13:551)

Hong Mai, an educated official, realizes that the charms were simple—after all, the semiliterate Liu Daochang could not have mastered the usual Daoist script for charm writing—but the effectiveness of his charms was what mattered to his customers. The local people respected him so much that they built a Zhenwu hall for him to live in. Performing *jiao* has often thought to have been limited to ordained Daoists who had received registers from someone in a Daoist line of teaching, but clearly the unlettered Liu was not such a man. In spite of his low literacy and corresponding ignorance of Daoist doctrine, he did everything ordained Daoists were supposed to. He was judged not in terms of his doctrinal knowledge, but, like a popular deity, in terms of performance. Hong reports that Liu could get results in the same day.

In *The Record* also appears one of Liu's Buddhist counterparts, Monk Zhang. After having a vision in the mountains of a goddess who gave him a text, Zhang abandoned his wife in Raozhou (now Poyang county, Jiangxi). He went to Fuzhou (now Linchuan county, Jiangxi), where there was a drought, and encouraged villagers to pray to him for rain. He promised that if it did not rain, they could burn his body. The local people piled wood on a pyre, and just as they were about to light it, it started to pour. Zhang was freed. Following his subsequent arrest for embezzling funds for road repair, Zhang went to Shaowu Commandery in Fujian, exorcised ghosts, and cured sick people there. Upon his death in 1134, the local people put up pictures of him and worshipped him (*Yijian zhi* 1:9:9:78). Monk Zhang defies easy classification: although not ordained, he still identified himself as a Bud-

19. A *jiao* (literally sacrifice) is a community festival in which offerings are made to the gods to reconfirm a covenant between the people and the gods; villagers summon Daoist practitioners to conduct the rite on their behalf. See Schipper (1974) for a detailed description and explanation of such a ceremony as it was conducted in 1969 in Taiwan.

dhist; his eclectic repertoire comprised the standard services of popular specialists; and he was finally worshipped as a god.

Buddhist and Daoist practitioners had to work within whichever tradition they identified as their own. If, after the people of Fuzhou had finished piling wood, they had set both the pyre and Monk Zhang on fire in order to bring rain, Monk Zhang could not suddenly have announced that he was going to perform a Daoist thunder rite. Switching religious affiliations would have been tantamount to admitting he was a fraud. But, if the local people had lit the funeral pyre and Monk Zhang had burnt up, but rain still did not come, they could have consulted a Daoist practitioner, summoned a spirit medium, or prayed to a dragon god.

I have followed Hong Mai's terminology in labeling Liu and Zhang as Daoist and Buddhist, but, as their biographies show, little of substance distinguished the two.[20] Both men began to practice after a vision and receiving a text. Neither was educated, and neither was familiar with Buddhist or Daoist doctrine. Why should either of these men—who had no training and were probably illiterate—have bothered to call himself Buddhist or Daoist? Identification with a religious tradition granted access to textual authority and so to a divine source of power. To persuade the unlettered populace that one was a Buddhist or Daoist, one had to be able to do what Buddhists and Daoists did: to chant Buddhist sutras aloud, to write Daoist charms, or to perform *jiao*. The illiterate could do little more than distinguish Buddhist rites, which usually consisted of reading of sutras or recitation of the Buddha's name, from Daoist rites, which involved the writing (and subsequent burning) of memorials to heaven. At the very least, an unschooled practitioner had to be able to mimic these different ritual acts well enough to convince the illiterate of his (or her) claims to cure the sick, bring rain, and perform miracles. And if he could cure the sick, bring rain, and perform miracles, then he could go from place to place, charging people for his services.

The increase in these less schooled practitioners led to a decrease in

20. The terminology used in the Song reflects the confusion of categories. Lay Buddhists both called themselves and were referred to as people of the way (*daomin, daoren, daozhe*) (Chikusa 1982f). Similarly, because some people (like Liu) became Daoists without having undergone rigorous training, the term "Daoist" (*daoshi, daojia*) came to be used increasingly loosely; often in the Song it refers to any religious practitioners who would more accurately be called fortune-tellers, spiritual healers, and so on. These labels should be viewed with caution. In some cases they denote individuals with full training in and knowledge of Buddhist and Daoist doctrine; often they denote the self-appointed specialist.

the cost of Buddhist and Daoist services. Hong tells of one Daoist practitioner in Hangzhou, a certain Master of Rites (*fashi*) Wang, who

> daily practiced the rites of the Celestial Heart (*tianxin fa*), conducted purification ceremonies (*jiao*) for the presentation of memorials to Heaven on others' behalf, and wore the star cap and ritual vestments. But he was not an ordained Daoist practitioner (*daoshi*). The people preferred him to real Daoists, as his rates were one-third of theirs, and they therefore often hired him. Each time he had his neighbor Li write the petition or present the official prayer. (*Yijian zhi* 9:6:12:1101)[21]

Clearly Wang was himself illiterate, as he had to depend on a neighbor to write his petitions for him, but he was able to convince his customers of his skills.

There were other ways to lower the cost of these rituals. In 1145, one man in Suzhou, after being wrongly executed, possessed the district magistrate and asked that he conduct a Buddhist rite to give food to the hungry ghosts on the land and water (*shuiluhui*) so that he could rest in peace.[22] The magistrate protests: "The cost is extravagant. I am poor and cannot do it." The ghost obligingly responds that the ceremony does not have to be on his behalf alone and that he is willing to have his name submitted with that of others in the same ceremony (Matsumoto 1983b:177–78; *Yijian zhi* 3:12:3:465–66). Hong Mai also tells of a thousand people from Raozhou (Jiangxi) joining together in 1198, paying 1200 cash in order to participate in a purification ceremony (*jiao*) of the Yellow Register (*huanglu*) (*Yijian zhi* 12:2:12:1319).[23] These bits of evidence suggest that the costs of Buddhist and Daoist rituals were lower by the Southern Song.

Hong Mai provides several telling examples of lay people who spent money to consult both gods and specialists. In Jiangxi, a man plagued by ghosts paid religious specialists to conduct an exorcism and itinerant Daoists to perform a curing ceremony; when they failed, he then summoned Buddhists who recited oaths, conducted an exorcism, and

21. I am indebted to Bob Hymes for this reference, and I follow his translation here (Hymes 1987b:35).

22. Holmes Welch (1967:190–91) translates *shuiluhui* as "plenary mass" and provides a description of this rite as it was conducted in twentieth-century China. He comments: "The purpose of the plenary mass was to save all souls of the dead on land and sea (hence the term *shuilu*), but as usual the merit arising therefrom was credited to the account of the deceased relatives of the family that was paying for it. They paid a great deal."

23. Schipper (1974:315) explains that Yellow Register ceremonies are conducted on behalf of the dead.

called on spirit soldiers. In Jinhua (Zhejiang) a sick girl's parents asked
both spirit mediums and Daoist practitioners to try to help her without
success. And in 1190 in Huzhou, an eighteen-year-old girl fell ill and
spoke as if whispering to someone. She failed to respond to the treat-
ment of doctors, but an itinerant Daoist practitioner, who was very
good at controlling ghosts, cured her. Most striking of all, a drought
occurred in Fuzhou (Fujian), and a respected member of the gentry led
a procession of Buddhist monks, Daoist practitioners, spirit mediums,
and three hundred peasants to pray for rain at a well thought to be the
residence of the local dragon (*Yijian zhi* 2:14:10:304–5; 10:3:12:1158;
8:2:12:982; 8:2:13:982–83). None of these people had qualms about
consulting specialists and gods associated with different traditions.
Their sole desire was to exorcise the ghosts, to cure the ill, or to bring
rain, and they all had enough money to pay the fees of these different
specialists.

In the Song people could select from among many different types of
religious specialists and deities when seeking help. How did they
choose between praying directly to a deity and consulting a Buddhist
monk, Daoist practitioner, or spirit medium? Presumably on the basis
of their reputations, availability, and cost. Yet deciding who cured an
illness or who brought rain could not have been easy. The sources say
nothing about these kinds of judgments.

If a mother prayed to one deity for her ailing child to recover and he
did, presumably that one deity got the credit. But suppose that many
people in a village prayed to different deities for rain, and it rained.
Which deity then received the credit? Or if it did not rain, then what
happened? Were an anthropologist to ask why a certain deity was popular, a Song devotee would have explained simply that the deity was
powerful. So the most powerful deities were the most popular.

It is at this point that one must go beyond the circular reasoning of
the believer to probe more deeply into the question of how people
decided which god was most efficacious. In the absence of evidence, I
suggest that such decisions were the products of a social process by
which the followers of each deity tried to garner the credit for the deity
they supported. Moreover, because the determination of efficacy was
a social process, any attempt to freeze the pantheon—be it by the central government or by Daoist clergy—was doomed to fail. The dynamics of efficacy ensured that the pantheon was always changing.

CHAPTER III   Understanding the Gods

Because the gods were thought to reason exactly like the human beings they had once been, their behavior was explained in highly anthropomorphic terms throughout the Song. One broad principle underlay all interpretations: people and gods were mutually dependent. As men needed protection and miracles, deities needed people to acknowledge and reward them. The gods lived, even vied, for human recognition. Temple inscriptions and *The Record of the Listener* all indicate how highly gods were thought to value paintings and sculptures of, temples to, and central government titles for themselves. Intensely concerned with the state of their own images, temples, and titles, they responded positively—with continued miracles—because they needed human recognition. Without it, they languished. The gods had powers that mortals did not, but they were thought to exercise those powers just as people would have, sometimes benevolently, sometimes humorously, sometimes vengefully. Accordingly, the Chinese gods, like their counterparts in ancient Greece and Rome, often seemed capricious.

Out of a conflicting tangle of dreams, natural events, and chance readings of oracles, a given deity's supporters spun tight, well-reasoned interpretations of divine behavior. They had no scriptures to guide them. Instead, they based their explanations on a body of orally transmitted knowledge. In this chapter I will first recount many of these anecdotes, which appear in both *The Record of the Listener* and temple inscriptions, and then parse them to reveal the unstated principles of popular religion. The original stories are theirs, the analysis mine. Because Hong Mai presents material from all over China, and because his book was available in different editions throughout south China, my examples come from all over the empire.[1] And because Hong Mai almost always provides capsule biographies of the people in his tales, it is possible to examine the extent to which people of different social strata consulted the gods. People from the lowliest peasant

1. I limit my inquiry here to Hong Mai's tales about this world. He also tells many stories of people's experiences in hell, where they are punished for various misdeeds, such as eating meat or killing fish, but these do not concern specific deities and their responses to human behavior. These stories, instead, reflect contemporary thinking about retribution and deserve study in their own right.

48

to the highest official prayed to, dreamt about, and used oracles to communicate with the gods.

As *The Record* suggests a range of participation among different social groups, so too does it hint at a range of attitudes from open disbelief to total faith in the power of the gods. Yet, because many of the entries in *The Record* are to some extent, and temple inscriptions even more so, testimonials designed to impress readers and listeners with the power of the gods, they exaggerate the extent of reverence for the gods. To counteract that tendency, this chapter begins with two sources that suggest that irreverence about the gods coexisted with belief. First, an entry from another of Hong Mai's works, *Notes from My Studio*:

> In the fall of 1173 in Ganzhou and Jizhou prefectures [both in Jiangxi], continuous rain caused flooding. I [Hong Mai] was prefect in Ganzhou and ordered many bags of earth to be packed at the city gates in order to prevent the water from entering the city. After two full days, the water retreated. When my superiors ordered me to pray for rain, I did not carry out their order but reported the actual situation.
>
> Then I heard that in Jizhou they had erected a Daoist platform in the small hall of the government office to pray for the skies to clear, while in the big hall they prayed for rain. When asked why, the prefect replied: "I asked for the skies to clear because this prefecture has been disastrously flooded. Praying for rain is an imperial order."
>
> The prefect did not realize that this shrewd tactic was almost an insult to the gods. On what were they in the underworld to base their decision? (*Rongzhai suibi* 4:3:651–52)

Hong Mai dared to disregard the imperial order to pray for rain, but his fellow official in Jizhou did not. He attacks the Jizhou prefect's inconsistency in praying for different outcomes simultaneously: if the magistrate believed the gods really could affect the weather, how could he ask for both rain and clear skies? Hong Mai continues:

> A book of village jokes tells that "two merchants entered a temple. The one traveling by land wanted clear skies and obtained the god's permission to offer a pig head. The one traveling by water wanted rain and obtained the god's permission to offer a sheep head. The god delegated a small ghost to say, 'On a clear day, I will eat pig head. On a rainy day, I will eat sheep head. What is

there to prevent me?' " This story is actually told. (*Rongzhai suibi* 4:3:651-52)

Each merchant may hope the god will respond to his own prayer for rain or clear skies, but, by juxtaposing their two requests, the joke-teller reveals his doubts about the god's ability to bring either. The god's purported rejoinder in this tale is instructive: he has no compunctions about accepting both their offerings, and he makes no promises about the weather. This joke is ambiguous. Either the god cannot control the weather and, like the travelers, must wait to see the outcome, or he will be completely arbitrary in bringing rain or clear skies. This joke circulating among the people suggests a degree of doubt on their part, but it also shows that an awareness of the gods' capriciousness did not necessarily prevent people from praying to them. The weather was something over which the two merchants had absolutely no control. An offering of a pig or a sheep head was a small price to pay for good weather for the trip. And if one man wanted rain and the other clear skies, who was to cavil over consistency?

The same tone also marks the appearance of an earth god and his subordinates in a Southern Song drama, *Zhang Xie Comes First in the Exams*.[2] The play is about a venal exam candidate, Zhang Xie, who meets, marries, and then abandons a young girl after he comes first in the civil service examinations. Only after a series of adoptions and deaths are the two reunited at the end of the play. Early in the play, the earth god reports that, even though he had sent a special cloud to protect Zhang, he was unable to prevent his being robbed. Then he sings:

> I live under Five Chicken Hill (Wuji shan). Those far and near have all heard of me. I have demonstrated my power for over eight hundred years, and three times has spirit money been burnt for me. I watch over tigers, leopards, and other wild beasts; I control beans, grains, and rice. How do I know what chicken tastes like? Where could I have ever eaten pork or mutton? When people wor-

2. I am indebted to Takahashi Bunji for introducing this play to me, for providing me with copious bibliographic information, and for giving me a crash course in early vernacular drama.

Although experts agree that this is the first surviving example of *nanxi* (Southern drama), they disagree as to the actual date of composition. Judging strictly on the basis of its publication history, the version incorporated into the Yongle encyclopedia in 1408 could have been printed any time between 1200 and 1400. In his thesis on *nanxi*, Tadeusz Zbikowski (1974:50–79) summarizes the arguments of different scholars using Ming sources in order to date this play. They arrive at conclusions of 1120, 1190, and 1260. The editor of the definitive edition, Qian Nanyang, argues from internal evidence that it is definitely a Southern Song play (preface to *Xiwen sanzhong* 1979:1).

ship me, they often offer bean-paste dumplings and rice cakes. (*Xiwen sanzhong* 54)

The beginning of his speech mimics many temple inscriptions, stating where the temple is, asserting the god's wide reputation, and exaggerating how long he has been worshipped. (In a later scene, the god says his power has been recognized for over a hundred years [*Xiwen sanzhong* 83].) Then, in a brilliant switch, the god laments that he has received money offerings only three times in all those years. Reverting to the language of inscriptions, he says that he watches over animals and governs crops and then, once again, shifts the level of discourse with a startling admission about the low quality of the offerings made to him. Longing for chicken, beef, or mutton, he gets only rice cakes and bean-paste dumplings.

The anonymous author continually pokes fun at the earth god; when the god admits that he has not been able to protect Zhang Xie, he pompously refers to himself as "the earth god of the hill in question," not in the first person (*Xiwen sanzhong* 54). Yet, for all his satire, the author does not challenge the basic precept of belief in the Song: the god's ability to perform depends entirely on the quality of offerings from his devotees. The god maintains, "If I am given four or five dishes of sesame cakes and one to two hundred paper cash,[3] then I can be very powerful and demonstrate my strength" (*Xiwen sanzhong* 83). The earth god's complaints about his meatless diet would have amused and struck a deep chord with the poorer members of his audience, who themselves ate very little meat.

The author's depiction of the god closely conforms to another convention prevalent in the Song: endowed with divine powers, the gods exercised them according to the most human of motivations—anger, envy, and desire for affection. *The Record of the Listener* contains one entry that illustrates the gods' dislike of criticism. An earth god at a monastery in Poyang county, Jiangxi (Hong Mai's home town), fails to keep thieves from breaking into a monk's room while he is out. The monk posts a poem on the temple wall:

> Disaster comes.
> Misfortune arrives.
> Neither at the hands of men.
> The earth god of the monastery is not efficacious.

That night the monk dreamt that the deity visited him, explained that he had been on guard duty at another gate, and implored him not to

---

3. Literally "paper money" (*zhiqian*), this refers to the spirit money used exclusively for offerings to the gods, and not real money.

broadcast his failure to all the local people. The monk took his poem down (*Yijian zhi* 10:7:2:1186). The earth god, like any human being in China, feared losing face.

In reading the pages that follow, remember Hong Mai's colleague who prayed for both rain and clear skies. Keep in mind the depiction of the earth god from Five Chicken Hill in *Zhang Xie Comes First in the Exams*. The people who talked to Hong Mai or who wrote in temple inscriptions about how powerful their gods were had little reason to depict doubt. Many of the people of the Song who approached the gods did so as a last resort; they were not sure the gods would perform. Even a slight chance of success would justify going to a temple, making an offering, and praying.[4] We can see this same coexistence of skepticism and belief in our own society. Not all the people with cancer who go on a macrobiotic diet or use biofeedback techniques are convinced they will be cured. They are, however, convinced that such treatments are worth trying. For people who had no other options, and for people who were desperate, it did not take a high success rate to convince them that praying to the gods might help. As in our own society, coexisting alongside the skeptics were believers whose faith would be not be shaken no matter how many times the gods failed them.

What the Gods Wanted, Part I: Statues

Because the gods were thought to behave and think just as people did, anybody could draw on his own experience and understanding of human motivation to account for the behavior of the gods. Neither education nor religious training was needed. Deities were thought to respond to prayers only to the extent that they were publicly honored. An inscription dated 1098 from a temple to the city god of Shaoxing offers the most explicit statement about the dual role of temple images:

> The temple has so many cracks and leaks that it is on the verge of collapsing; it is not enough to satisfy the god. The statue is falling down and is of poor workmanship; it cannot suggest the god's grandeur. Dust has gathered on the image's face; its clothes are dark and torn. Those who visit only cursorily look at the image. Nothing conveys the mystery or the power of the god. (*Liangzhe jinshi* 7:4b)

4. See Jordan and Overmyer (1986:266–70) for a discussion of this issue in contemporary Taiwan.

Images shaped the devotees' perception of the deity at the same time they affected the deity himself. If his image was in poor condition, then he could not perform miracles.

Given the emphasis on new images and refurbished temples, it is not surprising that few examples of popular religious art survive from the Song. Much more is known about people's ideas about images and temples than about what they actually looked like. No temples from the Song to popular deities exist in south China; only a few survive in the north.[5] The Goddess Mother Hall (Shengmu dian) at the Jin shrine (Jinci), a temple complex just south of Taiyuan, Shanxi, was built in the eleventh century and contains forty-three clay statues probably dating to the time of the temple construction; these are among the very few images from the Song still in place. The relative scarcity of stone statues (compared to the Tang) and the many wooden statues of Guanyin, the goddess of mercy, suggest that people tended more and more to favor cheaper materials of earth and straw or wood over stone. Laurence Sickman, one of the few art historians to work on this topic, characterizes twelfth- and thirteenth-century sculpture saying, "In this new style the gods become far more human than at any previous time. They retain the full-bodied fleshiness of the mature Tang style, indeed they become more portly, and the modeling of the faces and hands is often rendered in a most life-like manner" (1971:189). The forty-three ladies in waiting from Jinci (Taiyuanshi Wenwu Guanli Weiyuanhui 1981: plates 46–70), the many wooden statues of Guanyin in Western collections (for example, those photographed in Thorp and Bower 1982:84, 91–92), and the Song paintings of Lohans in Japan confirm his comment (Miyazaki 1981:159). These depictions exude a human warmth lacking in earlier, more emotionally remote pieces. Given Song ideas about the gods, it is not surprising that they should have been shown in such life-like poses.

Not merely depictions of a deity, portraits and statues were thought to actually be inhabited by the gods, who usually did not give direct evidence of their presence. But, on rare occasions, Hong Mai tells us, they made their statues bleed in front of an official in Tai'an county, Shandong, cry in sympathy for someone who had not been appointed to office in Hezhou, Anhui, and offer a coin to buy beans from a small boy in Changzhou (now Wujin county), Jiangsu (*Yijian zhi* 5:1:5:714–

5. See Siren (n.d.) and Soper (1948) for descriptions of Song temples in Kaifeng and Datong, which may have been renovated since. Dazu in Sichuan and Yongle Temple in Ruicheng, Shanxi (by the Yellow River), date to the Yuan. More temples may survive in Shanxi, but descriptions have not yet been published; these remote areas are not normally open to tourists.

15; 4:15:13:668; 13:8:9:1446; 15:12:3:1653). People believed they could communicate their desires to the gods through their images, hence the common practice of praying to a deity's statue or portrait. People of all social strata put up images in their own homes. In Fenghua county, in the great commercial center of Ningbo, the great families (*daxing jia*) and rich people (*fumin*) prayed to a local god, the God of Three Chambers (Santang shen) at household altars. In Suzhou, a beggar over eighty years old saved her money in a bottle to buy a picture of Guanyin (*Yijian zhi* 15:15:8:1693; 7:3:4:898–99).

The accuracy of these depictions assumed great importance because they provided devotees, especially those who were illiterate, with the only sure means of identifying the deities. Often dreamers retained only hazy memories of mysterious figures in their dreams, and temple images granted their memories a specificity they may well have originally lacked. *The Record of the Listener* is full of dreams in which the deity who appears cannot at first be identified. When he can be, it is because he states his name, or, more often, because the dreamer recognizes the deity. Sometimes the dreamer is able to make the identification immediately; sometimes years pass before he sees a picture that matches the figure of his dreams. Those having this type of experience span all levels of society. In one entry from *The Record*, an official identifies a god he had dreamt about in his childhood on the basis of five images in a temple; in another a villager's wife does so when she sees three images in a nearby monastery (*Yijian zhi* 12:10:9:1379–80; 8:7:5:1021).

The Record of the Listener shows to what lengths individual deities would go to ensure that their portraits were accurate. In Xiazhou (now Yichang county, Hubei) lived a man who fervently worshipped Daoist immortals and the Buddha. He held a gathering to worship Lü Dongbin, which was well attended by both Daoists and lay people. Just as the ceremony ended, an elderly soldier appeared at the house and asked for food and drink. After consuming a prodigious amount, he said:

> "If the immortal Lü were to come here himself, you would not recognize him." The host pointed to a portrait on the wall, and the guest looked at it carefully. Smiling slightly, he said, "I actually met Lü once. He looked totally different from this. Give me five feet of silk for me to use to capture his likeness for you." The host gladly gave it to him. The guest took the silk and did not grind any ink. He just crumpled the silk in his hand, suddenly spat, and then wiped away the excess.
>
> The host was initially disgusted by this and then concluded the

soldier was already drunk and nothing could be done. . . . After a while, the soldier put the silk in an empty bottle, smilingly bowed, and left. A young boy picked up the bottle and pulled the cloth out to get a better look. The immortal's image had already formed. He wore clothes and boots and was just like the guest. The people then realized that the immortal Lü had descended to earth. (*Yijian zhi* 5:6:3:755–56)

Of the many tales Hong Mai tells about Lü Dongbin, this one not only captures his playfulness but also reveals how important it was that depictions of him give a good likeness. Lü cared enough to bestow a spitting image of himself. Had the host in the tale possessed a portrait that looked like Lü, he would have been able to recognize the immortal.

In another entry from *The Record*, a doctor from Xiangyang (Hubei) challenges what he is told because it does not accord with the iconography he knows. He dreams that he and his wife visit the underworld, where he asks who one figure is. An attendant replies, "That is the King of Hell (Yanluo Tianzi)." Zhang replies: "When I look at him, he looks different from the pictures of him circulating in the world. In fact, he looks more like Qingyuan zhenjun [Erlang]" (*Yijian zhi* 4:17:4:679). Once again, Hong Mai is having fun. No two gods could have looked more different than the old, wizened King of Hell and the young, virile Erlang. If the depiction of the King of Hell was so inaccurate, then most of the portraits circulating in the world were equally misleading. This anecdote, though humorous, suggests that a gradual tightening up of iconography occurred in the Song: certain people must have acted as arbiters, determining which images really resembled the god in question and which did not. These tales may have been designed to impress upon devotees the risks of entrusting the painting of their god to an uncertified artist, to one who was not familiar with the approved iconography.

The deities of *The Record of the Listener* were thought to pay close attention not only to the accuracy of their images but also to their upkeep. Damage to the image wounded the deity; likewise, repairs helped him. Let me cite a few examples from the many Hong Mai offers. In Fuliang (Jiangxi) the local people commissioned an artist to paint two door gods on the temple of the city god. Miffed at the low pay, the artist used only black ink. The gods then appeared in a dream to complain to him that his painting would not inspire reverence on the part of the people. In Ganzhou (Jiangxi), the local people replaced temple doors that had been damaged in a storm, but they forgot to put two statues of horses back. The deity appeared to the local magistrate in a dream and complained that whenever he wanted to go out, he had no horses to ride. In each of these cases, the deity in question appeared in a dream, complained about his mistreatment, and gave his followers a chance to make amends (*Yijian zhi* 9:10:10:1133–34; 8:3:2:984–85).

The deities were not always so forgiving:

> For generations, Wang Huan of Shuangdian in Raozhou had worshipped a benevolent god whose image he placed in a niche in his house. His five-year-old son broke the deity's middle finger while playing. Wang dreamt that a deity wearing golden armor told him, "I have protected your house for years now, and I have never allowed even the slightest misfortune to befall you. How could you allow your child to break my finger?" Wang agitatedly apologized. In the morning when he went to examine the statue, it was as the deity had said, and he ordered workmen to repair it. His son fell ill that day. A boil grew on his middle finger and hurt constantly. When it healed, his hand curled into a fist which he could not open. (*Yijian zhi* 3:6:13:418)

This tale underlines the strict reciprocity governing the relations between men and gods. If the hand of the image is hurt, the god then hurts the hand of the child.

Gods were thought not only to inhabit images and to reason like human beings; Hong Mai and his informants even credit them, like the gods of classical Greece, with the ability to assume human form. One god in Raozhou takes on the body of a young boy, gets drunk at a festival, and then, the next day, the local people find his image has fallen to the ground (*Yijian zhi* 11:6:12:1269).[6] Perhaps the most startling instance of gods assuming human form (and human desires) is when they have sex with their admirers. Hong Mai tells of one prostitute in Chengdu (Sichuan) who visits a temple and is attracted to a handsome image. Then a man resembling the statue comes to see the woman several nights. He weeps and says that because he has missed his guard duty he is to be beaten and exiled the next day; he asks the prostitute to burn money for him. When the appointed time comes, a man with his wrists bound, face covered with blood, and forehead tattooed with the exile order, passes by her house. She sets up an altar

---

6. The gods took nonhuman forms as well. When a visitor asked about lights appearing on Lake Dongting, a boatman explained that the deities frolicked on the lake at night. A skeptic shot a slingshot, and suddenly all the lights went out. On visiting the temple the next day, the visitor found the image split open with a pellet lodged in it, sure proof that the deity had been on the lake the previous night (*Yijian zhi* 8:8:3:1029).

with offerings, burns money, and sobs as she sees him off. On another day when she visits the temple, the image she had originally admired had fallen to the ground (*Yijian zhi* 1:17:2:146). The very humanness of the gods coupled with their ability to take human form meant that the distinction between gods and people was a fine, even blurred, one.

What the Gods Wanted, Part II: Temples

Because temples served the same function for gods as houses did for people, the quality of the dwelling was thought to affect the god's well-being and so his (or her) power. When a temple was beautiful and new, the occupant could perform miracles. When his abode was old and decrepit, the neglected inhabitant could no longer bring rain or cure illness. Because temples were so important to them, the deities who appear in *The Record* often helped their followers to secure the necessary materials to build a temple for them. They mysteriously provide money; they cause a storm that brings ready-felled trees to the temple site; and they clear and level a large tract of land overnight (*Yijian zhi* 7:9:5:950–51; 7:1:7:883–84; 11:6:9:1266–67).

One account about Hongzhou (now Nanchang county, Jiangxi) shows how deep a god's attachment to his temple could be. The local magistrate ordered the earth god's temple moved from its original site near a toilet to a more suitable setting within the temple of the god of walls and moats. Just as construction of the new hall was completed, the assistant magistrate dreamt that the earth god appeared and identified himself. Then he said:

> I have been worshipped on this site for a long time in this region. Although it is close to the toilet, no harm is done. If suddenly you move my temple, then all my followers, both young and old, will have no one to depend on. If I stay in the great deity's house, it will be inconvenient to enter and to leave, or to move and to rest. Please tell your superior that I would like to continue living at the old site. (*Yijian zhi* 9:4:13:1084–85)

This deity preferred the house to which he was accustomed to a new, more glamorous house largely because his devotees could visit him on the way to the toilet. If he had moved, then they would have had to make a special trip. For the earth god, as for all gods, human recognition was crucial to his well-being—even more so than a new dwelling.

Because deities were thought to inhabit their images and temples, people adorned them when they sought help. By the same token, when prayers failed, they coerced the deities by threatening to harm or by actually harming their images and temples. Bandits who failed to get a favorable moonblock reading to their request to burn down a city tried to drown the two main images in the temple. When the images had spasms and resisted, the frightened bandits fled (*Wuxing jinshi* 12:21b). When asking for rain, local officials often summoned images to their offices. Sometime between 1068 and 1083, a local magistrate brought an image to his office, locked it up, and vowed, "If it does not rain in three days, I will destroy your temple" (*Taizhou jinshi* 5:5a). Officials elsewhere used similar threats to bring rain or recover stolen wine (*Liangzhe jinshi* 2:14a–15b; *Kuocang jinshi* 2:1a; *Yijian zhi* 4:3:13:560–61; 15:15:2:1686–87). The Chinese gods were so human that officials could address them as equals, or even as their inferiors. Their clear and direct threats were couched in no uncertain terms.

Tales about these temples reveal much about contemporary attitudes toward temples but little about the size, tax obligations, or landholdings of popular temples. A popular temple could start as just an alcove in someone's house, and even a small temple did not require much upkeep. Many temples were located on the grounds of Buddhist or Daoist monasteries. For example, an 1197 inscription from Suzhou tells of an image "residing temporarily" (*yu*) in a Daoist monastery. Following a rainstorm, which the magistrate attributed to the deity, a new temple was built on the grounds of a Buddhist monastery (Beijing library, Gu collection 925). These popular temples had no land but were permitted to occupy a plot courtesy of the monastery.

Some temples did have land of their own. A 1227 inscription from a temple in Yixing county, Jiangsu, to a Jin dynasty hero, Zhou Chu,[7] offers rare insight into one such temple.[8] The organizer[9] begins by explaining that the temple had fallen into disrepair, and that the local people had decided to raise money to buy land to restore it: "The respect of the people is endless. But this temple has never had any endowed lands. To subject the god to having to ask for offerings from people cannot be called the meaning of reverence and worship. Today

----

7. Zhou Chu became a folk hero in later periods. As a youth he was a bully, but one day he suddenly reformed and asked the local elders how he could help them. At their bequest, he killed a wild beast that was threatening their village and then for three days and nights grappled with a dragon (*jiao*) before strangling it. He later served as a general and was killed in battle (*Jinshu* 58:1569–71).

8. See below for a discussion of an 1186 inscription from the same temple that describes the creation of a new set of divination sticks.

9. He is called donation-solicitor devout practitioner (*muyuan fenxiu daoshi*). The use of Buddhist terminology (*tanyue*, "donor," from the Sanskrit *dānapati*) and links to this popular temple suggest that *daoshi* does not mean ordained Daoist, but merely religious practitioner.

we want to set aside some land in perpetuity" (*Jiangsu jinshi* 15:22b; Beijing library, Gu collection 946). As other sources indicate that this temple was founded by 1119, if not before, it is reasonable to conclude that, lacking a fixed income, the temple had survived for over a hundred years on the basis of offerings from devotees (*Jiangsu jinshi* 11:38b–40a; *Xianchun Piling* 14:13a–14b). The next eight lines concern the deity's need for worship, money, and food; packed with references to Mencius, Chan Buddhist texts, and official histories, they suggest a high level of erudition, quite possibly self-conscious, on the part of the organizers. One line sums up their argument: "Because there is no permanent land, this means there can be no permanent devotion." A list of seventeen donors and their contributions, totaling thirty-two *mu*, follows (*Jiangsu jinshi* 15:22b–24a).[10] The high social level of the donors as well as the convoluted language of the text suggest that Zhou Chu's temple was better endowed than most.[11]

Even richer was King Zhang's base temple in Guangde Commandery (Anhui), possibly one of the largest in south China.[12] A 1262 inscription reports that the government granted 130,000 cash and 680 *dan* (64,500 liters) of rice to repair the temple. At the end of the reconstruction, thirteen halls (*dianyu*), thirty-five two-story buildings (*louyu*), six towers (*ge*), and five hallways (*langwu*) totaling 148 rooms were restored (*Cishan zhi* 10:28a). Although the temple gazetteer for Temple Mountain does not mention landholdings, so many buildings must have occupied considerable space, presumably on land belonging to the temple.

An official notification granting a tax exemption to a Suzhou branch temple to King Zhang in 1270 provides the only extant information about the tax status of popular temples (Beijing library, Gu collection 968-1). The monk in charge had petitioned the prefect, saying that because the four plots of over ninety *mu* the temple owned did not generate enough income to pay its taxes, it had to borrow money every year.[13] The document is addressed to a tax official in a monastery, suggesting that the temple was under the jurisdiction of the same office

10. A *mu* was a measure of area equal to 5.66 are in the Song (Ogawa 1968:1224–25). (An are is equal to 100 square meters, or 119.6 square yards.)

11. See Hansen (1987a:36–37) for details about the income generated by the land and the social standing of the donors.

12. See chapter 6 for more about King Zhang.

13. This document is from one of six prefectures in south China where the public field system (*gongtian fa*) was implemented. This reform, instituted in 1263, limited the total holdings an individual could possess. Whether or not it also applied to temples is not clear (Sudō 1954).

regulating monasteries. In the Song, a few monasteries were granted tax exemptions by the emperor, but most paid land taxes as well as a head tax on monks who did not perform corvée labor (Liu 1982: Chikusa 1982d). Similarly, the granting of this one exemption suggests popular temples did not enjoy tax-free status, but of course in the many cases where they had no land, they did not pay taxes.

Paucity of data prevents sweeping conclusions, but the landholdings of popular temples seem to have ranged in size, with most temples having little or no land, and a few, like King Zhang's base temple, having a great deal. Zhou Chu's temple with thirty-two *mu* and King Zhang's Suzhou branch temple with ninety *mu* fall in the middle range. One local history from a county in Ningbo gives landholdings for both Buddhist monasteries and popular temples (*Dade Changguozhou* 7:1–17a). Although dated 1297–1307, slightly after the end of the Southern Song, these figures offer the only basis for direct comparison between the landholdings of temples and monasteries.[14] The monasteries in the same county averaged holdings of 658.8 *mu* of paddy, 353.5 *mu* of dry land, and 1,340.1 *mu* of mountain land.[15] In sharp contrast are the small holdings of popular temples: the temple to Wenchang, a god who became an important regional deity in the Southern Song, had slightly more than 16 *mu*. The gazetteer lists several other popular temples without mentioning their landholdings. Very possibly they had none.

It would be foolhardy to generalize about the landholdings of popular temples on the basis of just these few examples, but several other indications suggest that, unlike many Buddhist and Daoist monasteries, popular temples usually rested on small plots. Temple inscriptions almost never list landholdings.[16] Government regulations required that a Buddhist monastery have more than thirty rooms before it could receive government recognition; no such requirement existed for popular temples. Most significant is that many stories circulating in the Song credited the gods with a desire for beautiful portraits, for accurate images, for refurbished temples, and for longer government titles,

14. Liu (1982) compares the figures contained in the two local histories from 1225–1227 and 1297–1307 and concludes that the monastic holdings of paddy land increased 27.5 percent between 1225–1227 and 1297–1307, and those in dry and mountain land, 155.6 percent.

15. There was, of course, a range, with 28 percent having under 100 *mu*, 65 percent between 100 and 1,000 *mu*, and 7 percent over 1,000 *mu*. The largest monastery had 12,408 *mu* of all types of land.

16. This may, however, simply be an omission on the part of those making the rubbings.

but never for land. No record survives in which someone dreamt that a deity asked for more land for his temple. This telling silence confirms that popular temples had little, if any, land.

The small size of temple endowments resulted in a greater dependence on regular contributions from devotees for their upkeep (a dependence that the man organizing the campaign to donate land to the Zhou Chu temple viewed as unseemly). This very dependence meant that in the absence of continued miracles, a popular temple would fall into disrepair. *The Record of the Listener* is legion with instances of gods appearing to people who wanted to occupy temples that were no longer active (*Yijian zhi* 5:9:4:781–82; 8:9:13:1034; 10:6:6:1182–83; 11:2:9:1235–36). Of course, no one wrote inscriptions for a temple whose god they no longer viewed as powerful: devotees simply stopped making offerings, and the temple declined. Popular temples, then, were fragile entities. Lacking land of their own, their upkeep was inextricably tied to the ability of the resident deity to perform miracles.

The gods' dependence on people resulted in a curious circularity. The gods who performed the most miracles were those most deserving recompense, so they had the most opulent images and the most lavish temples. According to the same logic, those deities with the most opulent images and the most lavish temples must have performed the most miracles. If an individual or a group wanted to start a new cult, or to increase support for a certain deity it backed, it had only to make new images and construct new temples. Doing so was thought to encourage the deity to perform more miracles. Such actions, not coincidentally, would also have had the effect of convincing others of the deity's power.

Communicating with the Gods

Although the Song gods were viewed as having many human qualities, and although people addressed them just as they would address other people, the gods' responses usually lacked the comprehensibility of human speech. One exception was spirit possession: some gods spoke with extraordinary clarity to mediums. Hong Mai tells of a medium from Chong'an county (Jiangxi) who was possessed in 1161 by a deity who said, "I must go far away and during this time will not be able to answer questions or cure illness." The medium responded, "For a long time I have depended on your power for my livelihood and have burnt incense and worshipped you without fail. I do not know why you abandon me now." The god explained that, because rebels were coming from the south, the city god had summoned him and many other local gods to fight them. When asked when he would return, he said sometime in the winter of the following year.

Subsequently a rich local man fell ill and sought the services of the medium, who beseeched the deity many times to no avail. In the twelfth month, the deity announced both that the rebel leader had been vanquished and that he had been released from his duties. He resumed his miracles (*Yijian zhi* 4:6:6:585). Little in this account distinguishes the god's interaction with the medium from a conversation between humans; he speaks clearly, responds to questions, and explains his behavior. The medium, although frustrated, is not confused by the god's absence. This ease of communication was rare; far more common was uncertainty on the part of devotees about how to interpret the ambiguous messages of the gods.

Deities frequently appeared to individuals in dreams and visions; at times, the recipient was sound asleep, at times, half-awake or in a daze. Some of these dreams were solicited: people would stay overnight at temples famous for enabling visitors to dream about a deceased family member or a deity.[17] An unvoiced dream could be intensely private, experienced by only one person,[18] but, as soon as he (or she) talked about it, it entered the public domain. And in a society like the Song, where people were constantly trying to interpret the behavior of deities, dreams offered a specificity that other sources of information did not.

Deities appearing in dreams often identified themselves and made their wishes explicit—as, for example, the King of Opportune Aid, who requested a stele. In 1109 an official named Lu Zao, who accompanied his brother to Ruijin county (Jiangxi), dreamt that

> he moored his boat on a river bank, climbed the northern shore, and saw an impressive temple. An imposingly dressed man bowed and said: "I am the King of Opportune Aid (Shunji wang). Why have you come here? My temple has just been built. You should note this down for me, then write it out."
> Lu Zao hesitated and then refused, saying: "If you want to make an inscription, you need to carve a stone. There are no suitable stones here. If you want to write a text, my characters are not

17. This is still true in Taiwan today. Zhinan gong, just outside of Taibei, is such a temple.

18. In unusual cases, two or three people had the same dream—as in the case of the two officials who dreamt that they were beaten for not giving enough to famine relief (*Yijian zhi* 15:9:5:1630).

suitable.[19] Furthermore, I am unknown and not qualified for such a task." Then he mentioned the name of a high-ranking court official, saying, "Your majesty can entrust him to do it."

The king, looking serious and sounding severe, said, "Who says that Nankang lacks suitable stones? Who says that I do not know famous officials at court? Just write down what I say with no further excuses." (*Yijianzhi* 8:1:1:968–69)

Two years later, when he was serving as an official in a neighboring district, Lu Zao dreamt again of the deity, and then a few days later the local people reported a strange apparition. They built a temple to the King of Opportune Aid, for which Lu Zao finally wrote the inscription. Not content just to see the text, the King of Opportune Aid knows both what kind of stone is necessary and what kind of credentials the author must possess. All of this information is imparted through a dream.

Such a dream was not unusual; judging from *The Record of the Listener*, encounters with deities in dreams occurred all the time. Because dreams lacking independent confirmation were subject to considerable skepticism, many, but not all, accounts about appearances in dreams include some external detail that backs up whatever the deity had said in the dream.[20] Hong Mai tells of the son of a vice-censor-in-chief (*yushi zhongcheng*) who, in 1116, on a visit to the Kaifeng temple to an important examination god named Pichang, saw one of the shoes his father had been wearing when buried. That night he dreamt that his father visited him, saying, "I have died and become a god, with a lot of power, no less than when I was alive and a commander (*shuai*). I know you are poor and hard-up; tomorrow I will send five hundred strings of cash to you." When the son awoke, not only did he find the money, but even a gift card as well, which said, "Great King Pichang sends Lord Xi three hundred strings of cash" (*Yijian zhi* 1:5:10:39–40).[21]

An 1124 inscription from a Guanyin temple in Jiangyin (Jiangsu) begins with the appearance in 1023 of a strange light that tailed an

19. Emending *gong* (work) to *qiao* (skillful).

20. An inscription from a Jiangsu monastery in Huating county, Xiuzhou, dated 1046, records that a deity appeared to a dreaming monk in 713, claimed he had originally occupied the site of the monastery, and asked the monk to build him a temple. On awakening, the monk discovered a buried inscription in the corner of the monastery grounds, just as the deity had predicted (*Jiangsu jinshi* 8:51a).

21. As Hong Mai offers no explanation for the missing two hundred strings, this is very likely a textual corruption, with subsequent editors mistaking three (*san*) for five (*wu*).

ocean-going boat. On the same night that the light appeared, a local man dreamt that a white-robed female figure appeared and asked him for an arm. When he protested that it would be very difficult to find one locally, she told him about a local merchant who had a block of sandalwood just the right size. The next day he went to inquire and heard the people in the market saying, "On the banks of the Yangzi river, Guanyin came in from the sea. She is several *zhang* tall." And when he went to see the image, she was indeed missing a left arm. Subsequently he obtained the block of sandalwood over five *chi* long from the merchant—and it fit perfectly (*Baqiong shi jinshi* 111:28a–30b).[22] Before going to market and consulting with others, the dreamer did not know who the white-robed woman was. The block of sandalwood that fit the image exactly provided the clinching piece of evidence.

In addition to dreams, other means of soliciting a deity's opinion existed, but what they offered in increased numbers of witnesses they lost in specificity. One relationship characterizes all Song records of communication with the deities: the clearer the message, the fewer the recipients. The more ambiguous—and as such the more open to interpretation—the utterance, the greater the number of witnesses. Either one person was sure he had encountered a deity or many people thought they might have.

Oracles allowed direct, public questioning of the gods, who would respond with moonblocks, spirit-writing, or divination sticks, but their responses were often difficult to understand. The most popular of these oracles, and by far the easiest to use, were moonblocks.[23] Cheng Dachang (1123–1195) in his *Extended Commentaries* says this type of prognostication originated with people tossing two oyster shells in the air and examining the way they landed. Later they made blocks from bamboo or wood, carved in the shape of a clamshell. In out-of-the-way temples, people sometimes made blocks from bamboo root. One shell face-up and one face-down constituted a positive reading (*Yanfan lu* 3:1b–3a).[24] Cheng's account of the origins of moon-

22. A *zhang* equaled 3.072 meters, and a *chi*, 30.72 centimeters (Ogawa 1968:1224–25).

23. Hong Mai consistently uses the term *beijiao*, but the high number of variants both the *Yanfan lu* and the *Daikanwa jiten* give for *jiao* suggests that this term was originally spoken and transcribed in many different ways. Either syllable (*bei* or *jiao*) is used in Mandarin to refer to the blocks.

24. See also Jordan (1982) about moonblocks and their use in Taiwan today. He points out that most people think three positive tosses constitute approval of the god and calculates that the odds of a positive reading on one toss are one in two; in three tosses, one in eight. Thus, to get a positive reading may require many tosses. Jordan comments,

blocks is speculative, but his description of their use and manufacture is clearly based on observation.

Surviving sources make it impossible to ascertain how often or why people cast moonblocks to solicit the gods' opinions, but their very simplicity assured their wide use. Even the totally illiterate could, by tossing the blocks, ask a god's opinion. If some people went to temples to ask for help on a daily basis, others went only at critical junctures; some may not have gone at all. A scene from *Zhang Xie Comes First in the Exams* suggests, however, that it was standard to consult the gods before marrying. The protagonist, an exam candidate who is robbed and beaten on his way from Chengdu to Hangzhou, takes refuge in the temple of a local earth god where he meets a gentle, beautiful woman, aptly named Poor Girl (Pinnü).

In one scene, the anonymous author pokes fun at the earth god (*tudi*) and his underlings whose only interest in the couple reflects their craving for the meat and wine that were customary offerings to the gods at a wedding. One subordinate says, "Probably Zhang Xie and Poor Girl will toss moonblocks. If so, they will marry. If so, they will be joined together. If so, there will be a thousand and ten thousand couplings." The earth-god replies, "If they have a pig head to offer, then I will show them a pig face and a dog face [one flat side and one convex side up, a positive reading]."

Poor Girl's heartfelt prayer to the gods contrasts sharply with their off-color jokes and longing for meat: "The gods are far off and their power incomprehensible. If they bestow a favorable moonblock reading, then I will be allowed to marry. If not, we will hurriedly part and not be joined eternally" (*Xiwen sanzhong* 83–85). Her earnest tone suggests that whatever the verdict of the gods is, she will accept it. After a favorable toss of the moonblocks, Zhang and Poor Girl spend the night together. Zhang's social status, that of the stereotypical impoverished exam candidate, makes it difficult to pin down his background. He comes from a family wealthy enough to have financed his education, but after he has been robbed, it is Poor Girl who raises the requisite funds to send him to the capital to sit for the civil service examinations. Her asking the gods for permission suggests that peasant families tossed moonblocks; his joining her, that wealthy did too.

In granting permission for them to marry, as in other cases, the deity could respond only in the affirmative or negative to those questions put to him. Excessively hemmed in by having to give yes or no re-

---

"As any worshipper knows, it sometimes takes a long time before you can get a god to agree to something" (1982:116).

sponses, the deities occasionally used moonblocks in more creative ways to express themselves. Hong Mai reports an instance sometime between 1127 and 1130 when a bandit leader, Ma Jin, repeatedly and unsuccessfully tossed moonblocks to obtain the deity's permission to conquer Xingguo Commandery (now Yangxin county, Hubei). The bandit grew angry and made up his own rules for the use of the blocks: "If I get a favorable reading of the blocks, I will butcher the city. If I get an unfavorable reading, I will butcher the city and set fire to this temple as well." He tossed the blocks again. One fell to the ground. The other disappeared. Suddenly the missing block appeared upright on the door jamb several feet way. The bandit, both surprised and terrified, bowed and took his leave (*Yijian zhi* 4:2:5:547). Ma's acquiescence, although belated and grudging, testifies to the seriousness with which people took moonblocks.

The oracle of the Purple Maiden (Zigu), like moonblocks, was originally able to give only affirmative and negative responses; by the Song, she had become the primary goddess of spirit-writing. A fifth-century text reports that the Purple Maiden was thought to have been a concubine hounded to death by her husband's first wife. On the anniversary of her demise, the fifteenth day of the first month, women placed small images of her by the toilet. She would respond to questions, which were often about the raising of silkworms. If she approved, then the figure danced, if not, it remained still (*Yiyuan* 5:5a; Jordan and Overmyer 1986:38). Shen Gua (1030–1086) reports that by the eleventh century, literati conducted spirit-writing sessions to ask the Purple Maiden questions year round, no longer limiting themselves to the fifteenth day of the first month (*Mengxi bitan* 21:685–86).[25] Another important change dating to the Song was that other gods, and even the spirits of dead people, began to convey messages through spirit-writing, a technique which had once been exclusively the Purple Maiden's.

One or two people held a brush or some kind of pointed tool which the Purple Maiden caused to move, either on paper or in sand. Someone then explained what the god had written. Su Shi (1036–1101) describes three different kinds of tools used in automatic writing: a clothed doll of grass and wood held a chopstick in her hands, a brush was clasped between two chopsticks, or a dustpan and broom were connected to a stick (*Dongpo quanji* 13:30a–b). By the Southern Song,

25. Several excellent studies of spirit-writing are available. See Xu (1941), Chao (1942), Kani (1972), and, most recently, Jordan and Overmyer (1986), whose study traces the history of spirit-writing and then situates it in the context of sectarian movements in modern Taiwan.

most common was a winnowing basket (*ji*), to which a stick or chopstick was attached; as the people holding the winnowing basket were possessed and jerked it around, the stick moved in dirt or sand in a tray beneath it (Kani 1972:62). Unlike other deities, the Purple Maiden did not have her own temple; spirit-writing sessions were held in people's houses or other buildings (as in the case of Sheriff Chen's consultation in chapter 2).[26] Several entries in *The Record* testify to the popularity of spirit-writing in the twelfth century, especially among literati who consulted the goddess about their chances of success in the civil service examinations (*Yijian zhi* 9:2:10:1065–66).

In the thirteenth century, Zhou Mi (1232–1298) devoted a section of his miscellaneous notes, *Scattered Talk from East of Qi*, to spirit-writing. He introduces the section, saying,

> In the case of spirit-possession, many people think that the person holding the winnowing basket is playing a trick on the observers standing by, or that people use already finished poems and claim they are the works of an immortal (*xian*). In fact, this is not so. It is just that those who are able to summon ghosts (*gui*) are those who are able to write.

Many of the responses from the Purple Maiden that Zhou cites in the supporting eight anecdotes are in perfectly rhymed five- or ten-character phrases: no wonder people suspected they had been composed before the session. Zhou's tone here suggests that spirit-writing in the Song resembled the ouija-board craze in America following World War II: the verb *xi* (to play) is regularly used to mean to consult the Purple Maiden. Once several concubines who belonged to Zhou's uncle asked the goddess to write a poem on a fan: the resulting oracle contained one of the women's names, confirming its power. Zhou concludes the section about spirit-writing with a tale in which the soul of a dead official took the brush: "I do not know whether or not this was true, but everyone who read the tale felt a chill." Some of the people consulting the Purple Maiden could have been completely in earnest; others, like the frolicking concubines, were not (*Qidong yeyu* 18:299–301).

Like moonblocks, spirit-writing afforded both the illiterate and the literate access to the gods; unlike moonblocks, spirit-writing required the services of at least a partially literate interpreter. The movements

---

26. There were exceptions: in 1112, following a particularly spectacular demonstration in Hubei when she wrote one giant character on two hundred pieces of paper, a temple to her was authorized (*Chunzhu jiwen* 4:64).

of the brush or chopstick produced an extremely cursive script—squiggles, really—bearing little resemblance to actual characters. The interpreter then had the job of deciding what the god had said. Although he had to know some characters, he did not necessarily have to have a classical education; he simply had to be a little more literate than his audience. A slightly educated practitioner who could read only a few hundred characters was liable to become the laughing stock of a literati spirit-writing group, but his services would have been more than convincing for a group of illiterate clients. Without a skilled interpreter, the Purple Maiden's messages would have remained squiggles in sand; with one, she could give crucial information about the exams.

Because one had to be able to read to use divination sticks, the illiterate had to consult someone, possibly a resident temple caretaker, to make sense of the information these oracles presented. Song sources mention divination sticks (*qian*) without actually describing them. If they are like those in use in Taiwan today, after shaking many thin sticks (often made of bamboo) in a can, one picks the stick that protrudes farthest. The stick is keyed to a chest containing fortunes; the fortune contains the answer to one's original question, often in obscure language. One 1186 inscription from the Yixing county temple to the Jin dynasty hero Zhou Chu (mentioned above) gives the most concentrated information about Song use of divination sticks. It also illustrates the complex interplay of different types of oracles—dreams, moonblocks, and divination sticks—in ultimately determining the god's will.

Zhou Rong takes down the tale of the local man (*yishi*) who designed the divination sticks in use at the temple, one Ma Xianmin:

> I passed by the temple in 1125-1126 and wanted to use Guanyin-type divination sticks,[27] but in the ensuing chaos of the Jin attacks from the north, I forgot my original intention. Four years later I dreamt that the deity Zhou Chu gave me two divination sticks and said, "I have heard that you wanted to use the sticks. Would you please explain these to me?" One was entitled "when *yin* meets *geng*, shoot a tiger," the other, "when *chen* meets *ren*, behead a dragon."[28] The characters were as clear as if one saw them in

27. The text does not explain how these might have differed from other types. It mentions three types in all: the Guanyin sticks, the Daoist sticks, and the new sticks.

28. These refer to actual events in Zhou Chu's life. *Geng* and *ren* were two of the ten celestial stems, and *yin* and *chen* were two of the twelve branches. These were usually used to generate a cycle of sixty, on which the Chinese calendar was based. Here, how-

broad daylight. When I awoke, I did not understand, but then I remembered my earlier impulse to visit the temple and wondered if this was somehow connected.

The next day, Mr. Ma went to the temple to cast moonblocks to get permission to use the divination sticks, but the blocks gave a negative answer. After consulting with some kind of resident specialist,[29] he realized that the deity would not permit him to use either the preexisting sticks or those of a Daoist type. He left the temple slightly perturbed and met a Daoist who, on hearing the tale, explained that the god wanted Mr. Ma to make a new set of divination sticks, incorporating the two he had seen in the dream. Mr. Ma went back to the temple, and all the moonblock responses were positive. After Mr. Ma had finished making the sticks, the deity appeared in a dream to another follower and asked that the sticks containing the taboo character *chu* ("place," which was the god's given name) be altered. Finally the sticks were ready to use (*Jiangsu jinshi* 11:38b–40a). Mr. Ma's perplexity colors the entire narrative; following his strange dream, he consulted two specialists. Only the second was able to provide an explanation that moonblocks subsequently confirmed.

Interpreters for the Gods

Mr. Ma's experience was probably typical of most: confronting bad reception, people would consult any available specialist in order to receive the gods' message more clearly. On certain rare occasions, as when Mr. Ma asked the Daoist about his dream, lay people might consult one of the Buddhist or Daoist practitioners mentioned in the previous chapter. More often they asked temple caretakers, literate acquaintances, or even just their friends and relatives for help in determining what the gods wanted. Various individuals, unnamed and behind-the-scenes, elucidated these different oracles. They were not necessarily educated, and they may not have worked full time, but they had the ability to unravel the tangled messages of the gods. The simplicity of the reciprocity principle and the highly anthropomorphized logic governing the behavior of the gods point to people who were not

---

ever, these refer to writing on specific divination sticks, which were marked with these symbols: according to the Daoist, all the permutations were used, resulting in a total of 120 sticks.

29. Unfortunately there is a gap in the text here, which reads *shi   zhe .qiu shen yi* (causing   type of person to seek the god's intention). I would supply *dao* (way) or *shu* (technique), which results in "Daoist" or "technician."

necessarily either highly educated or familiar with Buddhist and Daoist doctrine. In some cases full-time religious specialists did the explaining, but the basic principles and simple logic could be used by anyone.

Other entries in *The Record* indicate how much influence these explicators wielded. Without them, people might simply have concluded that a given god was no longer powerful. An exam candidate in Ganzhou (Jiangxi) went to a temple hoping to have a dream; in the middle of the night he heard a cry, "On the second examinations held in Ganzhou, you will attain the rank of prefect." Although the voice used the Tang dynasty term, *cishi*, the man assumed the god meant he would become a prefect (*junshou*). He subsequently developed heart disease. Ten years later he fell while going up the stairs to an outhouse and died. Hong's informant explains that the deity had spoken in a muffled voice and that the man had therefore mistaken the word for toilet-death, *cesi*, as the word for prefect, *cishi* (*Yijian zhi* 14:1:3:1469). Surely the person who concocted this explanation was a devotee of the temple in question. And surely Hong Mai relished this tale because it was so funny.

The word-play in this story may seem laughable, but it raises the issue of theodicy: how to account for death and suffering given the presence of the gods. An inscription from a temple to two local officials in Huzhou provides further insight into this problem:

> In 1240 the bodies of famine victims lay in disorder—as if strewn on a battlefield—in two corridors of the temple. It was very dirty. A disgusted monk burnt incense and prayed to the deity. That night the deity told him, "The poor people have no homes to return to. They are staying under my roof to avoid the wind and rain. If I send them away, then who can they depend on?" From this incident one can clearly see the deity's deep compassion. (*Wuxing jinshi* 12:21a)

No irony seems intended here. Unlike the toilet-death incident, the failed harvest, the ensuing famine, and mass deaths cannot be explained away as a misunderstanding of the god's garbled speech. One can easily understand the despair of the people; they certainly must have questioned the gods' power to protect them. We do not know whether or not they were convinced by the monk's dream; we do know that the temple survived the famine year and that the gods later resumed performing miracles (*Wuxing jinshi* 12:21a–b). This inscription, unlike most, indicates who was doing the interpreting: the resident monk in the temple, who certainly had a stake in encouraging the people not to give up their worship of the two gods.

Accounting for disaster taxed the explanatory powers of a deity's supporters to the fullest. When a local magistrate in Jing county (Anhui) took office, the head clerk told him he should visit a local temple within three days. The official, a Daoist practitioner of the thunder rites, refused. After his office was flooded in a terrible storm, soaking all his documents, the local people concluded the god was punishing the official. In another case, in spite of a boatman's repeated urging, another official failed to make the requisite offering of a pig to a Suzhou dragon deity, commenting irreverently, "He's eaten my pigs continuously. Surely he's stuffed." A sea squall resulted during which many people drowned. And in 1173, an official leading a convoy of horses ignored the advice of a soldier and failed to enter the Hanyang (Hubei) temple to the god of walls and moats. About half the horses died (*Yijian zhi* 6:8:1:853; 2:15:11:314; 7:7:1:932). In each of these cases first a calamity occurred: a storm, a sea squall, the mass death of the horses. Then an explanation was worked out: the officials who ignored the counsel of a local person to worship a local god brought disaster upon themselves. The appearance of a common topos in places so far apart suggests a common pool of interpretative mechanisms—all variations on the principle of reciprocity—available to those interpreting the acts of the gods.

When calamities occurred, people looked for someone to interpret the behavior of the gods. Similarly, when oracles pointed in several directions at once, as when moonblock readings contradicted other sources of information, people often consulted specialists to help them decide which kinds of evidence to weight more heavily. An exam candidate in Jianyang prefecture (Fujian) asked a local deity if he should sit for the local exams and received three negative moonblock readings. The candidate took this to mean that he should not, but then he dreamt that the deity told him, "When your honor visited, I had just gone to Yan mountain to attend a banquet. My wife, who is not qualified to examine [the moonblocks], mistakenly caused the three negative responses." When the candidate visited the temple again, he received all positive responses and subsequently passed the exams (*Yijian zhi* 4:5:10:578). Hong Mai does not mention whether or not the candidate consulted with anyone, but it seems likely that he talked to other people—maybe a full-time specialist, maybe just his wife or a friend—about the negative readings and what his dream meant.

Because people viewed certain natural events, especially rain, as under the control of the gods, they prayed to them for rain or clear skies, much as they asked for a sick child to be cured or for protection from rebels. Dramatic changes in weather, like oracles, were viewed as responses to prayers. How did people decide which deity was responsible for bringing rain? One topos recurs throughout twelfth- and thirteenth-century temple inscriptions. After unsuccessfully praying for rain at all the other local temples, the local magistrate goes to the deity who is the subject of the inscription and prays. And when the rain comes, it confirms that deity's power. One 1240 inscription from Shaoxing offers slightly more detail than the standard line about having fruitlessly prayed to all the other gods: "The local officials prayed to the city god (*siyong*)[30] but there was no response. The elders prayed to the village gods with no response" (*Yuezhong jinshi* 5:45a). The deities who fail to perform are almost never referred to by name, perhaps to avoid humiliating them and so incurring their ire.

One is supposed to infer that the deity most recently prayed to must be the one responsible for the rain. These texts suggest a deceptively orderly process, in which everyone prays together at one temple, waits, then when there is no rain, prays at the next temple, and so on. Reality must have been much more complex. In times of severe drought, people probably prayed at several temples at once—and they prayed both as individuals and in groups. The Chinese liked to cover their bets and saw nothing wrong with simultaneously consulting different religious specialists or deities (as I have argued in chapter 2). Under such circumstances, with people praying at the same time to different deities, sorting out the claims was far from the simple process the inscriptions suggest it was.

Because inscriptions record attributions only after they were made, no evidence survives concerning the negotiations leading up to consensus. Allow me to suggest that conflicting claims could be resolved only as the result of a social process. Followers of different deities, working in concert with religious specialists, constructed different explanations for why it was their deity who had brought the rain. And whoever constructed the most compelling explanation persuaded others of that deity's power. Surely in some instances followers of rival deities maintained claims to the same miracles.[31] Usually, however, one claim came to prevail, and that claim is the one appearing in the historical record. Incorporating all information—from dreams, oracles, and natural events—into a seamless narrative was similar to the

---

30. Literally the four walls, meaning the four walls around the city. The walls are a metonym for the city, and here, by extension, the city god (Victor Mair, personal communication, November 1986).

31. See chapter 5 for one example.

task of those who originally interpreted the oracles and dreams; the authors of the final, polished versions in temple inscriptions have edited out all the confusion and doubt in order to demonstrate the deity's power. These interpreters not only constructed explanations, they actively propagated them. Groups well-organized or rich enough had different means of publicizing a deity's exploits and downplaying its failures: using word-of-mouth, building and refurbishing temples and erecting images, carving laudatory inscriptions, printing pictures of the deity, sponsoring theatrical troupes, and seeking government titles.

Some of these activities generated more material evidence than others. Word-of-mouth itself left no trace but ultimately resulted in the compilation of *The Record of the Listener* and other miscellaneous notes. Travelers traded local products as well as tales about the accomplishments of deities; some, like Hong Mai, wrote down what they heard. Temple inscriptions were carved to establish a permanent record for the benefit of both people and the gods. Although few original steles survive, rubbings and transcriptions by subsequent generations of epigraphers make them available today. These sources underpin the above account of popular religious ideas.

The development of wood-block printing in the Song made it easier for people to print sheets of paper with pictures of the gods on them. Their fragility meant that few survived. Hong Mai reports that two devotees of Guanyin used printing to recompense her for her miracles. In 1175, following the death of his only son the year before, a man from Leping county (Jiangxi) visited a monastery in Shuzhou (now Huaining county, Anhui). A monk there advised him, "I have a picture of Guanyin that is very efficacious and powerful. I now give it to you. If you can have wood blocks carved to print and distribute the picture, you will definitely get what you pray for." A year later the man's wife gave birth to a son. Similarly, in Ningbo, sometime between 1190 and 1194, a young widow fell deaf and dumb. "Barely literate, she could only write on a piece of paper every time she needed something." Within a month of her nephew's praying to Guanyin, she was cured. The nephew subsequently printed an account of the miracle in order to publicize it (*Yijian zhi* 8:1:3:969; 8:1:2:969).[32] Hong Mai does not tell us the source of the tales, but it may have been the flyers themselves. Both the monk who advised the bereaved father and the

---

32. These tales may be derived from the Buddhist idea that one way to generate merit is to commission the hand-copying (or later printing) of sutras.

nephew who prayed to Guanyin realized the importance of printing as a way to publicize miracles and generate support for the goddess.

Like printed pictures of deities, theatrical performances at temple festivals left few traces. Zhu Yu (1048–c. 1102), a native of Canton, gives one of the few available descriptions of theater in the Lower Yangzi:

> Also they [the worshippers of deities in Jiangnan] use puppets to amuse the gods. They call the job of the exorcist doing a play. Whenever there is a troupe, they allow them to put up several tents for plays. At the time of the religious procession, they perform music and manipulate puppets. At first they burn spirit money and incense to pray. *It is just like worshipping a god.* When they perform, there are dirty jokes which cause the crowds to laugh. Anything is liable to happen. The villagers gather to observe and to drink. When they become intoxicated, they get in fights. (*Pingzhou ketan* 3:13a, emphasis mine)

The ubiquity of popular religious theater startled Zhu, whose comments about the religious nature of the performance confirm Piet van der Loon's (1977) suggestion that the plays done at temples performed a similar function to that of the Daoist *jiao*: both were purification rites designed to cleanse the community. After his retirement from government service, Lu You (1125–1210) wrote many poems about being old and going to the theater for amusement (Iwaki 1963). In one, written around 1200, he says:

> In the north of the alley I observe the shrine to the earth god.
> In the east of the village I see the theater.
> Who knows the meaning of their being side-by-side?
> (*Jiannan shigao* 80:5)

If I may go where Lu You fears to tread, temples and stages are linked because, like inscriptions, the plays were directed at an audience consisting first of the gods, and only secondarily of people.[33] As all of these means of honoring the gods—building temples, putting up images, sponsoring plays, printing pictures, and carving inscriptions—

---

33. Modern practice in Taiwan certainly suggests this. Stages are constructed just opposite of temples, so that the gods sit in the seats of honor, and people watch from the side. Barbara Ward (1985:165) says of Hong Kong theater: "Unlike the secular shows, the primary object of the festival performance is neither commercial nor artistic; it is to please a deity or deities." Archeologists working in north China have excavated several stages from the eleventh, twelfth, and thirteenth centuries on temple grounds (Idema and West 1982:89–90).

cost money, those who had disposable income definitely had an advantage over those who did not. Although little evidence survives about the activities of the poor on behalf of their deities, presumably they were also honoring the gods as much as possible within the limitations of their resources.

Changing Conceptions of Divine Power

The religious system described in this and the previous chapter lacked a fixed body of written doctrine. Lay people chose among practitioners and gods on the basis of efficacy, and they accounted for the doings of the gods by generalizing from their knowledge of human nature. The very supple nature of Chinese popular religion granted devotees and practitioners ample room for innovation: whoever provided the most compelling explanation could persuade others of the power of the god he (or she) worshipped. This flexibility meant that popular religion was especially sensitive to the developments taking place in the lives of devotees. Nowhere is this sensitivity to social and economic change clearer than in the changing understanding of divine power in the twelfth and thirteenth centuries. Of course, the expression of divine power continued to take certain forms throughout the Song and even into the twentieth century. The gods were thought to cure illness, to enable women to conceive, to bring rain and clear weather, and to protect communities from locusts, pillaging troops, and epidemics. But a few temple inscriptions and entries in *The Record* indicate that the gods acquired a new commercial expertise and began to perform different kinds of miracles in the Southern Song.

Two temple inscriptions from Zhejiang, the region that witnessed the most dramatic economic changes in the Song, illustrate this godly diversification. Zhao Bing (a magician from the Han dynasty), the deity of the Efficacious Abundance (Lingkang) temple in Taizhou (Linhai county, Zhejiang), had demonstrated his power in usual ways: repulsing the Jurchen invaders, protecting the emperor in a storm, and bringing rain and good harvests. Sometime before 1131, his district was hit by famine. Traditionally deities would send rain or a good harvest or somehow alleviate the suffering of the dying. But Zhao assumes human form and appears to grain merchants in Fujian and Guangdong, telling them: "My name is Zhao. I am a rich man from Taizhou. The price of grain in Taizhou is high. If you ship grain there, you will make profits." No doubt the price of grain was high, as it was during a famine. When the grain-bearing merchants arrived ten days later, they sought out the merchant who had advised them to come to

Taizhou, but the only person of the surname Zhao was the deity (*Taizhou jinshi* 5:5a). The deity has capitalized on market dynamics. By serving as a broker of information in a time when news of commodity prices traveled slowly, he helped the people of his district to avert starvation. This miracle suggests that Song people both understood that prices varied among different regions and valued up-to-date price information.

An 1160 inscription from Yin county, in the commercial center of Ningbo, tells of a similar diversification. Although the local deity, the Broadly Efficacious (Guangling) King, has protected the district for over a hundred years, helping in times of drought, flooding, famine, and epidemics, the local people have allowed his temple to fall into disrepair. A Buddhist monk[34] appears and prays to the deity, saying, "If you, the King, can bring our district repeated good harvests, I will definitely and energetically work to rebuild the temple." The inscription continues, "Subsequently an excellent crop came onto the market and the profits of fish and salt merchants increased tenfold. Those who had had difficulty obtaining food and clothing themselves were transformed immediately into the rich" (*Liangzhe jinshi* 9:10a–b). Gone is the phrasing of earlier inscriptions—here there is not just rain and a good crop, but a tenfold increase in profits! The terms of religious discourse are shifting to include the more commercialized language of the marketplace.

The range of events prompting supernatural explanations broadened throughout the twelfth and thirteenth centuries. For example, Hong Mai reports in 1183 in Fuliang (Jiangxi), one peasant tried to make rice wine. The first batch was ready to be sold at New Year's. After he ladled it out, he added water in order to feed the leftover grain to pigs. Two days later the brew gave off a fragrance and turned out to be a delicious wine. He subsequently added more water and got more wine. The neighbors initially thought he was tricking them, but once they visited the wine-making site, they decided a deity was protecting him, and they extended their congratulations. But subsequently all the wine turned to water, a development Hong does not explain (*Yijian zhi* 8:7:7:1022–23). Still, this man's neighbors evidently credited the gods with a knowledge of wine-making that they themselves had yet to acquire.

Hong Mai also tells of a family outside Jianchang (Nancheng county, Jiangxi) who consult the spirit-writing goddess, the Purple

---

34. This monk was probably an unordained religious specialist like those mentioned in chapter 2.

Maiden. She has advised them where the price of tea is high and which districts are short of rice, enabling them to make a profit. Then she tells them that a beggar will arrive and that they should treat him kindly. When the beggar appears, they offer him clothes and a bath and hold a spirit-writing session. Sobbing in response to the Purple Maiden's question, "Have you forgotten the incident of the Azure Wave Hall?" the visitor admits that there he had drowned a prostitute with whom he had eloped. The family gives him several hundred taels of silver and sends him off. From that time on they stop worshipping the Purple Maiden (*Yijian zhi* 1:16:7:140). Even though her predictions were startlingly accurate, the family has lost money by following her advice; Hong Mai provides no explanation for why the Purple Maiden instructs them to give the beggar money. And in an age of commercialization the issue was not just whether the deity could perform but whether she brought profit. Commercial farmers who were growing rice and tea for the market did not reward the deity for correct, but costly, advice.

Like the Purple Maiden, Lü Dongbin, who appeared earlier in this chapter as a connoisseur of his own portraits, reveals a growing commercial acuity. In 1158 a reed-mat merchant, who is going by boat from Huating county (Jiaxing) to Hangzhou with a full load of mats, reluctantly gives a ride to a Daoist, who, on arrival, bids him farewell, saying, "I will enable you to get twenty thousand to reward you." The merchant does not understand, but, just at this time, because the demand for reed mats in Chengdu is so great, there are not enough in Hangzhou, where a major imperial ceremony, the suburban sacrifices, is to be conducted. The Hangzhou governor is so frightened by the prospect of a shortage that he orders the government to pay an extra two cash to any merchant surpassing his quota. The government buys all the merchant's mats, and he makes twenty thousand cash. At the bottom of the pile of mats on the boat is a note from the Daoist saying, "Lü Dongbin rode in this boat" (*Yijian zhi* 15:12:6:1655–56). Were this tale told in more traditional terms, Lü Dongbin would have arranged for the money to be delivered to the merchant directly; here he combines his knowledge of the dynamics of the national market in mats and of the government's purchasing system to give the merchant money. Lü is well-versed in the ways of entrepreneurs.

The story does not end here. Lü Dongbin, famed for his sense of playfulness, appears the next day at market selling ginger. The mat merchant bows to him and says, "As you are Master Lü and can change things into gold, you can give me more money." Lü smilingly replies, "Watch this ginger for me, and I'll go back to my store to get the gold." The merchant waits until sunset, and when Lü doesn't reappear, he takes the ginger home in a handcart. Lü Dongbin is having fun here; when met with a demand for more money instead of gratitude, he leaves the merchant stuck with his ginger. And Hong Mai too is poking fun at the greedy merchant, whom he calls an idiot. In this tale a sharpened awareness of profits meshes nicely with the more traditional values of reverence for the gods.

Little that has been described in this chapter will surprise those familiar with nineteenth- and twentieth-century Chinese popular religion. Many of the assumptions underlying popular worship, especially concerning reciprocity between men and the gods, predated the rise of the Song and postdated its fall. Their very simplicity contributed to their longevity. Only one perceptible change occurred: the gods acquired the financial expertise necessary to manipulate the increasingly complex Song economy. As the market system expanded, the gods became more commercially acute and began to diversify. Or so contemporary observers thought. It would be more accurate to say that, as their followers were drawn into increasingly large market systems, they brought their gods in with them.

CHAPTER IV   The Granting of Titles

According to the precepts of popular religion as reconstructed in the previous chapter, devotees expressed their reverence for the gods by making new or refurbishing old images and temples. Starting in the late eleventh century, a third form of recognition—the granting of titles by the central government—became more and more common. Of the many ways of recompensing deities for miracles, only title-granting involved officials each and every time. The officials awarding titles worked on the same assumption as did the devotees who built temples and erected statues: the gods needed human recognition in order to continue to perform miracles. Because bureaucrats forwarded petitions for titles, conducted investigations into a given god's history of performing miracles, and made recommendations as to whether the emperor should award a title, an enormous number of documents concerning this sphere of activity exists.

Following the award of a government title, the local people sometimes put up a stele with both the text of the government grant written by the Imperial Secretariat (Shangshu sheng die) as well as their own version of events leading up to the grant (ji).[1] The reports of the Imperial Secretariat usually quoted extensively from local officials and allow a glimpse of how local government functioned at the grass roots. At the end of their reports, they attached the edict bestowing the title; it was very short, stating the title to be given and that it took effect upon arrival. In addition to these inscriptions and *The Record of the Listener*, I also use the administrative law code, *The Collected Important Documents from the Song (Song huiyao)*, which I will refer to hereafter as *The Important Documents*. By comparing official prescriptions with records of grants from temple inscriptions and *The Record*, this chapter will assess the actual role the state played in popular religion.

Figure 1 is a graph of the annual frequency of title granting based on the lists contained in *The Important Documents*. Although by my reckoning the total number of temples in Huzhou awarded titles in the Song was ninety-one (see table 4), these lists mention only seven.

1. *Ji* literally means record; however, in the case of temple inscriptions, it is used to denote texts that do not accompany the grants of government titles.

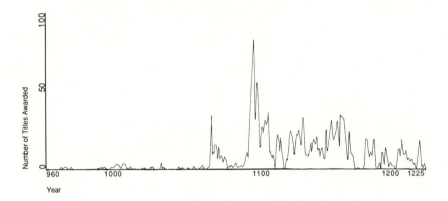

FIGURE 1. Titles Granted to Popular Deities Year by Year

Clearly they are not complete, and this figure cannot be read as an accurate count of all the titles granted to deities in the Song. Still it does show general trends: a sudden increase in the number of titles granted in the 1070s and a sharp spate of activity in the early 1100s under emperor Huizong, followed by continuous grants through the twelfth century. The official history confirms this trend, saying the period of greatest activity took place at the end of the eleventh and in the early twelfth centuries (*Songshi* 105:2562). It is impossible to determine whether the number of titles issued actually declined in the twelfth century, or whether the coverage of later periods is just not as good as that of earlier ones. *The Record of the Listener*, published 1157–1202, gives no sign that title granting diminished; nor does the epigraphical literature, which, as this chapter shows, continues down to the end of the Southern Song. Very possibly, then, the awarding of titles began on a large scale in the late Northern Song and continued throughout the Southern Song.

The Song emperors were not the first to give honors to deities. Like so many things in China, title granting had classical precedents. The *fengshan* sacrifices to earth and the heavens conducted on mountain tops by emperors certainly dated to the Qin (221–207 B.C.) and Han (206 B.C.–A.D. 219) dynasties, if not to the sixth century B.C. In making these offerings, rulers staked their claim to be emperor (Granet 1959:101–102). And as they awarded fiefs (*feng*) to their human subjects, so too did they give them to deities, thereby acknowledging their power but relegating them to subordinate roles. Temple inscriptions record grants from Han and Six Dynasties rulers, and the Tang emperors and the rulers of the various Five Dynasty kingdoms also awarded certain mountain gods titles (*Tang huiyao* 47:833–35; *Wudai huiyao* 11:192). The early Song emperors continued the practice of previous dynasties and granted titles to mountain deities, as in 1008 when the emperor Zhenzong climbed Mount Tai in Shandong, granted the God of the Eastern Peak a title, and had inscriptions carved to mark the occasion (Ye 1980:91–92).

As figure 1 makes clear, the incidence of title granting before 1075 was low. Even if more grants were awarded than listed in *The Important Documents*, long stretches of time at the beginning of the dynasty seem to have elapsed with no awards at all. In fact, during this time, the Song government concentrated on certifying Buddhist and Daoist religious institutions.[2] In the early years of the Song, recognition of deities took many different, unstandardized forms. The government allotted money for temple repair, granted titles, or added the deity to the register of sacrifices. On occasion it did all three, but there was no fixed pattern. Although the emperor ordered the repair of all popular temples on an empirewide basis in 1047 and the reporting of the names of all deities who brought rain in 1050, the response to these edicts remained negligible (*Song huiyao*, *Li* 20:2b).

Then in 1074, the emperor issued another edict calling for local officials to report the names of gods (*Song huiyao*, *Li* 20:2b), and this time in response to his call he received the names of many deities; in 1075 an unprecedented thirty-seven titles were issued. The timing will surprise no one familiar with Song political history. The 1070s were, of course, the time of the New Policies under Wang Anshi, whose activism extended to giving out loans to peasants, reorganizing the army, and strengthening systems of local authority. The activism of the reforms on the mundane level was matched by that on a supernatural level.

The sudden increase in the number of titles granted prompted the need for greater standardization of policy. In 1080, Wang Gu, then a low-ranking staff member (*boshi*) at the Court of Imperial Sacrifices (Taichang si) petitioned the emperor, saying:

2. In a thorough study of this topic, Chikusa (1982b) concludes, on the basis of materials in local histories, that most of the grants to monasteries were made during the reigns of Zhenzong (998–1022) and Yingzong (1064–1067). By the Southern Song the number of grants to new monasteries declined so sharply that the government did not issue new titles but reissued titles from defunct monasteries. To receive a government grant, a monastery had to meet several criteria: to have thirty or more rooms, to have a resident monk in charge, and to have merit (*gongde*).

Grant temple plaques (*e*)[3] to all temples with no noble titles (*jue-hao*). Add titles (*fengjue*)—first marquis (*hou*), then lord (*gong*), then king (*wang*)—to those temples that already have plaques. For those who held ranks when alive, let them keep their original rank. For females, first give them the title lady (*furen*), then consort (*fei*). These titles should first contain two characters and then four more can be added.

If one does like this, the bestowal of titles will govern (*yu*) the deities and the system of granting imperial favors will be orderly. (*Song huiyao, Li* 20:6b–7a)

Wang Gu makes the interesting point that the Song system did not consist simply of one instance of recognition by the central government. The system of titles allowed the government to recognize continued miracles in two ways: by promoting deities—first from marquis to lord and then to king—and by increasing the number of characters in his title from two to four to six. Wang does not distinguish between awarding titles to the deities or to their temples. The conflation of a deity with his temple, which characterizes all Song documents, probably resulted from the close identification of the two (chapter 3).

As time passed, Wang Gu's system did not allow enough flexibility, and in 1129 an edict raised the maximum number of characters to eight (*Baqiong shi jinshi* 117:5a–b). Throughout the Southern Song, an eight-character title was the longest a deity could hold.[4] And once a deity had attained this rank, the government began to award titles to his family members—usually first to his wife, then to their sons, then to their daughters-in-law. They too could be promoted or receive an increased number of characters in their titles. What this meant in practice was that deities—actually their supporters—were always looking to the central government for promotions. And many, many instances occur where a promotion follows only a few years after the initial grant of a temple plaque and where strings of promotions are punc-

---

3. Song officials constantly use this term, but it is not entirely clear what they meant by it. The word *e* originally referred to a piece of wood bordered on four sides; gradually it took on the broader meaning of a quota, of something fitting within the allotted space. In the Song, the central government issued a document that authorized the temple in question to put up a wooden plaque with the temple's name on it. In 1138 one temple petitioned for a replacement following the loss of the original authorization in a fire (*Song huiyao, Li* 20:73a)

4. Hong Mai reports that following the promotion of the God of the Eastern Peak to emperor (*di*), other gods also received this title. Hong petitioned requesting that the god of the Yangzi river also receive this rank, but his petition was rejected, and the god only received two more characters in his title (*Rongzhai suibi* 1:10:128–29).

tuated by pauses of only a year or two. (See the case of the Eternally Efficacious temple in the next chapter.)

It is not entirely clear what form the register of sacrifices (*sidian*) actually took. In 1095 Huang Chang petitioned: "Please order that all prefectures list all temples within their jurisdiction and make a book, called the register of sacrifices of such and such prefecture." His petition was approved (*Song huiyao, Li* 20:9b). Clearly there were individual registers of sacrifices in each locality, which the local prefect could consult. But there was probably also a register of sacrifices for all the government-recognized temples in China; the lists from *The Important Documents* must be the remnants of the originals.

The sudden increase at the end of the eleventh century in the number of titles granted prompted a series of petitions by bureaucrats about abuses in the system. In 1101, one official objected that many of the deities in the register of sacrifices had not really performed miracles; he suggested that local officials reexamine all claims (*Song huiyao, Li* 20:7a). And in 1111, the director of the palace library (*bishu jian*) He Zhitong complained that many of the deities in the register of sacrifices bore multiple titles: "How can one being have temples in two places with different titles?" He recommended that the higher title be taken as the standard (*Song huiyao, Li* 20:10a). The opposite case also occurred: two deities with the same title. Zhou Bida records two instances where this duplication prompted the issuing of new titles (*Zhou Bida wenji* 98:8a–b, 11a–b).

At one point, possibly long before the Song, because a title was meant to embody the deity's nature, the assignment of appropriate characters in a deity's title was probably a matter of great symbolic import. The same would have been true of posthumous titles awarded to officials, which were also awarded by the Court of Imperial Sacrifices (Taichang si). But by the Southern Song, at least judging from surviving records, the Court of Imperial Sacrifice's greatest concern was merely to keep track of the many titles they awarded and to avoid duplication or obvious blunders, such as giving a title that violated name taboos.[5] As the whole bureaucracy of title granting expanded, the issuing of titles took on certain aspects of mass production. Inscriptions harp on the number of characters in a title, regularly using such terms as "four-character marquis"; they almost never discuss the significance of the characters themselves.[6] With the huge number of dei-

5. For example, no god could have a title containing a character from his father's name.

6. Certain characters were reserved for certain types of deity. For example, *ji* meaning salvation and containing the water radical was used for dragons. *Lie* denoted martyrs.

ties receiving titles, the Court of Imperial Sacrifices was hard-pressed to keep up with its workload, and just maintaining up-to-date lists kept it occupied.[7]

What did inclusion in the register of sacrifices mean? Most important from the point of view of the bureaucracy was that once a temple was listed there, local officials went to that temple twice a year in the spring and autumn to conduct rituals as prescribed in *The Book of Rites*. Although many sources mention the biannual observances, they do not say how much money was spent (*Wang Shipeng wenji* 22:1b–2a). The government spent money not just on ritual observances but also on the upkeep of these officially recognized temples. An edict of 1127 specified that the prefecture where an officially recognized temple was located should allocate money to fix temples that were in disrepair, and that they should under no circumstances be allowed to fall into ruin (*Song huiyao, Li* 20:4a). An 1130 edict was more specific: the government instructed the counties to use leftover money in their budgets for temple repair following the Jurchen attacks (*Song huiyao, Li* 20:4a–b). An 1170 edict also specified that should a temple become dilapidated, the local officials could use any savings to work on the temple, but the amount of time allotted for such repairs could not exceed one month (*Song huiyao, Li* 20:1a).

So here are several edicts specifying the use of government funds to repair temples. Is there any evidence that such activities actually took place? Although authors of temple inscriptions generally employ hyperbole to say how much money was spent, they rarely give exact figures, and even more rarely the breakdown of how money was spent. This omission may well be the product of transmission; succeeding generations, more interested in prose-style or calligraphy, simply may not have bothered to transcribe these details, which, of course, are of major importance to the historian. One exception to this trend is described later in this chapter.

Suppression of Popular Cults

Previous analysts have seen the system of granting titles primarily as a means of control—that, because any temple lacking official sanction could be stamped out, only temples with government approval could survive.[8] Thus, according to this view, only two categories of temple

7. Remember that the number of grants per year given in figure 1 is probably only a fraction of the total number of grants awarded in a given year.
8. For the classic statement of this position, see C. K. Yang's "Ethicopolitical Cults: Guidance by the Way of the Gods" (1961:144–79).

exist: those in the register of sacrifices and those outside it. Those outside it are by definition licentious (*yin*). In fact, during the Song, the
term *yin* simply meant unofficial or unauthorized; only in the mouths
of critics did it take on the meaning licentious. Inclusion in the register
of sacrifices was the final measure of accreditation for a cult. Recall
Commander Fan (chapter 2). Only after his cult had attained a wide
measure of popular support, as evidenced by the erection of a temple,
did it receive government recognition.

One Song official's petition from 1111 shows the fallacy of dividing
all deities into two rigid categories: the ins and the outs (that is, those
in the register of sacrifices and those outside it). The director of the
palace library, He Zhitong, mentioned above, suggests making a new
list of the temples in each district and tallying it with that of the magistrate. Once the list is accurate, he proposes dividing the deities into
three categories: (1) those who have received either a temple plaque or
a title; (2) those without titles or plaques who have demonstrated merit
(*gonglie*) as well as the power to perform miracles; and (3) those to
whom the common people have built temples but who have no merit
and those things the law labels licentious cults (*yinci*) (*Song huiyao, Li*
20:9b–10b). Presumably those in the second category should be included in the register of sacrifices while those in the third should not.
He does not specify what should be done once these categories of analysis are established, but it is significant that he sees a large middle
ground between government-approved cults and those that the government should suppress.

Because suppressions of cults occurred only in certain localities and
not on a nationwide scale, it is difficult to assess their overall impact.
In 1109, for example, the emperor ordered 1,038 licentious temples in
Kaifeng to be torn down and the images in them moved to other temples (*Song huiyao, Li* 20:14b–15a). The edict specifically singles out
three cults whose temples are to be destroyed and whose worship is
henceforth forbidden. Yet, even this suppression, occurring at the
height of the Daoist revival, if carried out at all, was limited to Kaifeng. In an 1153 petition to the emperor about the danger of unauthorized cults, a registrar commented that deaths associated with such
worship had recently occurred in the more settled regions of the Lower
Yangzi and Sichuan, and not in remote areas as had been the case previously; the emperor approved his request to tear down temples not
listed in the register of sacrifices (*Wenxian tongkao* 90:8a–b). Isolated
examples of an individual official embarking on a campaign to suppress licentious cults occur throughout the Song; such activities are
often mentioned in funeral inscriptions. Zhou Bida tells of one official

in Gongzhou (Pingwu county, Sichuan) who in 1168 ordered the people to stop sacrificing cows in their attempts to cure illness (*Zhou Bida wenji* 34:7b). Although activist officials could attempt to condemn popular practices at any time, the cumulative effect of such suppressions was limited.

Clearly the category of licentious cults existed, as it had even before the Song (Stein 1979). The thrust of Song government policy, however, was not the suppression of cults outside the register of sacrifices, but, rather, the recognition of powerful gods. One could view the register of sacrifices as a means of co-optation or manipulation, but the sources do not encourage this reading. They speak in terms of recognizing a deity's accomplishments and so enabling him to continue to perform miracles.

One 1090 inscription from Huolu county, Hebei, provides an unusually detailed explanation of the register of sacrifices. Only government-approved cults should be in the register of sacrifices, explains the author, but an exception could always be made:

> Previous generations had the register of sacrifices to list the multitudinous deities. Thus temples were able to stay intact. How was this so? The performance of sacrifices was the basis of ruling the nation, and nothing in the conduct of rituals was more important than the worship of the gods. Is it not to establish ten thousand generations of merit and extend endless benefits?[9]
>
> There are also temples outside the register of sacrifices. Each one is prayed to by the people of a district. There are many examples. They exist because the people respect the ancient people, those who competed to be upright and virtuous, who are heroic and honorable. (*Changshan zhenshi* 12:13a–b)

The author then explains that, although most of the deities not in the register of sacrifices are not good, the worship of the few who benefit the people should be continued. And of course the deity in question, whose temple inscription he is writing, belongs in this second category. This logic applied on a universal scale meant that every deity one supported oneself belonged in the register of sacrifices, whereas unnamed others did not. In theory, the register of sacrifices may have been viewed as exclusive, but it was, in reality, open to all gods who had proved themselves powerful.

Like the author of this text, Hong Mai also reports that temples outside the register of sacrifices existed. At the end of the twelfth century

9. Both are the obligation of the emperor.

one temple on the border between Zhejiang and Fujian attracted many poor people who would pray and then find a little cash upon scratching the ground. In identifying this temple, Hong Mai gives its geographical location and mentions that, although it is not in the register of sacrifices, it is still very popular (*Yijian zhi* 12:8:8:1363). The same is true of a temple in Shaoxing. Hong says, "It is very large. Although it did not host the fall and spring rites, the common people were still very devoted" (*Yijian zhi* 12:8:11:1364). As mentioned above, inclusion in the register of sacrifices was the final step in the history of a cult from its inception to its acceptance by the government. To think that all temples were in the register of sacrifices is to envision a situation with only fully developed cults; in their incipient stages most cults simply were not eligible for inclusion.

Hong Mai's anecdotes are particularly valuable because they indicate the flexible nature of the register of sacrifices. In one instance Official Xiong from Chongren is appointed prefect of Leizhou in Guangdong. On his arrival a clerk tells him to go and pay his respects at the thunder temple. Xiong replies, "I know there are the gods of earth altars and those of hills and rivers, and rites at schools, that is all. How can there be worship at the thunder temple?" He uses the precise terminology of government cults; he will brook no temple that lacks official approval, and he certainly will not pray at one. That night there is a terrible storm, and from the sky falls a wood plank, which his family used to cover their granary. It has Xiong's own handwriting on it. He immediately goes to the temple to offer money, incense, and his apologies. This tale brings out a crucial point that recurs throughout Hong Mai's tales: the register of sacrifices is just a formality when compared to the reality of a given deity's power. Subsequently, in 1167 when Hong Mai was an official in the Secretariat Chancellery (Zhongshu sheng), he petitioned to get the god of thunder a title. He concludes his tale, saying, "The temple was then listed in the register of sacrifices. How can it be overlooked?" The thunder god had demonstrated his power with the miracle of the wood plank; it was only right to recognize him (*Yijian zhi* 7:9:11:955).

Hong Mai tells another tale with the same theme of a reluctant official being won over by a demonstration of the deity's power. An official in Suzhou, upon hearing a loud celebration in the streets, is told that it is the local god's birthday. Suspecting that the deity is not in the register of sacrifices, he wants to report the temple, which is located in the yamen, to his superior and have it torn down. That night the deity appears to a low-ranking military official (*bingma dujian*) and explains:

I am not of this world but am he who is called the Hundred
Flowers Great King (Baihua dawang). I have long received offerings in the courtyard of the government office. Although I do not
have a title from the court, I have always to the best of my ability
brought men good fortune and prevented disasters. I have never
dared to do anything wrong. Now the prefect is about to destroy
my temple. . . . Please have a word with him.

On hearing of this appearance, the official was surprised to hear that
the god knew of his unvoiced idea; he abandoned his plans to tear
down the temple and even helped to repair it (*Yijian zhi* 15:15:1:1685–
86).

In both these tales Hong Mai shows that the issue is not whether a
deity is in the register of sacrifices, but whether he is powerful. The
Leizhou deity brings a storm and causes the plank of wood from the
official's home to fall from the sky. The Suzhou deity reads the prefect's mind and appears in dreams to register his objections to having
his temple torn down. A 1216 inscription from Qingpu county,
Jiangsu, takes Hong Mai's logic one step further by applying a startling
bureaucratic metaphor to the register of sacrifices, beginning with a
play on words. The first line divides the two characters *si* and *dian*,
which together in a compound mean register of sacrifices, and uses
their individual meanings—*si*, to perform a sacrifice, and *dian*, ritual.
In the next sentence, *dian* is used in its other meaning, register.

Sacrifice (*si*) is the great ritual (*dian*) under heaven. Those whose
power does not cover things, and whose virtue does not reach the
people, are not in this register (*dian*). . . . Any time there is flood,
drought, plague, or locusts, then the deity of that place is to be
dismissed from the register. Otherwise those in the register would
be collecting their salaries as they shirk their duties. (*Jiangsu jinshi*
14:47a)

This is the language and the logic of the bureaucracy applied to the
heavens. If an official does not perform his job, he should be dismissed,
and likewise if a deity fails to protect his district, then his name should
be deleted. The register of sacrifices is explicitly equated with the civil
service register. A deity's salary, although not explained here, must
have been thought to have consisted of recognition, in the form of
having sacrifices performed at his temple and of having his temple
maintained by the government. So here again the register of sacrifices
is viewed in entirely functional terms: as long as a deity protects his
district, he is to be kept on the list.

Were any deities ever excluded from the register of sacrifices? If the main criterion for inclusion was the power to perform miracles, rejection, then, would be on the same grounds: the failure to perform miracles. The historical record is understandably almost mute on this topic. People who happily recorded miracles and instances of government recognition would have certainly remained silent about the denial of a title by the court.

One of the few exceptions is an epitaph to an official, Yang Wei, whose nephew unsuccessfully attempted to start a cult to him. The followers of the would-be deity explain to Chao Buzhi (1053–1110), "When alive, he was virtuous. When dead, he demonstrated his power. His existence will never be forgotten. Whether or not we can erect a temple to him, making unauthorized offerings on an annual basis will be enough to console us." In addition, they ask Chao to record Yang's life as well as his nephew's vision. Soon after his death in 1087, Yang appeared to his nephew at dusk and identified himself as a judge in the court of the underworld who ruled whether or not people had been loyal ministers, filial children, righteous husbands, and faithful wives. The uncle and nephew spoke freely until nighttime. Bystanders saw only the nephew bowing and talking to himself. Just as the apparition was about to go, two purple-clad servants said, "He likes the stone platform at the foot of Mount Fan. Why not build a temple to him there?" The nephew awoke from his trance and told many people. He also commissioned an image that, although crude, was so like Yang that people thought he was probably a deity.

The lifelike quality of the image seems to have been the main indication of Yang's apotheosis; no miracles are mentioned. Because Yang was not powerful, there was no one willing to petition the emperor for a title for him. The result was that the shrine was not built, and the cult was stillborn (*Jile ji* 63:6a–9a).[10] Although Chao says that "many people" came to ask him to write about Yang, the only person evincing any real interest in the god is his nephew; he was unable to launch the cult on his own.

Over one hundred years later, in 1196, the price of rice in Xiangtan, Hunan, soared and all the villagers, who earned their livelihood making different kinds of bamboo products, had difficulty obtaining food. In the previous year, the bamboo trees had flowered and produced a type of grain, nine parts of which could be added to one of rice to make

---

10. Hong Mai paraphrases the epitaph, only slightly embellishing the tale, and, ever the careful historian, adds a note. After consulting many accounts of trips to hell, he has determined that the office Yang Wei claimed to hold in the underworld bureaucracy did not exist (*Yijian zhi* 3:14:7:485–86).

a fragrant soup tasting just like all-rice soup. Because they had this bamboo-grain, the local people survived the rice shortage. Some of them thought this unusual grain was a miracle worked by a deity whose temple was right in the middle of the bamboo-growing region. An advanced degree holder (*jinshi*) requested a temple plaque for the deity from the prefectural government, but his request was denied. Hong Mai does not explain why, but he quotes elders who say that the bamboo trees had flowered once before in 961 (*Yijian zhi* 13:8:13:1448). This is a rejection even more telling than that of Yang Wei; the petition is made but not forwarded to the fiscal intendant or the court. Contrary to what one might assume, recognition did not automatically follow a petition.

In telling us about deities who were refused titles, Hong Mai's emphasis on their failure to perform miracles echoes that of the imperial government—in every edict asking local officials to report the names of deities to be included in the register of sacrifices, the main requirement is that they be powerful.[11] Powerful deities who can perform miracles belong in the register of sacrifices. Weak ones do not.

At regular intervals in the Southern Song, as in the Northern, the emperor requested that local officials report the names of powerful deities to him so that they could be included in the register of sacrifices. The most often-cited regulations in the reports of the Imperial Secretariat were those of 1129 and 1187. The 1129 regulation was usually given in abbreviated form: "In the event that a temple is the site of miracles, then it should first be given a temple plaque and then promoted to marquis."[12] The edict then gives the number of characters to be bestowed at each rank, ranging from two to eight (*Baqiong shi jinshi* 117:5a–b). The 1187 edict, in its shortened form, says, "Today and in the future, should a temple be the site of miracles in response to prayers, the fiscal intendants of all circuits are commanded to follow correct procedures to report to the emperor in order to obtain an edict to promote the deity in question" (*Liangzhe jinshi* 12:39b). The originals of these two edicts are not extant; they survive only as they are cited, often in truncated form, in inscriptions.[13]

11. Hong Mai does mention one incident in which a deity failed to receive a title because the Board of Rites and the Court of Imperial Sacrifices determined that the petition had been submitted past the filing date of one year as had been specified by the emperor in his original request. Hong recounts the incident in order to poke fun at the bureaucratic mindset of the government and explains that he obtained permission to have an inspector sent to the district in question. In due time the god received his title (*Rongzhai suibi* 2:16:212).

12. Note the language used here: the temple, not the god, is to be recognized.

13. Here is a partial list of edicts by year as they are cited in Song sources: 1050: *Song huiyao, Li* 20:2b; 1074: *Song huiyao, Li* 20:2b; *Jinshi cuibian* 138:3a; c. 1121: *Liangzhe jinshi*

The Southern Song witnessed an important change in bureaucratic procedure: the introduction of a complicated system of double-checking to confirm that the deity had indeed performed the miracles he was supposed to have. An 1135 grant of a title to the Eternally Efficacious (Yongling) temple in Huzhou (see chapter 5) records that once the county magistrate had approved the petition, he sent it to the fiscal intendant. Because the fiscal intendants were in many ways the de facto regional government of the Southern Song, it was natural that the awarding of titles should be part of their task, in addition to taxation, supplying the armies, and keeping peace (Lo 1974–1975). In this case, the fiscal intendant of Liangzhe circuit sent two officials—first a registrar (*zhubu*) from the neighboring county of Jiaxing and then a sub-official functionary (*ganban gongshi*) from his own office. When they had both attested to the deity's miracles, he sent the petition to the central government (*Liangzhe jinshi* 8:36a–37a).[14]

The law code of the Qingyuan era (1195–1200) transformed what had been standard practice into law; if there had been earlier edicts of this nature they do not survive, and they are not quoted in inscriptions.[15] As the late twelfth-century law is cited in inscriptions, it reads:

> The prefects should report and guarantee to the fiscal intendants the claims of all the temples and Buddhist and Daoist practitioners of each circuit who have performed miracles in response to prayers and who should be given titles and plaques. The fiscal intendant will send an official from a neighboring prefecture to check the claim personally. Then he will send another official who is not involved to double-check the claim. When these checks are completed, he will report the actual situation to the emperor. (*Wuxing jinshi* 12:4a; *Liangzhe jinshi* 12:39b)

Surviving inscriptions confirm that these bureaucratic procedures were indeed carried out on the local level. Once the circuit intendant concluded that a god was genuinely powerful, he then petitioned the emperor to award a plaque or a title.

Once such a petition arrived in the capital, it progressed on a determined route from one central government office to another. The fiscal

---

8:1a–b; 1129: *Jiangsu jinshi* 15:26a; *Liangzhe jinshi* 8:36a, 12:40b; *Baqiong shi jinshi* 117:5a–b; 1187: *Liangzhe jinshi* 12:39b; 1214: Fu Ssu-nien library, rubbing 02288; 1241–1252: *Liangzhe jinshi* 13:24b; 1257: *Liangzhe jinshi* 12:38a.

14. For similar examples of double-checking by neighboring officials, see *Liangzhe jinshi* 8:39a; *Wuxing jinshi* 9:18b.

15. Thirty-six of eighty chapters of this law code, *The Classified Laws of the Qingyuan Era* (*Qingyuan tiaofa shilei*) (edited 1203), survive, but not those dealing with the granting of titles to local deities.

intendant's petition to the emperor was automatically forwarded to the Imperial Secretariat, who sent it to the Board of Rites to check the claim one more time. Once they approved it, they sent it to the Court of Imperial Sacrifices to receive a provisional title (*nifeng*). The Court of Imperial Sacrifices then sent it back to the Board of Rites for approval; they then sent it back to the Imperial Secretariat who drafted the edict bestowing the title as well as a full report documenting all the investigations which had taken place on the local and national levels (*Liangzhe jinshi* 13:25b–27a). Because there were no major restructurings of the central government after the eleventh century, it is likely that this was the order throughout the twelfth and thirteenth centuries.

The procedures necessary to grant a god a title were both expensive and time consuming. It cost money to send officials to neighboring prefectures to check on miracles; it also took them away from their other duties. The services of many officials in the capital were also involved. Why was the government so concerned? First, because the government took the granting of titles seriously, believing that such grants could extend the power of deities, it did not want to make any undeserved awards. And, second, it may have suspected that county officials, pressured by local elites to recognize the deities they supported, could not be counted on to be entirely objective in their judgments about miracles.

Several tales in Hong Mai's *The Record of the Listener* enable us to see how the system of recognizing deities actually worked in the second half of the twelfth century. Outside the prefectural seat of Huzhou lived a boatman infamous for his lack of filial piety. He was alleged to have stood by watching his mother drown until a bystander saved her. In 1174 just as he had set off from shore, a man on foot called to the boat, and the boatman, wanting his fare, went back to the shore to get the passenger. There were so many people on board that some sat under the fishing platform. Suddenly someone spoke:

> "I am a god and not a person. Because you are not filial, heaven has sent me to attack you."
>
> The boatman was not especially scared and replied, "Since you are a deity from heaven, I will give the money back, and you can go." Just as he finished speaking, there was a clap of thunder and he died.
>
> At that moment, the god was not to be seen. The people in the boat, both horrified and frightened, told the sheriff of Wucheng county, Mu Bing, who came to investigate the matter. (*Yijian zhi* 15:1:9:1556)

Hong Mai does not identify the people in the boat; possibly the passengers were not of high rank. All murders had to be reported to local officials. At least in this one instance few obstacles stood in the way of people reporting what appeared to be a miracle. The local officials, in fact, may have been grateful for the tip that would have helped them respond to the emperor's request for information about powerful gods.

Two anecdotes suggest the readiness of officials to report the names of powerful deities to the emperor. During Hong Mai's maternal uncle's term in office as the governor of Xiazhou (Yichang county, Hubei), 1119–1125, no rain fell one summer. Prayers to a local deity brought rain, and the deity appeared to the uncle in a dream to identify herself. Hong comments, "Before he could request a temple plaque, he was transferred to another post" (*Yijian zhi* 3:14:2:483). Similarly in 1184 in Gutian county, Fujian, an official spotted a dragon while praying for rain. His superior reported the event to the court, and the emperor ordered that the deity be promoted and a temple built to him (*Yijian zhi* 9:1:12:1057–58). So here too it seems that officials would not hesitate to report a deity who had demonstrated his powers.

Like the title grants, *The Record* also mentions that the fiscal intendants actually sent inspectors out, but whereas the inscriptions usually repeat their certifications of the deity's miracles in the terse bureaucratic language of the time, Hong Mai tells one anecdote suggesting that these inspections were more than rubber-stamping of the original petitions. A sheriff is sent to Dexing county, Jiangxi, to check up on a temple to the Five Manifestations (see chapter 6). When he arrives, he suddenly remembers a dream he had had as a child in which he had entered a temple with five glimmering images in official clothing. He is aroused from his revery by the arrival of a clerk; he reports his experience to the fiscal intendant, and the deities are promoted (*Yijian zhi* 12:10:9:1379–80). Hong Mai implies both that the sheriff's positive report helped the gods to get their promotions and that these inspectors had the power to influence the outcome of petitions to grant titles.

Perhaps the strongest indication of the degree to which the title-granting system had permeated local society was the fact that, by the twelfth century, people thought deities wanted titles just as they sought images and statues. Hong Mai tells of three dreams in which deities spoke in these terms. As early as 1102, twenty-five years after the sudden increase in government titles, and during the peak period of government grants, in Ningdu county, Jiangxi, a local man named Sun dreamt that a white-haired elderly man came to his house and asked him: "How can I get a title?"

Sun realized that the man was a deity and responded, saying, "You must execute virtuous deeds, and you cannot hurt people."

The man replied, "How could I be one who hurts people? I'm the receptionist at the gate of heaven, and each day I determine the fortune and misfortune of people living in this district. You should ask others and check what I've said to you; I don't cause anyone to suffer."

Sun answered "The people are most concerned about the rainfall each year. If you can use your power to help, then the district magistrate and the prefect will petition the court, and you'll receive a title immediately."

Five years later, the local people prayed to the deity during a fire, and the fire suddenly ended, just as though someone had put it out. The deity was then granted the title he had so longed for (*Yijian zhi* 4:10:8:622). In 1130, Erlang, who had a temple in Langzhou county, Sichuan, appeared in a dream to an official and said:

> I formerly received the rank of king. I descended to deal with worldly things; accordingly, my post was to govern everything, good and bad fortune, winning and losing. Since 1110, the emperor changed my title to immortal. Although the name was pure and reverent, my power was dissipated. No one has come to ask me about the myriad affairs of man. I have been worshipped until today and only now feel shame.

Upon awakening the official immediately petitioned to restore the deity's original title. And from then on the deity recovered his former powers (*Yijian zhi* 3:17:3:508–9). Only after his rightful title of king had been restored to this deity could he resume his work. Finally, sometime before 1171, a local deity appeared to an administrative supervisor (*lushi canjun*) in Yongzhou (now Lingling county, Hunan) and said, "I am just the earth god of this area, that's all, and I am not a king or a marquis." He then asked for a curtain so that he would not have to vacate his temple every time the prefect went by; it would not be respectful for him to face the prefect (*Yijian zhi* 3:1:7:371).

The system of government ranks had so penetrated people's consciousness that they conceived of deities intensely aware of which title they held and whose powers were affected by those titles. It was not just deities or devotees who had this view; so too did many of the officials making these decisions. All the people Hong Mai tells about were officials. Rather than view their acts as co-opting the gods, one should take them at their word and view them as trying to harness the deities' power on behalf of the government.

By the late twelfth and thirteenth centuries, the granting of titles had become so extensive that one way for a group to enhance its status was to seek a title for the god it supported. These groups needed the assistance of local officials because only they could petition to the fiscal intendant for titles. Local officials, dependent on the cooperation of these elites to collect taxes and to keep order, may have supported these same deities in order to elicit that cooperation. Also, sheer proximity to these temples meant that they would hear of the local gods' miracles. Because county officials and local elites shared some of the same interests, an informal alliance between them took shape.

Song Social Strata and Temple Inscriptions

Who were the groups that achieved this consensus? The unusual format of inscriptions and petitions helps to identify those supporting certain deities. On occasion the names of the different people who helped to make the stele are known: the author of the text, the man who did the calligraphy or wrote the seal script heading, and the person who organized the funding. The texts sometimes mention donors who gave money or land, or individuals who supervised the construction or reconstruction of a temple. Similarly, officials petitioning the emperor to grant a title may give the names of the people who originally approached them or those who testified on behalf of the god to the inspectors.

The analyst who attempts to assign social categories on the basis of labels used in inscriptions must do so with caution. For one, the labels may have reflected desired as opposed to actual status.[16] Not imposed by higher authorities, these labels are especially significant, however, because they show how individuals referred to themselves in a local context. People might give themselves more glorious-sounding appellations than they deserved, but they had no incentive to downgrade their social status. The authors of inscriptions place people into four categories: commoners without office or title, those holding *lang* ranks but not office, those holding advanced degrees (*jinshi*) or in some stage

16. Also, the same word may denote different statuses in different regions or in different periods. However, because the inscriptions I use here span 150 years and the region of the Lower Yangzi, it seems likely that the terms are used consistently.

of the degree-granting process, and actual officeholders. All but the commoners usually possessed official household status (*guanhu*); they were exempt from village service obligations, could evade some taxes, and had a privileged legal position (McKnight 1971:27).

Commoners are referred to as "elders," by their positions in the village service system, or more generally as villagers or township residents. Historians debate the actual meaning of the term "elder" (*fulao*, *qilao*). There are those who, like David Johnson (1985:420), argue that the elders were not necessarily old, but just powerful: "Who were the 'elders'? Logic suggests they they were not village greybeards, but eminent commoners resident in the city. They were called 'elders' because that was the most respectful way of referring to men who had neither rank nor title." In twentieth-century Hong Kong, however, the term "elders" is actually limited to the "village greybeards." On reaching his sixtieth birthday, a man is inducted into the council of elders.[17] The label is made even more ambiguous by the fact that "elder" was sometimes the title of a position in the village service system (McKnight 1971:23, 75). Similarly, the terms superior guard leader (*dubao zheng*), assistant superior guard leader (*fu dubao zheng*), and guard chief (*baozhang*) all denoted positions of responsibility within the village service system, which varied from region to region and changed over time. For all the ambiguity of these terms, they characterize those commoners who, lacking official household status, had duties in the village service system.

Above these commoners were those with official household status (*guanhu*), some of whom held only a *lang* rank. The central government bestowed these ranks on those who had passed the exams but who had not yet received an assignment, on those who qualified for office under the *yin* privilege, on those between postings, and on those who had donated large amounts of grain (often in famines). The different ranks denoted specific sub-grades within the nine ranks of the military, administrative, or executory service of Song officialdom; those appearing in the inscriptions are almost always from the lower ranks of seven to nine and often from the military, suggesting they received their titles via the *yin* privilege.[18] In 1213, only 2.2 percent of

17. James Watson, personal communication, February 1987.

18. See Miyazaki (1974) for charts giving the ranks of the different *lang* titles. The Song bureaucracy was divided into two streams: civil (*wen*) and military (*wu*). The civil stream was divided into the administrative (*jingchao guan*) and executory (*xuanren*) classes, which had separate selection bureaus and different career paths (Kracke 1963; Bol 1986:13, note 8). Those in the military service slightly outnumbered those in the

those holding civil ranks had purchased them; 39.3 percent had entered through *yin* privilege. Similarly, 52 percent of those with military ranks had received them via the *yin* privilege (Chaffee 1985:25; Lo 1983:129). The different routes to becoming a *lang* mean that it is impossible, without further information, to pin down the social class of these men with certainty. Still, the holders of these *lang* ranks, whatever their qualifications or ties, were men of official household status.

Several terms are used to denote those at various stages of the examinations. Those who had passed the first round of local exams but not the second in the capital are called tribute scholars (*xianggong jin-shi*).[19] Those who passed the exams in the capital received an advanced degree (*jinshi*); this label is used in the inscriptions to refer to someone who had not yet received a duty assignment. The relatives of officeholders who received an advanced degree without having taken the exams are called exempted advanced degree holders (*mianjie jinshi*). Several other terms are used to denote students; these men hoped to pass the exams and probably studied full time. Some overlap existed among the different categories of those with advanced degrees and *lang* ranks; they were all official householders who had not been appointed to posts.

Above those with advanced degrees of the rank of *lang* were officeholders. The most frequent to appear in inscriptions were prefects (*zhizhou*), county magistrates (*xianling*), sheriffs (*wei*), assistant magistrates (*cheng*), and registrars (*zhubu*)—all local government officials. The rule of avoidance was not enforced in the Song, so many of these men held office in their home districts. These county officials forwarded petitions for a title to the emperor; they also were donors. Local men who held higher government positions were often asked to compose temple inscriptions to a god from their home district; although sometimes resident elsewhere, they drafted the requested texts, possibly in return for payment or as a favor to people they knew.

Whereas county officials needed the cooperation of local elites to collect taxes, to administer justice, and to keep order, these elites desired recognition from the central government. The recurrence of the

---

civil; often they did not serve in the army but held law-enforcement roles such as sheriff (Lo 1983; Umehara 1986).

19. Once they had gained this preliminary exam status, they could retain their eligibility for the round of exams in the capital without having to sit for the local exams again. This group probably totaled thirty thousand at any time in the course of the Southern Song, which was roughly .15–.25 percent of the population of sixty million. In the Ming and Qing this group of licentiates (*shengyuan*) swelled to 1–2 percent of the population (Chaffee 1985:31–33).

terms *lang* and "advanced degree holder" as well as the enormous
number of men taking the examinations (maybe as many as 400,000 in
the thirteenth century) show that local elites valued official household
status highly. Indeed, they may have valued it more highly than service
in the bureaucracy, which was widely and accurately perceived as a
minefield of factional divisions. The same people who coveted official
household status also canvassed vigorously for titles for popular deities. The most telling finding from the temple inscriptions is that
members of the four major categories—commoners, bearers of *lang*
ranks, advanced degree holders, and officials—often joined together in
an informal alliance to secure titles for local deities.

Several inscriptions show how these alliances worked in different
places. The first to be discussed are from Taizhou (now Linhai county,
Zhejiang) and do not specifically concern the granting of titles. But
because these texts give detailed financial information about the relative contributions of government officials and local people to the rebuilding of a temple, they reward close examination. In 1181, when
Tang Zhongyou, later to become famous as the target of Zhu Xi's
attacks, came to Taizhou as prefect, the temple to Zhao Bing (a Han
dynasty magician) had fallen into disrepair. Tang, who wrote this inscription, organized the renovation of the temple to reward the god
both for sending a good harvest and for preventing a fire from spread-
ing. The work took five months and required the services of 1,082
workmen. The entire temple was refurbished, and the images and
equipment were replaced. Total expenditures: 270,000 cash in official
funds and 250,000 from donations by the people. The enormous number of craftsmen and the presence of a county magistrate and registrar
who supervised them suggest that they were not paid, but were fulfilling their corvée obligations (*Jiading Chicheng* 31:8a–9b).[20] Only one
other person is named; he holds the rank of *dengshi lang* (executory 9a)
and helps to oversee the work.

Fifteen years later the river next to the temple flooded and damaged
the temple. This time, a total of 18,000 laborers were used; this number is so large as to strain belief, as does the author's next claim that
the laborers "were paid in money and recruited in the market place;
people did not think of it as corvée." Perhaps. But it seems likely that
the 18,000 were also fulfilling their corvée obligations. In this instance,
the local magistrate organized a rebuilding effort and gave 200,000

20. The use of corvée labor to maintain temples may have been common. In 1105,
five families were exempted permanently from their corvée obligations to maintain a
temple to the Dragon King of Opportune Aid (Shunji longwang) in Hangzhou (*Song
huiyao, Li* 20:3a).

cash[21] of a total of 1,500,000 spent. It is not clear if he made this contribution in a personal or, as is more likely, an official capacity. Following his name is a list of donors. One is the same as in 1181; he is joined by two men who hold the rank of *digong lang* (executory 9b), one with the rank of *jiangshi lang* (also executory 9b), and seven holders of advanced degrees (*Taizhou jinshi* 7:14b–17a). These men were very likely members of the local elite. The Taizhou inscriptions are unique in offering information about the financing of temple restoration. Government officials not only reorganized the rebuilding, but also funded the work, supplying more than one-half the budget in 1181 and one-eighth in 1192, as well as a huge number of laborers.

The tendency for local elites and officials to work together in the quest for titles did not go unobserved at the time. Chen Chun (1153–1217), whose other criticisms of popular cults I will examine at length in chapter 6, defined the term "licentious cults" in a dictionary of Neo-Confucian terms that he compiled:

> It has not been long since the time of Lord Di [Di Renjie, a Tang official who tore down 1700 licentious temples], yet licentious cults have proliferated to an enormous extent. This is all unenlightened belief that is concerned only with this world. The common people love strange things. Originally country folk, ignorant of the system of making offerings, supported these cults. Then many lowly people, aided by the rich and powerful of the villages, carried on their efforts. Thus, the village good-for-nothings and those without occupation falsely schemed to use these cults to extort money from the people to feed and clothe themselves. There is no prefecture or county, no village or settlement, that lacks a temple.
>
> Many of the ritual officials of the court [meaning those who carry out the inspections] are stupid and ignorant. The local people negotiate with them about the titles. By this means, those deities who have no antecedents all can get titles. And those with titles grow more influential each year. If one wants to consider heterodoxy and orthodoxy, this makes no sense. (*Beixi ziyi* 2:31b)

Chen's critique partially reflects his Neo-Confucian background; he was one of Zhu Xi's most ardent disciples, and certainly his most acerbic. He felt people should work the land and not earn a living by tricking honest farmers. But Chen, an acute observer, is right about many

---

21. Emending *jin* (gold) to *qian* (money) (Paul Smith, personal communication, February 1986).

of the Song deities; they did not have the noble pedigrees of their predecessors. Neither emperors nor generals, deities like Commander Fan (chapter 2) were springing up all over the empire, and Chen thought they were not deserving of worship. Even more importantly, Chen saw that the system of title granting fostered collusion between officials and locally powerful people. Because the local people could influence the inspectors, and because the inspectors were stupid, the wrong kinds of deity—commoner deities—were awarded titles. Chen also acknowledged the importance of a title: once a deity has one, regardless of his merit, his cult will flourish.

Several inscriptions from the late Southern Song indicate that Chen Chun's suspicions of collusion were well-grounded. The thoroughness of these inspections—so much like canonizations of saints being conducted in Europe at the same time—meant that cooperation between local elites and officials could do much to smooth the way through the bureaucratic maze leading up to the award of a title. One title grant from Wuxi county, Jiangsu (rubbing 02288 in the Fu Ssu-nien Library, Academia Sinica, Nankang, Taiwan), provides an extraordinary amount of detail about each step of the inspection process but little biographical information about the deity himself. The fiscal intendant addresses the report to the central government and explains what steps have been taken to verify the deity's power. He is responding to the petition of the county magistrate, who in turn is responding to a request by a local elder, an exempted advanced degree holder, and five to seven other people whose names and ranks are not given.

The first step to getting a title was testifying orally (*liezhuang*) to the magistrate about Grand Guardian Wang 33. The deity's appellation—Grand Guardian (*taibao*)—was an ancient title not in use in the Song and was clearly designed to indicate respect for the deity, who had lived in the late twelfth century. His name 33 perhaps suggests lower-stratum origins; commoners may not have had real names in the Song.[22] These men then cite a 1214 edict calling for the submission of

22. The phenomenon of giving numbers as names was widespread in the Song and is still not very well understood. In some cases it has clear legal implications, as in many court cases where people are referred to by number rather than by name. Because people of the same surname tended to live in the same place, the authorities used numbers to avoid confusion. Yet number-names may also have been the way that person was actually referred to; they occur frequently in *The Record of the Listener*. Wu Han (1961:52–54) suggests that in the Yuan and Ming commoners may not have been entitled to have their own names; he cites an edict where Ming Taizu, the first Ming emperor, bestows names on two of his supporters. Wu also describes areas in modern Shaoxing where parents added their ages at the time of their child's birth to arrive at a name for him. This may have been the case with 33.

names of powerful deities, summarize the biography of the deity and the history of the temple, and conclude that the god has always responded to prayers for rain or clear skies. They continue, "All Daoist and Buddhist monasteries, neighborhoods, and homes of gentry and common folk contain paintings or images of the deity they worship." In 1214, following the failure of the local people to capture a horde of locusts, the deity caused the insects to disperse. In 1226 he stopped heavy rains, and in 1228 he protected the people from plague. Thus they petition for a title.

On receiving this petition, the county magistrate sent all the leaders of the mutual surveillance groups (bao) and their deputies to check the claim. At the same time he dispatched someone to the Buddhist and Daoist monasteries to see if miracles had occurred at these places. Once they had reported back favorably, he delegated one of these group leaders to the first sector (du) in the district to do likewise. There, an elder and a leader of a mutual surveillance household (baohu) of the district, He Dedai, and some type of student (bu   xuesheng), Gu Duanming, reported that the deity had been born in 1186, and that the miracles of 1214, 1226, and 1228 had actually taken place. The county magistrate then gives the names and ranks of nineteen religious officials who vouched that Grand Guardian Wang 33 had never failed to perform miracles when offered incense and prayed to in monasteries and in villages: among the nineteen were nine supervisors of Buddhist monasteries (si zhishi seng) and one supervisor of a Daoist monastery (guan zhishi congshi).[23] Their testimony provides striking confirmation of the eclectic religious attitudes described in chapter 2; they saw no conflict between their positions as Buddhist and Daoist clergy and supporting a popular deity.

At this point, having examined local government officials, elders, and village authorities, the county magistrate petitions the fiscal intendant to give Wang 33 a title. This inscription provides just as much detail about the succeeding stages of the investigations; amazingly enough, it even records the names of the people to whom the inspectors spoke. The fiscal intendant dispatched a registrar from Changzhou (Suzhou) to go to the village and summon the elders and people of the neighboring villages. The superior guard household head (dubao hu) of Kaiyuan canton, a superior guard leader (difen baozheng), and the head of the temple to the God of the Eastern Peak all testified on behalf of the deity. The second inspector, from Zhenjiang prefecture, uses the usual bureaucratic formulas to confirm the deity's miracles; as was al-

23. I am very grateful to Ihara Hiroshi for copying part of this text for me.

most always the case, he does not give the names of the people he spoke with.

This inscription, written in 1230, gives the most detail about the different investigations that went on. Of the original petitioners, one was an elder and one was an exempted advanced degree holder. The other petitioners' names and ranks are not given; presumably, if they had held office, they would have been. It seems fair to conclude, then, that these men were the locally powerful but did not hold office. And in seeking recognition for the deity, they wanted both to increase his power and to bask in the reflection of his glory. In this instance, the eminent people of Wuxi allied with the local clergy to present Wang 33's case. Because if any of them had contested his miracles, the magistrate might not have forwarded the petition, it was of the utmost importance to present a united front to the various officials who arrived to conduct the investigations.

A petition from Jiaxing submitted in 1264 by one tribute scholar and five holders of self-styled advanced degrees (*daibu jinshi*)[24] gives further insight into the social level of people petitioning for a title for their deity; it is particularly noteworthy because none of the petitioners was an official. Only one of the six had passed the first round of examinations. But in spite of the fact that none held office, they had access to the magistrate, who forwarded their petition to the prefect. The prefect sent a registrar who summoned the guard leader (*baozheng*) Shen Chun and the elders, Ji 41, Li 38, Wu 76, and Zhang Little-three (*xiaosan*), to the side of the temple. They testify that they are residents of this sector, live in the vicinity of the temple, have seen the deity since he was nine and became a deity. Over a hundred years have elapsed since the founding of his temple. All the people of the district have been fortunate, and the deity has always helped them in times of flooding, drought, illness, and trouble. The bureaucratic procedure was exactly as stipulated in the Qingyuan regulations. This sequence of events confirms a point that Hong Mai makes in his *Record of the Listener*: one did not necessarily have to be of high rank to approach the magistrate about a title for a god.

Once those speaking on behalf of the god have finished their list of miracles, their testimony departs from familiar ground: "Subsequently the officials (*guanyuan*) present in the city, who numbered more than ten, prepared money to buy incense and candles and to pay for the

24. Ruan Yuan, the editor of the epigraphical collection containing this inscription, comments that this term appears on no other inscriptions and that these men must have made it up (*Liangzhi jinshi* 13:27b).

recitation of sutras in the temple in order to pray for rain. The result was that rain fell continuously" (*Liangzhe jinshi* 13:24a). The shift they describe is not sudden, yet the cult has changed from one backed by local people to one enjoying official support. The deity was powerful, the local people worshipped him, and eventually local officials also came to pray at the temple—even though it was not in the register of sacrifices. In fact the officials' unofficial support may have been one of the factors contributing to the eventual recognition of the cult; after all, it is they who must petition for a temple plaque.[25]

An inscription from South Bank (Nanxun), Huzhou, in 1270 tells of another temple that enjoyed official support before receiving a temple plaque. Here, too, the governor of the township petitions the central government after receiving an oral deposition from the local people about two local deities. In the next chapter I will discuss their petition in detail, but here let me just note that an official, the emissary of the imperial intendant (*yuqian tiju suo shichen*), and an elder present the petition. In explaining how it is that these two deities are not in the register of sacrifices, they say: "Before [South Bank] had been made a township, it was a special village (*te xiangcun*), that's all. It had no rank to speak of. Now it has been a township for about twenty years. Several times a year officials of the township pray, and there have been frequent responses" (*Wuxing jinshi* 12:22a). So the officials pray at a temple not in the register of sacrifices. And the petitioners make an extremely important point—if a temple happens to be located in an out-of-the-way place, it may have trouble attracting the attention of officials who can petition for a title for it. Only after South Bank had been designated the lowest unit of government, a township, were officials based there, and only they could apply for a title to give to these deities.

Conclusion

The system of recognizing deities can best be understood by taking seriously the professions of officials and authors of inscriptions: they viewed titles as a means of both rewarding the deities and enabling them to perform further miracles. The register of sacrifices listed all the gods who, by virtue of having passed the government's exacting

---

25. Hong Mai's tales about the disasters that ensued when officials did not make offerings to local gods, recounted in chapter 3, suggest that officials did visit temples, even those not listed in the register of sacrifices. Low-ranking clerks probably told newly posted officials about local cults, regardless of whether or not they were approved, when the officials arrived to take up their posts.

canonization procedures, were thought to have conclusively demonstrated their powers. Also an important consideration, bureaucrats gave titles to satisfy the local people, who supported the deities and believed that they needed recognition.

But not everyone shared the same positive view of the bureaucracy of title granting. Chen Chun's objections, quoted above, are the most telling: he does not view the deities of the Song, gods like Commander Fan or Wang 33, as deities deserving recognition. In voicing his criticisms he identifies a practice that no one will talk about in a temple inscription: collusion between county officials and specific people, whom he disparagingly labels good-for-nothings. Authors of temple inscriptions call these same people elders, holders of advanced degrees, and bearers of *lang* ranks. And because they have the ear of local officials, they can garner titles for their deities.

Other evidence supports Chen's point that specific groups were acting behind the scenes to obtain titles for gods. In the four cases examined above from Taizhou, Wuxi, Jiaxing, and Huzhou, powerful men asked the resident officials to petition for a title on behalf of a deity. Here, I suggest, was the final stage of a competition among deities and their backers. As long as different deities maintained claims to the same miracles, it would have been impossible to satisfy the many inspectors of one deity's power. But only when a deity had emerged victorious and been acknowledged by all as the most powerful deity would he have been able to fulfill the central government's exacting requirements.

Because the Song government wanted to make sure—doubly sure—that the deities it included in the register of sacrifices were powerful, it conducted a series of investigations that ensured that those gods whom the people thought at the time were powerful would be included in the register of sacrifices. No other god would have been able to pass the stringent canonization procedures. What many officials and the people saw as a way of rewarding the gods proved also to be an efficient way to rule. By awarding titles to deities who commanded the allegiance of local elites, the Song government was able to keep its finger on the pulse of local society. Magistrates, sheriffs, and registrars depended on local elites to keep order, but they had little to offer in return. What they could, and what they did, offer was recognition of local deities.

CHAPTER V　Popular Deities in Huzhou

Previous chapters have discussed the general principles of interacting with the gods and the process by which the government granted titles to deities. This chapter shifts vantage points to examine deities in just one prefecture, Huzhou in Zhejiang province, on the south bank of Lake Tai and adjacent to Hangzhou (see map 1).[1] As should be obvious by now, the illiterate common people of the twelfth and thirteenth centuries did not themselves produce records, but the temple inscriptions they commissioned provide otherwise unavailable insights into the changes they experienced during the Song. Other prefectures in China may have rivaled Huzhou in terms of commercial importance, and places farther from Hangzhou were arguably more typical. But Huzhou offers what very few other places in the Southern Song do: a continuous run of local histories. The first extant local history from Huzhou dates to 1201. From then on, through the twentieth century, new editions were compiled that contain both lists of temples and the texts of temple inscriptions.[2]

Huzhou was undergoing considerable change during the Southern Song, and the kinds of changes it was undergoing were also taking place elsewhere. As Shiba Yoshinobu points out, "In terms of topography, Huzhou was a microcosm of the whole Lower Yangzi valley" (1975a:33). Because Huzhou contained both highland and lowland areas, it provides an ideal site to examine their different rates of development. The western half of the prefecture is mostly hilly land; the eastern, more fertile lowlands suitable for paddy cultivation, with almost no hills at all. The contrast is sharp, and the county borders fall along the differences in elevation, with Anji, Changxing, and Wukang counties in the west, and Wucheng, Gui'an, and Deqing counties as well as Huzhou city in the east. In fact, the eastern and western halves

1. Although the name of the prefecture was changed to Anji (which was also the name of one of the six counties it contained) in 1225, I will refer to it as Huzhou. The city of Huzhou, which was the prefectural seat during the Song, is now located in Wuxing county, Zhejiang.

2. Accordingly Huzhou in the Song has already been the subject of several studies (see in particular Shiba 1975a, 1975b, 1976; Chikusa 1982c, 1982f). The local histories I have consulted are listed in the bibliography.

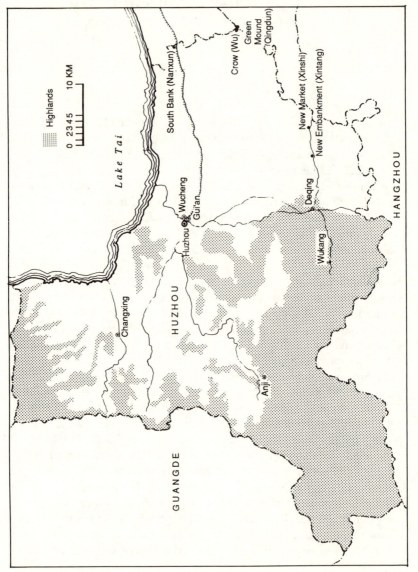

MAP 1. Huzhou Prefecture

originally belonged to separate prefectures and were first joined together in the Six Dynasties (Shiba 1975a:33).

Contrary to what one might expect, the highland regions of Huzhou were settled before the lowlands. The lowland areas were not fertile river valleys suitable for agriculture; they were malarial swamps. Only after a base had been established in the upland areas, starting in the Han dynasty (206 B.C.–A.D.219) and extending through the Tang (618–910), did the early settlers first drain and then move down into the river deltas. Previously, historians have thought that polder fields in the lowlands fueled the Tang–Song commercial revolution, but it is likely that the mountainous areas continued to play an important role in the regional economy. Shiba notes that throughout the region surrounding Huzhou, the northern Zhejiang highlands, steady population growth occurred in the Song, although little new land was available for exploitation: "It may be that, while there were few areas where the population could expand by cultivating new terrain, the production of hilly specialties [tea, silk, lumber, paper, stationery, dye, lacquer, and minerals] in the hinterland, along with lowered transaction costs, made it possible for the area to sustain a thriving economy for several centuries" (Shiba 1986:38).

Now a sleepy little town a few hours' bus ride from Hangzhou and only recently (1985) opened to tourists, the county seat of Huzhou today gives little indication of its importance in the Southern Song. Yet in the Song, the prefectural seat of Huzhou was a thriving metropolis. Endowed with a beautiful landscape and easily accessible by water, Huzhou prefecture attracted many people, even some long-time residents who maintained their household registers in neighboring Hangzhou. The prefecture contains several major rivers as well as a spur of the Grand Canal running from Suzhou into the mountains west of Huzhou city. In addition to these major waterways, a network of small streams and channels, many of which are navigable, criss-crosses the region. The variable winds across Lake Tai made it less useful for shipping than these rivers and the spur of the Grand Canal.

Huzhou's network of waterways contributed to its importance as a commercial center in the Song. In 1077 the commercial tax receipts from Huzhou ranked, by Shiba's count, twentieth in all of China (*Song huiyao, Shihuo* 16:8a, unaggregated figures; Shiba 1975b:226). Overall the population of Huzhou increased throughout the Northern Song and the first fifty years of the Southern Song and leveled off after 1180. The decade of the 1120s was a difficult one for Huzhou: in the 1120–1121 uprising of Fang La, one of his followers actually took over the prefectural seat (Kao 1963:33), and the Jurchen armies continuously raided the area just south of the Yangzi. Of course, one of the major factors contributing to Huzhou's growth in the twelfth century was the transfer of the capital from Kaifeng, after the fall of Northern China to the Jin in 1127, to the south. In 1138, Hangzhou was made the official temporary capital (*xingzai*). About 20,000 high officials, tens of thousands of clerks, and 400,000 soldiers and their families moved to Hangzhou and its environs at the time (Shiba 1975a:19). With this shift Huzhou prefecture was suddenly right next to Hangzhou—eighty kilometers separated the prefectural seat of Huzhou from the capital city, whose burgeoning population provided a market for Huzhou goods and crops. And in 1163–1164, the most populous county in Huzhou prefecture, Wucheng (in the lowlands along the Grand Canal), ranked fortieth in China (Shiba 1975b:226).

As one thirteenth-century observer, Fang Hui, pointed out in an essay about the productivity of land, the life of those in the lowlands was very different from those in the mountains. He drew the contrast neatly:

> I have seen tenants carrying rice—sometimes one *dou*, sometimes five or seven, three or four *sheng*—to their store where they exchange it for incense, pictures of gods, oil, salt, soy sauce, vinegar, rice noodles, flour, bran, noodles, pepper, ginger, and different types of medicine. The storeowners all use rice as the basis for prices. In one day, they obtain several tens of *dan* of rice, and as soon as they reach a hundred, they ship the rice by boat to Hangzhou, Xiuzhou, Nanxun, and Suzhou, where they exchange the rice for money, which they use to buy goods to sell on their return. The tenants in the watery regions are like this.[3]
>
> Those in the hills are different. If you want to know their annual budget, it consists only of foodstuffs and what they plant in paddy and mountain fields, minus the rent they pay to the landlord. They do not know of military service or of corvée. And so they resignedly eke out their lives by working diligently. (*Gujin kao* 18:698–99; Miyazawa 1985:73)

Those living in the lowlands obtained food at the market; strikingly, they did not use money but instead bartered for goods, whose price was set in terms of rice. Money crossed hands, not where the peasants went to local market, but at bigger marketing centers. Nanxun (South

---

3. *Sheng, dou,* and *dan* are all units of volume. One *dan* equaled ten *dou*, which equaled one hundred *sheng*, with a *sheng* in the Song equal to .9488 liters, a *dou* equal to 9.488 liters, and a *dan* equal to 94.88 liters (Ogawa 1968:1224–25).

Bank) was a market town in Huzhou established during the Southern Song; one of the cults discussed in this chapter was located there. Hangzhou is, of course, the capital; Xiuzhou (Jiaxing, Zhejiang) is located on a spur of the Grand Canal which joins it at Suzhou.

Whereas people in the lowlands lived close to navigable rivers and had easier access to markets, those in the hills did not. In the lowlands, people lived in the interstices of the crisscrossing rivers and streams. They raised rice in irrigated fields and commercial crops, which they traded at markets, sometimes to obtain even foodstuffs. They went by boat to market, and they hosted people who came by boat from other regions. Yet, even as late as the thirteenth century, people living upland continued to grow their own food. The rest of this chapter will analyze the pantheons of Huzhou, looking first at the mountain regions, then at the lowlands, in order to suggest how life, as reflected in temple cults, varied between these two areas.

The Mountain Counties

The local pantheons of Huzhou reflected the accretion of different types of deities over time.[4] Because the details of a given historical figure's apotheosis are often lost, the origins of cults to classical heroes who lived in pre-Han or Han times are, of necessity, less clear than those to gods who lived in the Song. Less clouded by the passage of time are accounts of Six Dynasties (221–586), Sui (586–618), and Tang heroes. The listings in local histories and inscriptions give more information about the feats these deities performed when still alive; they frequently borrow from the biographies in the official histories to do so. In the longer-settled mountains in eastern Huzhou, in Wukang and Changxing counties, were clustered most of the temples to ancient deities: to the legendary settlers of Huzhou, the Fangfengs; to Fuchai, the younger brother of the ruler of the pre-Qin Wu kingdom, who organized irrigation works; to Supervisor Zhao, a Han official in charge of mining copper who pitied the workers and who was killed in a rock slide; and to a Han figure, General Fan.

Although these gods were said to have lived in much earlier periods, local histories usually date the founding or reconstruction of these temples to the Six Dynasties period. One Five Dynasties inscription to

4. See tables 3 and 4 for a full list of gods in the Huzhou pantheon and explanation of the different types of deities.

the Fangfeng temple in Wukang county comments that, although there are many conflicting dates given for the founding of the temple, it was definitely rebuilt in the period 806–820, the date of an inscription no longer extant (*Liangzhe jinshi* 4:35b). Some of the evidence mustered to support a claim to an early founding was weak; one Song commentator notes that, because the images in the Supervisor Zhao Temple in Wukang have Tang-dynasty style clothes, the temple must have dated to the Tang (*Quesao bian* 2:21b). The paucity of evidence from pre-Song periods characterized many of these mountain temples. Although the deities lived in the Han or even pre-Han times, records of the temples go back only to the Six Dynasties or the Tang periods. This is, of course, when the bulk of China's population began to move south. Little is known of Huzhou before then; very possibly the deities, their achievements, or their connections to Huzhou were all legendary.

In an inscription from Wukang county, dated 1101, Mao Pang, the county magistrate, gives the history of a temple that goes back at least to the Tang, if not earlier. In 1101 there has been no rain and the use of the Indian drought method (*Xizhu ganfa*) has failed to bring any. "The elders of the county said, 'Eight *li* to the west of the county was Responding Echo Mountain, and a dragon lived at the foot of the mountain in the middle of a pool. Why don't you go ask him for rain?'" Mao checks the local history (*tudie*) and sees that the dragon previously brought rain in the Tang at the request of the local magistrate.[5] Interestingly, Mao comments, "In recent years I have heard that many places have slacked off in their tax payments. Only Wukang has remitted its taxes to the local officials on schedule" (*Dongtang ji* 9:15b–16a). Mao has mentioned the county's history for a reason: because without rain the county cannot pay its taxes, it is in the government's interest to bring rain and to reward the dragon for doing so. When the dragon brings rain, Mao applies for a temple plaque for him. The plaque is awarded (*Song huiyao, Li* 20:66b).[6] Mao says that "originally there was no temple so the local people, responding to the kindness of the emperor, contributed money to construct a building of twenty rooms" (*Dongtang ji* 9:15b). The absence of a temple strongly suggests that it was the site itself—the mountain and the pool—that was important, not the temple, as was usually the case with popular deities. The

5. The *Yongle dadian* (2281:14a) gives the date as 813.
6. Both Mao Pang and *The Important Documents* refer to this temple as the Deep Response (Yuanying) temple, whereas the 1201 gazetteer calls it Deep Virtue (Yuande) temple.

dragon temple provides a good example of a deity whose miracles were agricultural, with possibly very early antecedents.[7]

The economy of the hilly region was not entirely agricultural, however. By 1112, the area was beginning to be pulled into the commercial nexus of the Lower Yangzi. In an inscription from Anji, a low-ranking official from another county, Peng Xiu, describes the erection of a temple to the God of the Eastern Peak begun in 1100 and completed in 1112.[8] He points out that Mount Tai was traditionally the most important of the five peaks in China and argues that it has the highest position in the register of sacrifices. Temples of the cult, based in Mount Tai in Shandong, have been located on steep mountains in other places, and Anji's terrain—in the western half of Huzhou—is mountainous with streams running through it.

> The land is rich in silk and hemp. People live off the profits. Big merchants from ten thousand li come to gather here. It is one of the great regions of the Southeast. The city's pattern is tall and imposing, with many luxurious buildings of decorated columns and floating pillars, which impart a sense of great depth. But to worship the god there is not an inch of spare land. (*Liangzhe jinshi* 7:26a)

Peng continues, saying that "every year people organize a small, impromptu association to welcome and send off (*songying*) the deity [the God of the Eastern Peak], that is all. . . . At the time of the festival those who have come by boat and land brush shoulders and step on each other's toes." This is a standard cliché for temple inscriptions; people's shoulders are always brushing, and they are always stepping on each other's toes. So too the use of ten thousand li, which cannot be taken literally. But the arrival of people on land and by water is noteworthy. The author of this inscription does not say much about the deity's miracles, commenting only that "whenever there is too much or too little rain or someone is ill, the local people pray at the temple" (*Liangzhe jinshi* 7:26a–b). The mention of textiles provides an

7. Even in ancient China people prayed to dragons for rain. With the introduction of Buddhism into China, the Indian concept of nagas—creatures with a dragon's body and a man's head who occupied underwater kingdoms—merged with that of the dragon. From the Tang through the Yuan people wrote prayers addressed to the reigning dragon on metal or stone tablets and tossed them into pools where a dragon was thought to reside (Des Rotours 1966:261–64).

8. Many temples to the God of the Eastern Peak were built in the early 1100s; they may have been linked with the imperially sponsored Daoist revival during Huizong's reign (see chapter 2). This particular inscription indicates, however, that the cult also commanded popular support.

important clue to the identities of those backing the temple; they could have been the Anji textile merchants. This inscription testifies both to the production of silk in the mountainous county and to the availability of transportation.[9]

Several inscriptions from a temple to a Tang hero, Li Jing, underline the harshness of the mountainous terrain of Anji and reveal the precarious existence of the people who lived there. The link between Anji and Li Jing was tenuous. He had occupied Danyang (Zhenjiang, Jiangsu) sometime during the period 619–626, and at that time Anji fell under his jurisdiction. There were temples to Li Jing in other places in China; the 1183 inscription cites one in Guancheng (Zheng county, Honan), but it does not seem to have had any ties with the temple in Anji.[10] This inscription notes that, "In the case that one year there was too little or too much rain, the people prayed at the temple. Rain or clear skies responded each time like an echo." Exactly the same phrases recur in many other temple inscriptions, but they suggest that Li Jing, like so many other gods, was an agricultural deity. Later the inscription says that, "When the silkworms and wheat were almost ready to harvest, excessive rain fell. Just as the people sighed and prayed, the sky cleared. In the fall the harvest was good." The god also protected the district from locusts in neighboring counties (*Liangzhe jinshi* 10:7a–b).

A 1247 grant of a title to Li Jing describes the county of Anji, saying, "The county has ten thousand mountains and one river. It is terribly dry." More of Li Jing's miracles are listed: bringing rain in 1200, preventing a locust attack in 1208, curing the ill, and preventing floods in 1209. Then in 1246, from the third to fifth months, "it did not rain and the seeds did not enter the earth." The prefect decides to summon Li Jing's image to his office in order to pray for rain. On the day he and his underlings visit the temple to get the image, it is so hot that everyone is sweating and panting. Just as they place the image in the palanquin, clouds cover the sky and it rains all night and the next day, stops, and then resumes two days later.

> This is because the hills are twisted and the land is inclined upward in Anji. When it is slightly dry, the land is totally parched. When the land is slightly damp, it is inundated. The King [referring to Li Jing by his title] accordingly made it rain and subse-

9. Writing in 1154, Chen Fu commented that some of the residents of Anji county were able to live off the proceeds of silk cultivation and that they did not farm (*Nongshu* 3:21, translated in Shiba 1970:116).

10. *The Important Documents* (*Song huiyao*, Li 20:31b) mentions two temples to Li Jing in Shanxi, but these also do not seem to have been linked with the temple in Anji.

quently clear up until the water had flowed down to the lower branches. Only then did he cause it to rain again because he was afraid of the rivers choking with too much rain or hurting the people. So wondrous is he for protecting the people in this way. (*Wuxing jinshi* 12:3a)

The people praying to Li Jing live off the land; they inhabit the harsh terrain with its uncertain rainfall. They see the staggered showers as proof that Li Jing understood the topography of the region. In fact, their crediting him with this knowledge reveals just how great their own understanding was. Their ingenious explanation highlights the importance of a deity's followers in recognizing his miracles.

The inscriptions from the temple to Li Jing and that of the God of the Eastern Peak in Anji county describe the same terrain, but they take very different attitudes toward it. The Li Jing inscriptions were written from the point of the view of the cultivators; his miracles have to do with rain and curing illness. Remember Fang Hui's self-sufficient hill-dwellers who do not go to market; people like them probably figured among Li Jing's supporters. But only three li away was the temple to the God of the Eastern Peak. Its supporters were not just people whose entire well-being hinged on the annual rainfall, but also merchants who traveled great distances by boat to trade silk and hemp.[11] And if Li Jing's followers worshipped him as a god with an intimate knowledge of the land they worked, the merchants supporting the God of the Eastern Peak selected a deity whose appeal was not limited to only those from Anji but extended to anyone who chose to come and trade in Anji. Li Jing's supporters bemoan the ratio of hills to rivers in Anji as ten thousand to one, but, for the merchants supporting the God of the Eastern Peak, that one river sufficed to get them and their boats to Anji and to the markets there. Again and again one sees this tension between deities who embody localism and those whose appeal is broader.

The Lowlands

In the highland areas, with the exception of a few temples to new, low-born gods,[12] long-established temples, like those to the Wukang

---

11. An 1117 inscription from another temple to the God of the Eastern Peak on Fu mountain outside Suzhou mentions devotees coming overland and by water from the Huai and Yangzi river valleys, Fujian, and Guangdong (*Qinchuan zhi* 13:44b). I am indebted to Barend ter Haar for this reference.

12. Of the three highland cults to the commoner gods, at least one seems to have been

dragon and to Li Jing, were common. In contrast, in the lowlands, temples newly active in the Five Dynasties period or the Song seem to have predominated. This difference suggests that the highlands were settled before the lowlands (Shiba 1976). Population data from Ming gazetteers confirm this impression, showing that much of the growth in Huzhou's population during the Song took place in the lowlands in the eastern half of the prefecture, in Deqing, Gui'an, and Wucheng counties (see appendix table 2). There are gaps and irregularities in these figures, but certain trends can be glimpsed. In the lowlands, the number of households in Wucheng county increased 160 percent, in Gui'an 68 percent, and in Deqing 202 percent in the period from 1008 to 1290. This growth must have been partially due to the improved agricultural techniques of the Southern Song, especially the erection of wooden barriers that allowed better control of water in polder fields. Not all the lowlands were already enclosed and intensively farmed during the Song. As late as the 1360s and 1370s, 94 percent of the fields in the prefectural seat of Huzhou were enclosed, but only 45 percent in Wucheng and 25 percent in Gui'an were (Shiba 1975b:236). So even in the heart of the Lower Yangzi, the area covered by polder fields was limited.

As the population figures from Yuan and Ming local histories indicate that more and more people were living in the lowlands, so too does the increasing number of new townships (*zhen*) in this area point to a greater concentration of population in the lowlands. The central government wanted to tap the increasing wealth of these areas and established townships (an administrative unit lower than county) to do so; tax returns from the eastern half of Huzhou continued to increase during the Southern Song, while those from the western half declined (Shiba 1975b:231). One prefect of Huzhou, Xue Jixuan (1134–1173), commented that, "Although Crow (Wu) and New Market (Xinshi) are called townships, the surrounding area is prosperous and the tax receipts are many. Many county seats [a higher administrative unit] cannot match them" (*Langyu ji* 18:19b).[13] Both population statistics

derived from an earlier lowland cult: a son, who like Filial Cao was executed in his father's place, was worshipped in Wukang county from 1253 on (*Kangxi Wukang* 4:25a). One man from Changxing county went to Shandong, died on his return in 1121, and became a god linked with the regional cult to King Zhang (see chapter 5 for more about Marquis Li) (*Jiaqing Changxing* 26:20a–21b). Wukang county had a temple to a man with the identical biography but a different name, about whom nothing else is known (*Yongle dadian* 2281:14a).

13. In the Song the units of administration differed from those in later dynasties. The largest unit was the circuit (*lu*), underneath it the prefecture (*fu* or *zhou*) or commandery (*jun*), and then the county (*xian*). The term *zhen* is often translated as garrison; yet be-

and the growing number of townships indicate that throughout the Song the center of gravity in Huzhou was shifting literally downward—out of the mountain districts into the lowlands.

This shift downward also is reflected in the distribution of temples to the commoner deities founded in the Song—gods, like Commander Fan, whose cults took off with incredible speed. Of the eleven temples to commoner deities in Huzhou, eight were in the lowland counties of Deqing, Wucheng, Gui'an, or the prefectural seat of Huzhou (see appendix table 3). One man in Deqing county gave away so much rice during a famine that he was impoverished and committed suicide: the local people built a temple to him at the time of his death in 1055 (*Deqing xian xuzhi* 2:5a). Filial Cao, who was executed in his father's stead at the turn of the twelfth century, was worshipped in three different places: Huzhou city as well as Wucheng and Deqing counties (*Jiatai Wuxing* 13:11a, 14a; *Qianlong Huzhou* 40:24a). The 1120s, which witnessed the Fang La rebellion as well as Jurchen attacks, gave rise to several new deities: one who died while trying to ship grain to the people of Deqing county (*Deqing xian xuzhi* 2:5a), one man from Gui'an county who distributed food during a famine and fought against Fang La (*Wuxing jinshi* 12:10b–12b), and two low-ranking officials who also donated grain to the people of Wucheng county in this period (*Wuxing jinshi* 12:20a–23b). Finally, in the late thirteenth century one man drowned while trying to save some people in an accident in Deqing county; he too became a god (*Yongle dadian* 2281:15b). These gods lacked noble backgrounds, and they tended to be local, even parochial figures, whose lives were cut short.

In talking about the highlands, I argued that the temple to the God of the Eastern Peak in Anji enjoyed the support of merchants partially because it was not associated with just one locality or one group of people.[14] An inscription dated 1134 from the township of New Market describes another temple to the same god. Between 1102 and 1106 the local people began to build a temple to the god, but unexpectedly there was a bad harvest and they stopped work. In 1127, with no other tem-

---

cause these settlements' commercial role outweighed their military importance, I translate the term as township.

14. Sangren (1980:214) makes a similar point about a town in contemporary Taiwan. In Daqi, families originally from Quanzhou and Zhangzhou in Fujian continue to worship local deities whose cults originated in the mainland. Yet, because the Hakka, a minority ethnic group, had so little success in getting posts, their deities were not former officials, but the Buddhist goddess of mercy, Guanyin, and the gods of heaven, earth, and water (*sanguan dadi*). Neither Guanyin nor the gods of heaven, earth, and water were associated with any one place in China.

ple to pray at, they gathered at the temple to ask for help against the invading Jin armies. The Jin did not attack Huzhou, and the 1134 reconstruction of the temple was paid for by one man who held the rank of *baoyi lang* (military 8a), one with the rank of *chengxin lang* (military 8b), one with the rank of *digong lang* (executory 9b), an advanced degree holder, and an assistant instructor (*zhujiao*), who was most likely the holder of a facilitated degree.[15] They commissioned a text from an advanced degree holder who had served in another county. All six men had different surnames. After describing the new temple, Yao Yi[16] says, "This is not a temple whose believers come from only one canton. In the first month of every year people brush shoulders who come from several hundreds of li away to give money and to make offerings" (*Tongzhi Huzhou* 53:14a). Note that Yao specifically says that not just local people come, but also those from farther away. It was very likely that, as in Anji, it was merchants who backed this interregional cult. They had the transportation to allow them to cover such great distances; they came not just to make offerings but to trade.

Halfway between the county seat of Deqing and New Market, right on the river that linked them, was New Embankment (Xintang) canton (see map 1). The local earth god there was a Six Dynasties hero, Lu Zai. New Embankment's advantageous location on the waterway would have made it logical for its residents to engage in trade. And an 1163 inscription reveals that is exactly what they did. After giving a version of the deity's biography very similar to that in the official histories,[17] the document suddenly shifts from the Six Dynasties to the Song:

> From 1119 to 1130, many bandits [alluding to Fang La] rebelled in nearby districts, and only New Embankment was not the slightest bit harmed. The locally powerful led the people to protect the area, and one of them dreamt that the deity sent spirit soldiers to help. People of other districts all fled their own lands and depended on the deity to keep them safe. Whenever this district encounters flooding or drought, and we pray, rain or clear skies always follow. (*Wuxing jinshi* 9:17b)

15. Facilitated degrees (*tezou ming jinshi*) were degrees granted to men over fifty who had failed the examinations in the capital several times. These titles had little prestige and did not grant the holder the right to extend protection to his kin. After 1079 the titles of *wenxue* (professor) or *zhujiao* were most frequently awarded to them (Chaffee 1985:24, 28).

16. Yao took his advanced degree in 1115 and served as the vice-prefect of Taiping zhou Commandery (*Xinshi zhenzhi* 3:5b, 11a).

17. See *Beishi* 68:2391.

Because this last line, or some variant, recurs throughout all temple inscriptions, it indicates only that agriculturalists figured among Lu Zai's supporters.

The next miracle is more revealing: "This district grows many lotus pods and roots. In past years, these were harmed by pests. When we prayed to the deity, one night a strong wind and rain swept the locusts entirely away" (*Wuxing jinshi* 9:17b). Lotuses were not subsistence, but rather commercial, crops, indicating that New Embankment had become part of the Lower Yangzi market network. The inscription bears this out:

> Many of this district's residents travel by boat to distant places to trade. On the day of departure, the people always pray to the deity and paint his image in their boats. They pray to him morning and night. When they travel on a river or lake, even when they encounter wind or waves, he provides them with safe passage every time. (*Wuxing jinshi* 9:17b–18a)

This god, then, is not just the deity of those who grow the crops for the market, but for those who ship the crops to market as well.

The last miracle recounted in the inscription also testifies to the importance of merchant support for the cult. In the year preceding the petition to promote Lu Zai (possibly in 1162), a thief stole a merchant's boat and two children who had been left on board to guard it. After taking the boat more than ten li away, he killed the two children. The sheriff and his bowmen prayed to the deity and set a deadline for him to help them find the murderer (*Wuxing jinshi* 9:18a). The inscription does not say so, but on the basis of other examples we can surmise that they threatened to hurt him (or his image) if he did not. The thief was subsequently caught within the allotted time in Suzhou, just where the Huzhou spur of the Grand Canal connected with the Grand Canal itself—a major artery of the Lower Yangzi river system.

Not just cultivators and not just merchants, but even local government officials supported this cult. The petition to the central government was sent by a low-ranking official in charge of maintaining the embankments and boat yards (*pai'an jian chuanchang*), and a man with the rank of *baoyi lang* (military 8a) paid for the carving of the grant onto a stele (*Wuxing jinshi* 9:16b–19a). The Song records give us no information about other temples in New Embankment, but given that the author of the petition refers to Lu Zai as the local earth god, it seems likely that Lu Zai was the dominant deity there. His appeal was limited to the residents of New Embankment, be they cultivators, merchants, or local officials, and it did not extend to people of other districts. This one document gives a needle-sharp image of a cult at one point in time—1163.[18]

Just down the river from New Embankment was New Market, an aptly named township. A 1525 local history explains the town's name, saying that it was founded in 308, after another settlement had been flooded, because of its proximity to water (*Jiaqing Deqing* 1:17b). An unequaled eight inscriptions spanning 1099 to 1235 from the Eternally Efficacious (Yongling) temple offer a look at the history of this cult through the Southern Song.

The first of these inscriptions, dated 1099, commemorates the rebuilding of the temple. The author, Taishi Zhang, gives the biography of the deity, a general named Zhu Si, who lived in the third century A.D., and then a history of the temple. Although Taishi signs only his name without giving any title, he was a local literatus who had passed the civil service exams in 1085 (*Xinshi zhenzhi* 3:5b). Several classical references in the text indicate that he had received a traditional education. He begins with a general discussion of deities, saying that "great deities preside over a nation, lesser deities only over a canton." General Zhu is one of the latter. Said to have been born in New Market, he is very much a local deity.

As Taishi's story, related in the introduction, about receiving the text from the mysterious old man indicates, General Zhu was a figure of doubtful historicity. No matter. His purported accomplishments, even if made up by the Song elders, provide insight into the concerns of his followers.

> In [A.D.] 239 there was a severe drought and everything the people had was scorched. They had no one to turn to. Just then, the general took big urns and put them in the deep places in the rivers and gullies in order to bring water and avert the danger. The people depended on him for salvation. At this time the general was also concerned about the possibility of repeated drought so for ten years he worked to clear the Yang river route. In all famine years the northwest wind drives water from great streams into the county and makes travel by boat possible.

The first deed shows that the people of New Market depended on a reliable source of water to irrigate their crops; the second, that they needed waterways to trade. In 953 drought struck New Market, and when General Zhu brought rain, his followers petitioned the Wuyue

18. *The Important Documents* lists both this grant and a further promotion in 1174 (*Song huiyao*, Li 20:20b; 21:40b).

kingdom (a regional kingdom that ruled the Lower Yangzi between 910 and 960) for a title. He was given the title "Keeping-the-Peace-General" (*baoning jiangjun*). Because the temple had fallen into disrepair in the intervening 150 years, several people identified only as people of the township (*zhenren*) contributed money for the repair of the temple and financed the carving of the 1099 inscription (*Tongzhi Huzhou* 53:8b–9a). It is perhaps not a coincidence that one of these people is named Zhu; the Zhus may have viewed General Zhu as their ancestor.

Only in 1135 did the central government, in response to a request by the elders of New Market led by Chen Xiu, award the temple its first plaque. The grant states that General Zhu helped to protect the district during the Fang La rebellion (1120–1121). Significantly, the grant refers to General Zhu as the earth god of New Market, further reinforcing his identity as a local god (*Liangzhe jinshi* 8:36a–37a). The activities of the elders on General Zhu's behalf did not stop there. In 1139, General Zhu was promoted to the rank of marquis.[19] This time his supporters are called elders and market householders (*shihu*).[20] The 1139 grant, also from the Imperial Secretariat, cites the 1135 grant concerning the deity's miracles during the Fang La rebellion; in 1137 the general brought rain in response to the local people's prayers, and in 1138 he brought clear skies after a period of too much rain (*Liangzhe jinshi* 8:39a–40a). An 1140 commemorative inscription recaps the deity's miracles to date and expresses the local people's gratitude to him. It was probably written to accompany the 1139 grant of a new title; perhaps it was carved underneath or on the back of the grant. Drafted by Sun Yujin, who identifies himself only as a local man (*yiren*), but who had been in fact a low-ranking official,[21] the inscription's calligraphy and heading in seal script were done by a Hangzhou man.

The 1140 inscription is of great interest and value because it gives a list of supporters at the end of the text. Of the nine people whose names are given, two hold no functional office but have the rank of *lang*: one is a *chengxin lang* (military 8b), and one a *baoyi lang* (military 8a). Two are tax officials of the township who seem to have been appointed on a temporary basis (*tianchai zhenshui*); one is in charge of taxes and fire-fighting (*yanhuo gongshi*). The remaining four are the county magistrate, the assistant magistrate, the registrar, and the sheriff. These men all had different surnames: Bi, Sun, Zhao, Nie, Cai,

---

19. Both grants are mentioned in *The Important Documents* (*Song huiyao, Li* 20:161a).

20. The leading petitioner's surname is given as Lu, his given name as Xiu. This is probably a mistaken transcription for Chen Xiu.

21. See his biography in *Xinshi zhenzhi* 3:11a. He served as administrator of public order (*silu canjun*) in Jiangzhou (Jiangxi) in the period 1127–1130.

Lu, Wang, Chen, and Liu (*Liangzhe jinshi* 8:40b–42a). None was from the Zhu family. The list of names is in reverse order of rank, with the highest-ranking at the bottom of the list; it is probably a list of donors, not just of those who financed the carving of the 1139 grant and the 1140 commemorative text, but probably of those who financed the petition to the government for the title as well. Very possibly the two men who held no functional office were the largest donors. Significantly, local officials not only submitted the petition for a temple grant to the central government but also contributed money to this cult, further suggesting ties between locally important people and the officials who served in their areas.

For about fifty years following this spate of activity in the 1130s, nothing happened to merit the carving of an inscription. Then in 1203, Chen Jian,[22] who had served as a member of the Bureau of Compilation (bianxiu ju) in Hangzhou in the 1190s, wrote a commemorative text following General Zhu's 1196 promotion to four-character marquis. In his history of the temple he says that in 1196 a man named Zhu Fu, who held the rank of *xiuwu lang* (military 7a), led the local gentry and common people to petition the government for a new title; in addition to General Zhu's promotion, his consort also received a title (*Xinshi zhenzhi* 5:2a; *Song huiyao, Li* 21:43a). Zhu Fu's brother, Zhu Ren, commissioned Chen to write the inscription.

In the section concerning miracles, Chen describes the local people's custom of putting lanterns up for three days to celebrate the deity's birthday. The splendidly decorated cloth and glass lanterns surpass those at New Year's. Previously people used to light reed mats as torches; Chen weakly asserts that the absence of any fires is due to the deity's power. Chen then argues that the lamps show General Zhu's devotion to Buddha and that lighting lamps is Buddhist (*Tongzhi Huzhou* 53:27a–28a). Lamps may have been Buddhist, but they were not exclusively so. The lack of any mention of Buddhism in earlier inscriptions suggests that the insertion of Buddhist ideas is entirely Chen's invention. Chen's inscription, with its contrived attempt to construct a miracle out of the reed mats and its forced efforts to link the general with Buddhism, hints at a falling off of popular support for General Zhu.

So too does the twenty-seven-year gap between the Imperial Secretariat's grant of two more characters to the general in 1196 and its being carved onto a stele in 1223. Such a delay would have been unlikely in the peak period of the general's popularity in the 1140s. This

---

22. See his biography in *Xinshi zhenzhi* 3:11b.

time, as in 1203, the stele was financed only by people of the surname Zhu: a man with a post in the village service system (*zhangwu bao*), one of his sons who held the rank of *jiangshi lang* (executory class 9b), one unranked son, and their wives and children. A nephew, who was an assistant sheriff (*fuwei*), wrote the seal-script heading (*Liangzhe jinshi* 11:18b–19b). The exact nature of the ties between the people named Zhu and General Zhu remains unclear. Just one person of the surname Zhu appears in the first inscription of 1099, and none in that of 1040. But by the 1200s, the sole people named as donors are Zhus. General Zhu seems to have become the god of the Zhu lineage and no longer that of all of New Market. We simply do not know enough about the activities of the New Market Zhus—whether they compiled a genealogy, conducted worship at their families' graves, or built an ancestral hall—to decide if they qualify as a lineage in modern anthropological usage (Ebrey 1986).[23] They did not use a common naming system for men of the same generation.

In 1234 General Zhu was given two more characters, so that he became a six-character marquis: this text, like the other grants from the Imperial Secretariat, summarizes the original petition from a local official in abbreviated language.[24] Unfortunately the original is not extant. The grant states, "In recent years the deity's power has been especially manifest. He caused locust pests to be swept by the wind into the water. He sent a dream showing where the bandit's lair was" (*Liangzhe jinshi* 11:34a–35a). These miracles bear more than a passing resemblance to those of the New Embankment local earth god, Lu Zai, as described in the 1163 inscription:

> One night a strong wind and rain swept the pests completely away. . . . The sheriff and his bowmen all prayed sincerely to the god [Lu Zai] asking him to bestow his help so that they could quickly capture him [the kidnapper and murderer of the two small

23. An undated entry from a gazetteer that predates 1408 (*Yongle dadian* 2281:15a–b) and the author of an inscription from 1507 (*Xinshi zhenzhi* 6:7a) may be citing earlier accounts when they note that General Zhu appeared in the dreams of his lineage members (*zuren*) and asked them to build him a temple, but because no Song account uses the word *zu* (lineage) to characterize the Zhus, it is more likely that they are presenting a later version of the temple's founding.

24. The final grant of a title in the Song was in 1234, but activity at the temple did not stop then. A new temple, also in Deqing county, was built between 1265 and 1274. Repairs on both temples continued through the Ming and Qing dynasties (*Xinshi zhen xuzhi* 1:6a). The high level of activity in later periods may help to account for the unusual preservation of so many inscriptions from the Eternally Efficacious temple in the Song.

children]. They then set a time and a day. The result was that they caught him at Pingjiang prefecture [Suzhou]. The timing did not vary from that in the original agreement. (*Wuxing jinshi* 9:17b–18a)

Admittedly there are differences between the two accounts. Lu Zai sent wind and rain to battle the locusts; General Zhu sent wind that caused the locusts to enter water. Lu Zai enabled the kidnappers to be caught in Suzhou, but no dream is mentioned; General Zhu revealed the location of an unnamed bandit's lair through a dream. The order of events in the two accounts is the same: first locusts, then defeat of bandits. The differences may well be due to changes occurring in the process of oral transmission.[25]

The resemblance is not accidental. General Zhu's supporters have had no new miracles to report since the 1140s; since 1196 they have only repeated standard phrases about bringing rain and clear skies, without mentioning any specific miracles. Chen Jian tried to link the general with Buddhism and argued feebly that the lack of fires during the lantern festival was tantamount to a miracle. The author of the original petition, which resulted in the 1234 grant, claimed the miracles of a rival deity as the deity's own. Lu Zai's temple was just down the river; his annual festival fell on the thirteenth day of the fourth month, just one day before General Zhu's on the fourteenth (*Wuxing jinshi* 9:17b; *Tongzhi Huzhou* 53:28a). His supporters must have come to New Market often to trade their lotus roots and pods. They traveled in boats decorated with Lu's image, and they must have talked about his miracles. The 1234 grant reveals that people in one place knew about the doings of other deities, that people compared miracles, and that the people of one place did not hesitate to claim the miracles of a neighboring deity as those of their own.

The supporters of earth gods from New Embankment and New Market were all drawn into the expanding market system. In these different communities people who made their money through trade supported local deities; they were able to exercise their influence with local officials to ensure titles for those deities. Part of what motivated them was a sense of place. These examples are from places where information about only one earth god survives; it is easy under the circumstances to suppose that the residents of New Embankment and New Market worshipped only their respective earth gods, and that no other gods existed in these towns. However, two temple inscriptions

25. I am indebted to the members of Philip Kuhn's document-reading seminar at Harvard for discussing this problem with me (April 1987).

from another new township, South Bank (Nanxun), right on the Huzhou branch of the Grand Canal, suggest that, although we frequently know about only the gods who received titles, there may very well have been other deities who were these earth gods' rivals but about whom no evidence survives.

In 1270, in the last years of the Song, the Imperial Secretariat granted the title Auspicious Response (*Jiaying*) to the two resident deities of South Bank, Li and Cui, in response to a petition from the emissary of the Imperial Intendant and the elders.[26] Alive in the 1120s, Li and Cui had organized South Bank's struggle against the Fang La bandits and personally had donated grain during famine years. After their deaths, the local people built a temple to them: "The clothes of the two images imitated that of two images of guardian deities who protected the district." The similarity suggests that the cult to the two men may have supplanted an earlier cult. A list of typical miracles follows: the deities brought rain and clear skies, cured illnesses, drove locusts away, allowed famine victims to rest on temple grounds,[27] and saved an official from drowning (*Wuxing jinshi* 12:20b–21a).

The later miracles shed more light on the identities of the two gods' devotees. In 1254 salt-smuggling bandits came to South Bank and tossed moonblocks[28] in order to get the gods' permission to plunder the city, "a place where many rich merchants gathered." The gods' subsequent refusal suggests that the deities' supporters, who had something to fear from the bandits, were the wealthy merchants the bandits had selected as their target. Conversely, it suggests as well that the bandits respected the deity just as much as the city dwellers did. And in 1261 there was danger of flooding: "Troublemakers urged the people to borrow grain. The householders of the city burned incense and prayed. Suddenly the thugs' boats surrounded the city. Not long afterward, they dispersed. Someone asked them, 'How is it that you came so quickly and went so quickly?' " The bandits explained that they had seen two apparitions who had ordered them to leave (*Wuxing jinshi* 12:21b–22a).

Here too it was the rich, those who had grain stored, who would have been threatened by the people's forcible "borrowing." This last miracle highlights a detail in the deities' biographies: while still alive, they distributed grain during famine years. Li and Cui held the rank of *chengshi lang* (civil 9a). They may well have received their titles as com-

26. This document is also discussed in chapter 4.
27. This miracle was mentioned in chapter 3.
28. This miracle was mentioned in chapter 3.

pensation for distributing grain and organizing the local militia; the central government regularly granted (or sold) titles to such men (Wei 1974). Their activities on behalf of the community indicate that they belonged to the locally powerful when they were still alive.[29] In both the 1254 and 1262 miracles the deities side with the rich against grain robbers and those who advocate "borrowing" grain. Their loyalty to the wealthy suggests that the locally prosperous, very possibly grain merchants or householders with large stocks of grain themselves, were the main supporters of the cult. Their interest in protecting their property coincided neatly with those of local officials who wanted to keep order. In fact, local officials came to pray at the temple even before the government had awarded it a plaque, and it was they who petitioned the government to recognize the temple.[30]

The petition then goes on to explain why the two gods should be placed in the register of sacrifices. The first reason is the usual statement, even platitude, about reciprocity between men and deities: placing the two deities in the register of sacrifices is a way of showing the gods respect and enabling them to help the people. The next reason is far more telling. In an unusually explicit outburst of local consciousness, the petitioners say:

> For example, New Market, in Deqing county, is also administered by this prefecture. The local god of that township [referring to General Zhu, the god of the Eternally Efficacious temple] has already been granted a temple plaque. Only South Bank has not yet carried out the procedures to get the earth god into the register of sacrifices. It really is a gap in the register of sacrifices. (*Wuxing jinshi* 12:22a)

They succeed in their cause: the temple was awarded a plaque that year. On the basis of this inscription alone, one might conclude that the

---

29. Two nineteenth-century sources offer thought-provoking, if entirely unsubstantiated, information about the deities' biographies; they may reflect the embellishments of later oral versions. Wang Rizhen, the editor of *A History of South Bank Township*, says Li and Cui *chengshi* are the same deities as Li and Cui *fujun* (lord of the prefecture) in Yuan drama. Although the deities' last names are the same, their different titles make this doubtful (Takahashi Bunji, personal communication, April 1986). Cui, Wang says, was an official in the Lower Yangzi; Li, originally from Huizhou, was a merchant who came to South Bank to trade (*Nanxun zhenzhi* 5:1b). Wang's information may be wrong, but it does suggest that an alliance of grain merchants and officials supported this cult. Lu Xinyuan, editor of *A Collection of Inscriptions from Wuxing* speculates that, as neither of the two deities' names appears in any other records, they may have purchased their titles (*Wuxing jinshi* 12:26a).

30. See chapter 4 for a discussion of how this temple received recognition.

locally prosperous and the government officials formed an alliance to which no rival existed. But a forged title grant to the Repeated Fortune temple (Qianfu ci) also in South Bank, dated 1275 but most likely from the early years of the Yuan, indicates that other cults were present in the township (*Nanxun zhenzhi* 26:18a–19a).[31] Mentioned above was the example in which the author of the New Market earth god inscription claimed Lu Zai's miracles as General Zhu's. That was a more subtle deception than this text, in which the author lifts whole sections of text from the 1270 title grant to Li and Cui, making only a few slight changes in wording. Many errors and a total lack of originality betray that this title grant was a forgery. The initial lines of this inscription match those of the 1270 grant to Li and Cui exactly except that one step of the bureaucracy is left out—that between the fiscal intendant and the prefect of Huzhou—and one character in one of the petitioner's names is changed. The deity, Zhu Renfu, like Li and Cui, lived at the end of the Northern Song and fought Fang La. He also distributed grain. In 1243, his grandsons, both holders of advanced degrees, built a temple by his tomb, where the local people also worshipped. The document concludes with the summary of the bureaucratic procedures that precede inclusion in the register of sacrifices.[32] Who would have gone to such great effort to forge this grant? And why?

The first hint is that the deity's two grandsons, Zhu Ran and Zhu Lin, erected the temple to him in 1243.[33] And in the early years of the

31. I am indebted to Sugiyama Masaaki for his help with this text. He suggests that during the first decade of the Yuan, 1275, the year before Hangzhou fell to the Mongols, would have been viewed as a more auspicious year than the first years of the Yuan (personal communication, April 1986).

32. The editor of the local history that contains this document, Wang Rizhen, has an absolute field day identifying ways in which this text strays from the standard format of grants from the Imperial Secretariat: the phrasing concerning Zhu's pre-apotheosis acts is incorrect; the concurrent use of two dating systems, one by year and the other by sixty-year cycle, never occurs; the month given for Fang La's rebellion is wrong; and one of the place names in South Bank is mistaken. There are others. Let me add one to Wang's list: the temple was purportedly granted a three-character plaque, Repeated Fortune temple (Qianfu ci). In the Song, temple names always contained an even number of characters, from two to eight, and the word for temple was not counted among them.

33. They also apparently put up a forged tombstone for him at the time (*Nanxun zhenzhi* 26:1a), which they dated to the third month of 1120, when he supposedly died. Here, Zhu Ran, identified as his son (not grandson), is called the Intendant of Tea and Horses in Sichuan, but he never held this position (Paul Smith, personal communication, November 1986), and Zhu Lin, identified as Zhu Ran's younger brother, is called assistant prefect of Jiankang (Nanjing). The text is dated the third month of 1120, but Fang La did not rebel until the tenth month. Zhu would have been hard-pressed to serve in the government campaign against Fang La, which took place seven months after his

Yuan it was two brothers who financed the carving of the forged grant. Zhu Fei was a student at the imperial university (*taixue sheng*), and Zhu Zao was also a student with a stipend (*shouci sheng*). Denied any chance of becoming officials during the Yuan, they may have invested in a popular temple as an attempt to shore up their social status. The four supporters whose names are given all have the same family name as the deity: that their first names use the same radical for each generation points to their membership in the same lineage.

Their attempt, obvious as it is now, to create a popular cult to their ancestor was surely not as transparent to contemporary observers. The very blatancy of the forgery reveals a low level of literacy in South Bank. The Zhus were trying to get support from people who would not—possibly because they could not—compare the forged text with the original stele. The Zhu lineage's efforts to create a rival cult indicate that the cult to Li and Cui did not include everyone in South Bank. Their attempt to start a new cult failed; the cult did not replace that to Li and Cui. The author of a 1922 local history (*Nanxun zhi* 16:1a) lists the Repeated Fortune temple under ancestral shrines and not temples, which suggests that, although the building survived until the twentieth century, it did so only because of the Zhu lineage's continued support. Even the forgery of the temple plaque augured poorly for the future of the cult; much shorter than the grant it mimicked, it suggests that the Zhus did not have the financial resources to launch a cult on the same scope of that to Li and Cui.

Conclusion

The inscription from the Repeated Fortune temple gives the lie to the Auspicious Response temple's claim to represent all the people of the township of South Bank; it also gives pause to the analyst who assumes too readily that any given cult represents every resident in a given locality. One can be sure that, if the Zhus, a powerful lineage with several office holders and money to spare, did not feel included in the cult to Li and Cui, others less influential than they may have shared their dissatisfaction.

In examining these new cults in the lowlands of Huzhou—in New Market, New Embankment, and South Bank—I have argued that an alliance of locally influential people banded with government officials to support these cults. These local people are variously referred to in

---

supposed death. This text betrays a carelessness even more extreme than the forgery of the temple grant.

the inscriptions as "market householders," "residents," and "elders." They commanded sufficient sway to argue that natural events were the doings of the deities they backed, sufficient influence with local officials to get their petitions forwarded to the government, and sufficient financial resources to pay for petitions for titles and for the carving of those titles on steles. Much of the development of popular cults in the Song was the product of this stratum's activities. Local deities embodied their sense of place, and local cults gave them an outlet for their boosterism. These men were the Lion's and Rotary Club members of their day.

The example of the Zhu lineage cult in South Bank reminds us, however, that we cannot assume these locally powerful had a monopoly on popular religious cults. There must have been cults supported by less powerful, less influential, and less wealthy groups. Housed only in rooms in their followers' dwellings, they received no mention in local histories. Because their followers could not afford to carve inscriptions or to petition the central government for titles, no records about them exist. These deities were clustered at the lower reaches of local pantheons, jostling for position, and occasionally performing startling enough miracles to attract the support of more prominent groups. Only then were their followers able to build temples, carve inscriptions, and petition for titles; only then did these cults leave their mark on the historical record.

But if little is known about the gods of the powerless, the failure of the cult to Zhu Renfu to take off suggests that powerful supporters alone were not enough to launch a new cult. Without popular support, the cult would have remained exclusively the domain of its supporters, which is exactly what the cult to Zhu Renfu did. As important as the wealth and influence of a deity's followers were, they were not everything. Without miracles a cult would ultimately languish. And without miracles, no supporters would come to the temple or attend annual fairs, dooming the cult to a fate like that of Zhu Fu in South Bank. Cults that succeeded, like that to Lu Zai in New Embankment, commanded the support of both locally influential people and the masses. The cults I have been talking about were vital exactly because they could not be manipulated by the powerful.

CHAPTER VI   The Rise of Regional Cults

The changes delineated in the preceding chapters—the diversification of the gods, the standardization of title-granting, and the alliance between county officials and local elites—were so gradual that contemporary observers rarely remarked on them. Not so the topic of this chapter: the dramatic increase in extralocal cults excited great controversy throughout the Southern Song. Unlike local cults, regional cults were not confined to a single locality but spread across space, so that their temples covered regions and in some cases the nation. At the beginning of the twelfth century, branch temples (*xingmiao, xinggong, fenmiao*) to a few deities began to turn up in towns far from the sites of their base temples (*benmiao*, literally "root temples"); by the end of the thirteenth century, such temples extended over all of south China. Local deities, who had just one temple in a village or city, were to constitute the vast majority of gods in different pantheons throughout the Song and up into the twentieth century, but it was in the twelfth and thirteenth centuries that they came to coexist with a new kind of god who appealed to larger groups of people dispersed over a greater area.[1] Four deities had just one or two temples at the beginning of the Song; by the end of the Song, temples to the Five Manifestations, Zitong, the Heavenly Consort, and King Zhang were found throughout south China. Their rise illuminates the process by which people of one place came to worship the gods of another.[2]

1. Some Japanese scholars have worked out a scheme of popular religious change in this period. Before the Tang–Song transition, they see only local cults to earth gods existing; after the transition, the pantheon as we know it is born (Kanai 1979; Tanaka 1970). This mechanical application of the Tang–Song transition is misleading because it suggests that a certain kind of deity existed in earlier times that had died out by the Song; it is more accurate to see a new layer of regional deities on top of the different layers of more traditional local deities.

2. Although there were temples to both Guanyin and the God of the Eastern Peak throughout China even in the Northern Song, neither began as local gods (individuals with a known biography who, after apotheosis, came to be associated with a place where they had lived). Originally linked with the Buddhist and Daoist traditions, Guanyin and the God of the Eastern Peak gradually took on qualities of popular deities. Guanyin, the Buddhist goddess of mercy, was originally an Indian god, not a Chinese human being. The Eastern Peak was a name for Mount Tai in Shandong, but the God of the

While some responded to this change by arguing fiercely that deities could enlarge their traditional domains to govern entire regions—even the empire itself—their opponents contended equally fiercely that only the gods of licentious cults would want to do so. This debate was not theological; like so many of the issues discussed by Chinese literati, it concerned policy. If deities could expand their realms, then it would be permissible for people of one area to worship the deity of another, and the government should extend recognition to those deities. But if not, then it should deny them titles and tear down their temples.

Traditional Views of the Jurisdiction of Deities

The gods of New Embankment, New Market, and South Bank, discussed in the last chapter, typify local deities: they had one temple each, were identified closely with the place they were from, and enjoyed the support of people only from those districts. Most saliently, the catchment area in which they performed miracles was limited to the towns where their temples were located. Their very localness constituted an integral part of their attraction; they came to represent the people of their districts by embodying their sense of place.

Two tales from the late tenth or early eleventh century illustrate what kinds of limitations on the power of these local deities were thought to exist. In a collection of miscellaneous notes, He Wei (1077–1145) tells of a sheriff in Yongfeng county (now Guangfeng, Jiangxi) who dreams that two deities enter his chambers. One of them presents him with a written statement:

> I am the earth god of this county's border. The deity of a neighboring district is showing his power immodestly and threatening my good fortune. He has invaded my territory in order to attract my people. Because of this, the people have built him a large temple. Daily he stuffs himself with meat offerings. There is not enough attendance at my temple. (*Chunzhu jiwen* 1:10)

Once the sheriff decides that the other deity is guilty of transgressing upon his territory (*yuejiang*), the two deities leave. On awakening, the official hears that the new temple had caught on fire and that the altar had been completely destroyed. The judgment he delivered in his dream has mysteriously been carried out, suggesting that it was correct.

Eastern Peak was not a Shandong regional deity. The mountain had come to represent the underworld, and he, the god presiding over it. Daoists thought of this god as the emperor of the pantheon, with city and earth gods serving underneath him.

This concept of transgressing upon another deity's territory is an ancient one. The earliest textual reference is from a fifth-century B.C. text, *The Zuo Commentary* on *The Spring and Autumn Annals*. In one passage, a ruler of Chu explains why he will not take the advice of a diviner (*bu*) to perform sacrifices at the Yellow River: "The making of offerings should not transgress the boundaries of one's own fief" (*Chunqiu Zuozhuan* 58:2162, Year 7 of the Ai reign [488 B.C.]). Much as the ruler has a fief to which he is entitled on earth, so too do the gods; as he can receive taxes and services from the people residing in his territory, the gods can receive worship only from the people resident in theirs. As the ruler of Chu, he does not have the right to perform offerings to a deity of Lu.[3] Because this passage stipulates that a ruler should not worship the god of another place, Southern Song critics of the cults regularly cited it to buttress their attacks on the extralocal cults; common people, like rulers, they argued, should not worship gods from other places. This conservative view of the jurisdiction of the gods continued to attract proponents throughout the Song: gods had specific realms over which they presided, and their borders could not be exceeded.

By the Song, most Chinese gods, with the exception of a few mountain and river gods, were apotheosized individuals; no longer aristocrats or generals, they were thought to reason like the human beings they had been before becoming deities. Motivated by a desire for recognition, the gods rewarded those who honored them by performing miracles. In the age preceding the commercial revolution of the Song, when most villagers grew their own food and stayed close to the land, the classical conception of a deity's realm would have made sense, even to those not familiar with the classics: as peasants led localized lives, so too did their gods. But, in the course of the Song, as people, especially merchants, journeyed farther and farther away from home, they confronted a perplexing situation: seemingly they could travel over greater distances than those ruled over by the deities they worshipped.

Another tale, also from a collection of miscellaneous notes, Shen Gua's *Dream Brook Notes*, illustrates this problem. Sometime between 1068 and 1077, a small dragon attached himself to one ship in an army convoy, which he protected on its voyage from Zhenzhou (now Yiwei county, Jiangsu) to Lake Dongting in Hunan. The boat master recog-

---

3. Interestingly, archeological evidence indicates that, even as early as the third century B.C., the rulers of Chu did not respect this proscription. Archeologists working at Mount Tai have discovered a cache of six bronze vessels, indicating that after 249 B.C., when they conquered Lu, the rulers of Chu did indeed perform sacrifices at Lu (Yuan 1954:128–29). I am indebted to Lothar von Falkenhausen for this reference.

nized the dragon, presumably because it, like the convoy, frequently traveled the same route. The men on the boat made an offering to him. Because of favorable winds, the convoy traveled quickly, covering several hundred li a day, and encountered no waves. The ship continued, but the dragon affixed itself to a merchant ship returning to Nanjing. Shen explains how it is that the dragon did not accompany the boat farther, "for legend has it that the territory of his fief stops at Lake Dongting. He has never gone south of the lake" (*Mengxi bitan* 20:654–55). Unlike the earth god mentioned above, this dragon's area of jurisdiction is quite large, encompassing the section of the Yangzi river extending from Nanjing to Hunan (c. 700 km), but there are still clear limits beyond which he cannot go and beyond which the commercial vessel can.

These two tales indicate that by the end of the eleventh century some devotees had already come to question the traditional view of a god's domain. Eroding this conception even further were the massive migrations south that took place when north China fell to the Jurchens in 1127. Not all of the approximately 500,000 people who fled were willing to leave their gods behind. One of the most popular gods in Kaifeng (the Northern Song capital) was Pichang, an earth god who received his first title after a spectacular cure in 1101. Promotions followed in 1104, 1107, and 1115. Candidates prayed to him before proceeding to the final stage of the civil service examinations, the palace exam (*Yanyi yimou* 4:7a–b; Morita 1984:401). In the late 1120s a devotee carried Pichang's image from Kaifeng to Hangzhou, where he built a pavilion to him overlooking the river (*Xianchun Lin'an* 73:7a–8b). People from the north also built a temple in 1130 to Erlang, a Sichuanese god with a temple in Kaifeng (*Xianchun Lin'an* 73:7a–8b). The late Southern Song gazetteer that lists these two temples records no qualms on the part of their devotees about worshipping gods in areas beyond their jurisdiction.

These changing conceptions eventually prompted some observers to argue that because the gods' realms could not be smaller than human ones, they had to expand. In 1211, Zhang Kan,[4] the magistrate of Green Mound (Qingdun) township (*zhen*) in Huzhou, wrote an inscription to commemorate the reconstruction of a temple in which he eloquently rejects the traditional view of a deity's jurisdiction. Slightly north and west of New Market, just on the border with Jiaxing, and on a major waterway linking Suzhou to Chongde and then Hangzhou, were two townships: Crow (Wu) lay just within the borders of Wucheng county, Huzhou, and smack across the river was Green Mound

4. See biographical note in *Wuqing wenxian* 9:11a.

in Tongxiang county, Jiaxing prefecture (Hayashi 1984). Each township had its own earth god (*tudi shen*). Two earlier inscriptions from 1176 (*Qianlong Wuqing* 6:1a) and 1187 (*Chongzhen Wucheng* 9:29b–31a; *Tongzhi Huzhou* 19:5a–6a) imply that the people of Crow and Green Mound worshipped their own deities separately and that, although the two places were so close to each other, their deities were not linked in any way. This pattern was not in itself surprising; it was common for each village to have its own earth god.

After describing the temple in Green Mound, Zhang explains that because of bad harvests, nine-tenths of the rich people's houses in his neighborhood are empty, forcing him to go to neighboring areas to raise money. This is a daring strategy. When one follower expresses doubts about the future of the temple, Zhang replies:

> Although the deities of the two temples divide the area in which they hold office, the transactions of the spirits flow the way water does through land. There is no place they do not go. They issue punishments and respond with miracles. For them, there is no difference between one territory and another. Only human beings wonder at this. (*Qianlong Wuqing* 6:1b)

Zhang has chosen his water metaphor carefully and aptly. The people to whom he addresses his appeal make their living traveling along waterways to sell their goods or trading with people who have come to Crow-Green Mound via those same waterways. Why should the jurisdiction of the deities be narrower than their own spheres of activity? Zhang's purpose, of course, is to justify his soliciting money from people from nearby areas to contribute to the most quintessentially local of all gods: earth deities. That he tries to do so—and, judging from the fact that the temple was rebuilt, apparently succeeds—testifies to the at least partial breakdown of exclusively localistic tendencies and the formation of regional consciousness in the Song. Here Zhang wants the people of one township to acknowledge a bond with deities of a neighboring one; as he says, "Do not let the people of the two townships divide into two groups who each say, 'I worship my god, that is all' " (*Qianlong Wuqing* 6:1b). Acknowledging ties with another god, and so with another place, is the first step on the way to the creation of regional cults. In the Song people do start to accept deities from areas other than their home districts.

Regional Cults

Judging from the temple listings in the extant Song and Yuan local histories, four originally local gods had come to be worshipped over a larger region by the end of the Song. Unlike local cults with only one original base temple, these cults had branch temples all over south China. The links binding a home temple with its branch temples varied in intensity. Some temples may have celebrated the deity's birthday on the same day, and perhaps even sent delegations of pilgrims to the home temple on an annual basis; in other cases the ties were more tenuous, consisting of no more than sharing the same name as the base temple. Maps 2–6 show the distribution of these temples in 1100, 1150, 1200, 1250, and 1275.[5] The four gods were the Five Manifestations, Zitong, the Heavenly Consort, and King Zhang. Before going any further, let me first give thumbnail sketches of these deities.

The Five Manifestations (*Wuxian*) were five men from Wuyuan county, Huizhou, whose identities are not known. With miracles dating to the late ninth century, each was made a two-character marquis in 1109, and they were called both the Five Transmitters (*Wutong*) and the Five Manifestations[6] (*Chunxi Xin'an* 5:2a; *Chongzhen Wuxian* 21:19b).

Zitong, later to become Wenchang, a god with very close ties to the civil service examinations, was originally from Zitong county, Sichuan (Morita 1984).

The Heavenly Consort (Tianhou, Tianfei, sometimes called Mazu), a fisherman's daughter (later to become one of the most popular deities in south China whose temples can still be seen all over Taiwan), was born in the late eleventh century in Putian county, Fujian. She was given her first title in 1123 and was associated with ocean-going trade (*Bamin tongzhi* 60:12a–13b; Li 1979).

5. Table 5 (in the appendix) provides the references for each temple plotted on the maps. It is divided by Song circuit and gives the prefecture or county, the name of the god, the date that a temple is first mentioned, and then the date and name of the source. Of course, the closer the two dates, the more reliable the source. These maps do not show the distribution of cults in the Song; they do show the distribution of cults according to extant local histories. According to these histories, by 1275 there were forty-two temples to King Zhang, thirty-five to the Five Manifestations, eleven to the Heavenly Consort, and ten to Zitong. As with any other information from such an early period, caveats are in order, but overall trends can be discerned.

6. Because each of the five titles in 1109 contained the character *tong* (to transmit), they were called the Five Transmitters. In 1174, they received new titles with the character *xian* (to manifest), hence the name Five Manifestations. *Wutong* had several meanings at the time. In addition to referring to these five gods, it also denoted the five possibilities for rebirth in Buddhist thought and always mischievous, occasionally injurious, spirits. On one occasion Hong Mai uses *wutong* to mean god or deity and names the specific god in the next clause. In another instance, he used the term in a parallel structure with hill spirit (*shanxiao*) (*Yijianzhi* 11:10:4:1295; 3:1:1:368). I limit my discussion to instances where the five gods can be linked with a temple or identified as coming from Huizhou. See Cedzich (1985) for more about these different cults.

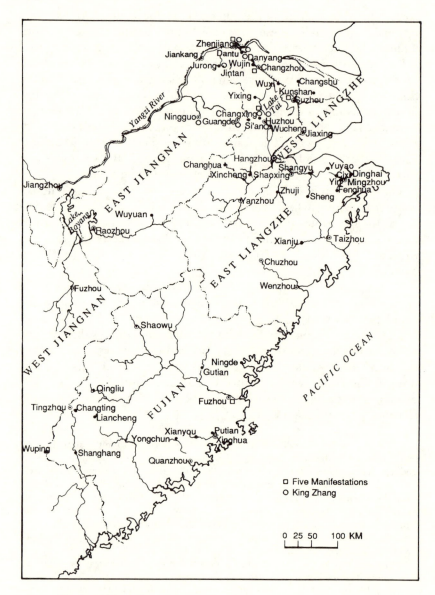

MAP 2. Regional Temples, 1100

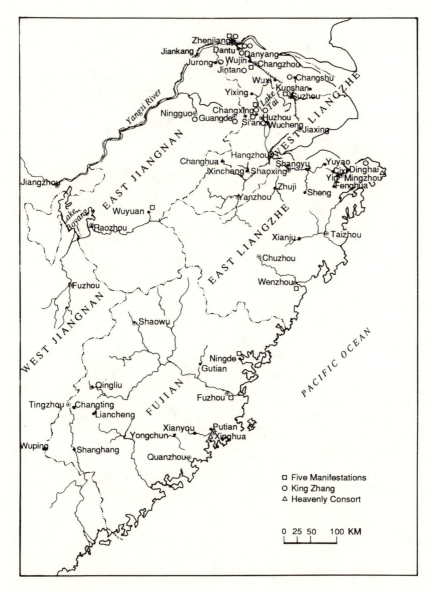

MAP 3. Regional Temples, 1150

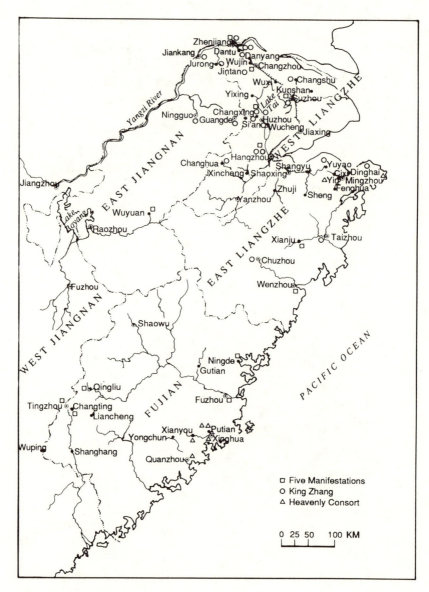

MAP 4. Regional Temples, 1200

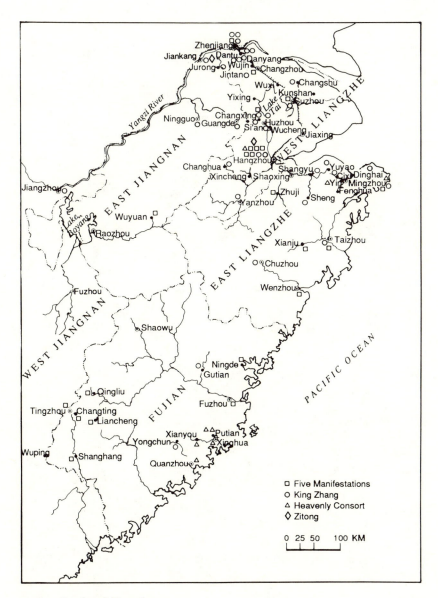

MAP 5. Regional Temples, 1250

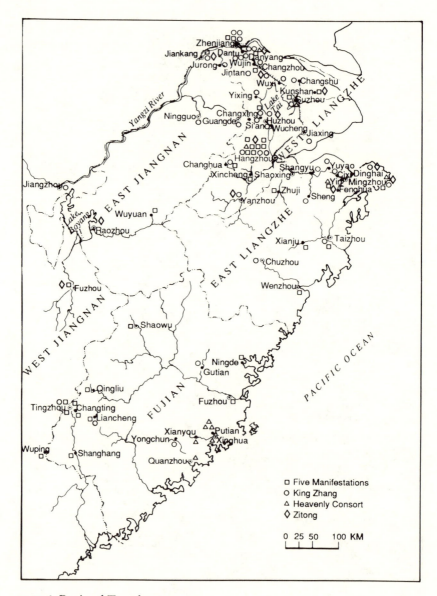

MAP 6. Regional Temples, 1275

King Zhang (Zhang Wang) was a Han dynasty hero, born in Wu-cheng county, Huzhou, who died in the neighboring commandery of Guangde, where his main temple was located (*Cishan zhi* 1:1a–3b; Nakamura 1972).

Although each of these gods had branch temples in widely separated places, the names of their home towns often served as epithets, as in Zitong of Zitong county, Sichuan, the Heavenly Consort of Putian county, King Zhang of Guangde commandery, and the Five Manifestations of Wuyuan county.

The maps clearly reveal that, whereas in 1100 only a few branch temples had been built, mostly along the Grand Canal north of Lake Tai and in the two coastal cities of Fuzhou and Taizhou (Zhejiang) (map 2), each fifty-year interval shows an increase in the distribution of regional temples. The only temples inland are the original base temples. By 1150 there are temples in more of the major coastal cities—Wenzhou and Ningde—as well as along the legs of the Grand Canal linking Lake Tai with Hangzhou, and Hangzhou with Ningbo (map 3). By 1200 one sees more temples lining the Grand Canal and along the coast, but also a few inland, especially in the interior of Fujian, in Tingzhou (map 4). In 1275, this trend is even more pronounced: there are temples inland in Jiangxi—in Jiangzhou, Raozhou, and Fuzhou, as well as even more along the coast and a very high concentration along the Grand Canal (map 6).

What can one make of this pattern of distribution overall? Most strikingly, these new temples all lie along waterways.[7] They crowd the banks of the much-traveled Grand Canal, with concentrations in Zhenjiang, Suzhou, Hangzhou, Shaoxing, and Ningbo; they cluster in the major coastal ports, with Taizhou and Fuzhou most prominent among them. Those inland all lay on rivers, either connecting them to the Grand Canal or leading down to the coast. This distribution of temples along waterways should surprise no one. Remember the people of New Embankment, who put images of Lu Zai in their boats and

---

7. Robert Hymes (personal communication, February 1987) points out that this distribution of temples indicates merely that the spread of regional cults was an urban phenomenon, as all cities in south China lay along waterways. So the most important supporters would have been those people traveling from city to city—officials and merchants as well as religious specialists. He also suggests that because the local histories may have been biased in favor of urban landmarks, such a pattern of distribution may just be an artifact of the sources. Still, although there may have been some regional temples in more rural areas, it makes sense that most of these temples would have been located in cities along water, for those were the places merchants and other travelers were going to, and where people would have been exposed to the deities of people from other places.

spoke of his miracles on their travels to trade lotus pods and roots. Throughout the Song merchants traveled greater and greater distances along these waterways, and they built temples to and related the miracles of their gods wherever they went.

How was it that people in south China came to hear of some deities' powers and not of others? It is worth keeping in mind that contemporary observers might have accounted for the rise of these particular deities by saying that they were the most powerful, but miracles—and deities' reputations—were extremely malleable. To answer this question one must look for information concerning the supporters of these deities. Because they rarely identified themselves, little direct evidence survives, but fortunately the distribution of the temples, biographies of the deities, and anecdotal evidence all give hints as to their identities. My discussion of the Five Manifestations, Zitong, and the Heavenly Consort will, of necessity, be brief; few sources reveal much about the devotees of these cults. Fortunately, because much more material about King Zhang is available, the history of this cult can be examined in detail. Here too his close ties with Huzhou provide a nice contrast to the deities discussed in the previous chapter who remained very much local gods. I have already alluded to the tensions between local and regional identities; the histories of these cults show that before the people of the Song could pray to deities from other than their native villages, they had to cast off the preconception that gods could only rule within the immediate vicinity of their home temples.

The Five Manifestations

The first branch temples to appear in other cities were those to the Five Manifestations of Wuyuan county, Huizhou. Branch temples were built in Taizhou (Zhejiang) in 994, in Fuzhou (Fujian) in 1004–1007, and in Suzhou in 1008–1016 (see map 2). No inscriptions remain from these temples, nor from the original temple, but the locations of these temples suggest that the merchants of Huizhou erected them in the different cities they traded in: Suzhou, on the Grand Canal, was a major trading city, and both Taizhou and Fuzhou were ocean ports.

Hong Mai recounts one incident that occurred at the base temple between 1102 and 1106. The local people commissioned an itinerant artist to paint the temple door and promised to pay him more if he could capture the likeness of a particularly striking horse. The artist gave the horse and its groom wine, and, as they slept, used a thread to measure their exact dimensions. On the day he completed the painting, the horse suddenly ran about crazily; his groom jumped on top of him, and the two drowned when the horse plunged into a local pond. Afterward the local people thought they sighted the horse at night, and they credited the boy with performing miracles (*Yijian zhi* 3:19:7:526). The actual feats the Five Manifestations themselves were thought to have performed are unrecorded, but the awarding of titles in 1123, 1132, 1145, 1167, and 1174 testifies both to continued miracles and to intensive lobbying on the part of their followers (*Chunxi Xin'an* 5:12a–b).

The formulator of the Neo-Confucian synthesis, Zhu Xi (1130–1200), provides an interesting description of the base temple of the Five Manifestations.[8] On his first trip to the site of his ancestral tomb in Wuyuan county, Huizhou, he visited a small village,

> where the so-called Five Manifestations temple was the most mysterious and strange (*lingguai*). The masses flocked there, saying that good and bad fortune could be immediately determined. Whenever the common people go out their doors, they take a piece of paper to ask the god's blessing and then they depart. The literati (*shiren*) who are passing by present a name card and say "disciple so and so is visiting the temple."

On the night of his visit, Zhu's relatives forced him to attend a feast where they offered animal entrails to the gods, and the next day a snake appeared. The people blamed Zhu Xi, saying that the gods were angry that he had not visited their temple; he responded that they had not liked the offering of entrails (which violated the classical strictures against making meat offerings). Finally Zhu Xi gave in and went to the temple, saying, "My ancestral tomb is very close. If you really have the power to determine good and bad fortune, then please bury me next to my ancestral tomb. It would be so convenient" (*Zhuzi yulei* 3:85).

This tale depicts a more human and a more humorous Zhu Xi than we are accustomed to. Zhu, long resident in Fujian, has gone to Huizhou to meet this branch of his lineage for the first time. Clearly the temple is the major local sight: the different offerings of paper and name cards suggest participation among both the common people and

---

8. Zhu Xi used the words for ghosts (*gui*) and deities (*shen*) to denote positive and negative manifestations of matter (Miura 1985; Tomoeda 1944:247–84). Zhu's own position about deities was very close to Confucius's as it appears in *The Analects*: the concerns of this world far outweigh those of the next. At one point, Zhu admitted to one of his students: "I have previously seen temples that were imposing and beautiful, but I usually do not like to enter temples to deities or even to view them. All this [popular religious worship] is for the stupid and ignorant" (*Zhuzi yulei* 106:4205).

the gentry. Zhu's relatives, proud of their local temple, want him to acknowledge the power of the Five Manifestations, but Zhu is both bewildered by these practices and surprised that some of the people advising him to go to the temple turn out to be educated. He reluctantly responds to the urgings of his relatives; because they have informed him that the gods can determine good and bad fate immediately, he challenges the Five Manifestations. Still his challenge is a light-hearted one: his remark that his ancestors' tomb lies nearby contains an element of sarcasm. The gods fail Zhu's test, but he does not expect the local people to stop visiting the temple. He ends his tale on a cautionary note: "When one is a local official, one must get rid of all licentious temples. If they are deities who have received government titles, then they cannot easily be got rid of" (*Zhuzi yulei* 3:85–86). Zhu may not believe in the Five Manifestations, but he realizes that all of his relatives, even the educated ones, do. Although critical of these cults, Zhu does not advocate extirpation; he is aware that tampering with them may result in even greater popular support.

The few fragmentary sources concerning the Five Manifestations reveal no doubts on the part of their followers about worshipping deities from other places. This may well have been because merchants were those who traveled the farthest themselves and who would have had the least knowledge of and, accordingly, the fewest qualms about ignoring the classics. It is not known how they justified the construction of temples outside Wuyuan county, Huizhou, but one can surmise that they wanted to take their gods with them on their journeys to trade lumber, paper, lacquer, and other products of the mountains they came from. In the initial stage of expansion, the merchants of Huizhou did not violate classical precedent by worshipping the gods of other places—they were just worshipping their own gods in new places. They probably assumed their gods could go where they did.

Although the paucity of information about the early stages of the cult makes identifying supporters especially difficult, Hong Mai provides evidence that the worship of the Five Manifestations spread to people who were not from Huizhou. In 1176 the gods also gave a prescription for medicine to a man in nearby Dexing (Jiangxi) (*Yijian zhi* 12:10:4:1378–79). People from more distant places also consulted them about commercial dealings. The Five Manifestations were said to inform secretly a peasant devotee in Fuzhou (Jiangxi) "in advance whether he would win or lose money in his dealings in money and goods" (*Yijian zhi* 4:15:12:667). Similarly, a seller of meat dumplings wrapped in lotus leaves lived in front of a temple to the Five Manifestations in Xinzhou (now Fuyang, Anhui). He began to worship them

after a chicken produced five dark pellet-like eggs; the family subsequently prospered (*Yijian zhi* 13:6:3:1427). Not only traders supported
this cult. In 1205–1207 a native of Ningbo built a temple to the deities
after his return from Huizhou where he had served as prefect (*Yanyou
siming* 15:12b). In an age when many popular deities began to perform
explicitly commercial miracles (see chapter 3), it seems that the success
of the Huizhou merchants rubbed off on the gods they worshipped.

Zitong

Zitong[9] was a deity closely identified with his birthplace, Zitong
county, in Sichuan—so closely identified, in fact, that throughout the
Song he was called only the god of Zitong, and his name Zhang Yazi
(Mute Zhang) was never used. Zitong established his reputation in the
Five Dynasties (910–960) and Northern Song by helping officials to
suppress rebellions in Sichuan. In 1001, following the end of Li Shun's
rebellion, he was promoted to king (*Xu zizhi tongjian changbian* 49:3a).
In 1132 he prevented another uprising in Luzhou (Sichuan) (*Jianyan
yilai xinian yaolu* 53:935; Morita 1984:398–99). Starting in the early
twelfth century several accounts (in *The Record of the Listener* and elsewhere) identify him as one of several gods who can accurately predict
the results of the civil service examinations.

Temples to Zitong alone—or as one of three gods from Sichuan[10]—
started to appear in south China only late in the Southern Song: in
Nanjing in 1235, in Hangzhou in 1236, in Suzhou in 1251, in Danyang
1253–1258, in Yanzhou in 1260, in Fenghua and Huzhou in 1261, in
Dinghai in 1264, in Ningbo in 1271, in Changzhou (now Wujin
county, Jiangsu) in 1274, and in Raozhou and Fuzhou (Jiangxi) by
1275. The first were built in major trading and political centers of the
Southern Song, then along the Grand Canal, and finally inland in
Jiangxi (see maps 5 and 6). By this time Zitong had firmly established
his reputation as an exam god: a 1261 inscription in Yanzhou says,
"Legend has it that it is he whom the Emperor has asked to oversee the

9. Because Morita Kenji (1984) has already traced the transformation of Zitong from
a local Sichuan god to the national god of the civil service exams, in this section I merely
highlight some of the points most relevant to this study. Only after I had finished this
manuscript did Terry Frederick Kleeman complete his study of the cult, "Wenchang and
the Viper: The Creation of a Chinese National God" (Ph.D. dissertation, University of
California, Berkeley, 1988). Accordingly, I was unable to incorporate his findings.

10. The other two were Erlang (see chapter 3), a god famed for constructing irrigation works in the Han dynasty, and the local deity of Shehong county, who, like Zitong,
was referred to by the name of his home county.

lists of successful candidates for advanced degrees (*jinshi*) and to determine the examination results" (*Jingding Yanzhou* 4:4a).

Inscriptions from Song temples make it possible to identify with
some certainty who propagated the cult; in every case we know about,
the supporters are, to a man, officials from Sichuan. The official Mou
Zicai, who organized the building of the temple in Hangzhou in 1236,
later led the Sichuanese in Huzhou to do the same (*Yongle dadian*
2281:9b). Yao Xide, who like Mou passed the exams in 1223, built the
temples to Zitong in Nanjing and Fuzhou (Jiangxi). Because these
men were officials and so were versed in the classics in a way that the
Huizhou merchants were not, they felt the need to resolve the issue of
the propriety of worshipping gods from afar. In his 1261 inscription
for the Nanjing temple, Yao begins, saying, "When the three deities [of
Sichuan] were worshipped, they performed miracles in Sichuan. This
is a fact. Can they accept offerings in Ye?"[11] This is a response to the
classical view already cited above: that the rulers of Chu should not
worship Mount Tai in the kingdom of Lu. But, like the other proponents of regional cults, Yao has found a classical citation suggesting
they can indeed worship the gods of other places: "*The Book of Poetry*
records, 'The power of the gods cannot be conceived of.' "[12] Yao then
provides his own explanation of this ambiguous line: "This means
their transformations cannot be fathomed. One cannot pin them down
to one place. Did not the gods of famous mountains and great rivers
always circulate everywhere?" (*Jingding Jiankang* 44:36a–37a).

These men from Sichuan started to build these temples just as the
Mongols were invading their homeland in 1236. So they were not in
the same boat as the Huizhou merchants who traveled long distances
to trade, who took their deities with them, and who were sure to go
home at the end of their journeys. These were men who had passed
the civil service exams and had originally expected to return to Sichuan
once their terms of office were up. But after 1236 they could not. Their
worship of Zitong took on added poignancy—that of exiles. Surely
Morita Kenji is right to see these men praying to Zitong to expel the
Mongols. In his Nanjing temple inscription Yao says: "Recently the
snarling Tartars bark in Sichuan. Inside and outside Liangshan commandery [now Liangping county, Sichuan], Wanzhou [now Wan
county, Sichuan], and Fuzhou [now Fuling county, Sichuan] people

11. It is interesting that he says Ye, which had been the capital of the Wei kingdom,
one of Sichuan's rivals in the Three Kingdoms period (222–265), and not Nanjing,
which had been the capital of the third kingdom of Wu. Sensitivity to the sensibilities of
the local people kept Yao from reminding them that they, too, had once been enemies
of the Sichuanese.

12. *Shijing: Daya Tangzhishen* 18:555.

cannot do anything.[13] Only the return of the deity will enable the emperor to broadcast his valor" (*Jingding Jiankang* 44:37a–b). Unlike the other extralocal gods, Zitong seems to have attracted primarily upper-strata devotees. In his 1274 description of Hangzhou, Wu Zimu reports that officials from Sichuan visit Zitong's temple on his birthday. He mentions no other supporters (*Mengliang lu* 19:181). The later career of Zitong was not without its ironies. Originally a symbol of Sichuan resistance to the Mongols, he became the acknowledged god of the civil service examinations in 1316, when the Mongol emperor appointed him as such (Morita 1984:410).

The Heavenly Consort

Like the Sichuan officials who built temples to Zitong, officials from Putian county, Fujian, were instrumental in introducing the cult of the Heavenly Consort in cities far from their native place; like the Five Manifestations who came to be associated with long-distance merchants, she was identified with an occupational group: those who made their living on the sea. A much-publicized miracle launched her career. In 1123 she appeared to an imperial envoy caught in a terrible storm on his way to Korea and brought him safely to shore (see chapter 2). She was given a temple plaque immediately. For the first hundred years her miracles—bringing rain, keeping pirates away— took place largely in Fujian or on the ocean nearby, especially in Xinghua prefecture, where her temples remained clustered (*Bamin tongzhi* 60:12a–13a). Hong Mai provides a description of her temple in Xinghua:

> All merchants who are going on ocean voyages must first come to pray at the temple. Only when they have used moonblocks and asked for her protection do they dare to depart. This is probably because in the past someone went on an ocean voyage and encountered terrible winds. As the boat was rocking, he prayed a hundred times and begged for help. He saw the goddess appear on the mast. (*Yijian zhi* 7:9:5:950–51)[14]

She was clearly a goddess for sea-goers. In 1200 it must have looked as though the Heavenly Consort was going to remain a Fujian goddess, enjoying support only in her home circuit.

Even the spread of her cult within Fujian evoked criticism. Chen

13. Emending *qian* (thousand) to *wan* (ten thousand), I take the three-character phrase *liang wan fu* to refer to the three prefectures in Sichuan of Liangshan, Wanzhou, and Fuzhou.

14. Hong Mai is referring to Xu Jing's voyage (see chapter 2).

Chun (1159–1223), one of Zhu Xi's most devoted disciples, never served as an official, but he did write one petition to the emperor about popular religious abuses. He lived in Zhangzhou county in Fujian, two prefectures south of the Heavenly Consort's home district of Xinghua prefecture. This was not a great distance, but as far as Chen was concerned, the people of his district should not worship alien gods. The dramatic increase in popular cults and especially their festivals did not escape Chen's observation; it accounts for the vehemence of his attack. "Moreover, she whom they call the Heavenly Consort is a ghost from Putian county. What connection does she have to this area?" Chen calls for placards to be erected specifying correct means of worship (*Beixi xiansheng daquan wenji* 43n.p.).[15]

Chen's critique had little effect. Just at the turn of the thirteenth century, devotees began to build branch temples to the Heavenly Consort in other places outside Fujian. A 1228 inscription from one of those temples, in Hangzhou, gives some indication of the mechanism by which the cult fanned out. The writer, Ding Bogui (1171–1237), was himself an official from Putian serving in the capital. He recounts the miracles of the twelfth century, which all occurred in Fujian, but, after noting her promotions in 1208 and 1217, says:

> Although she is from Putian, she enriches all the world. Therefore all those who welcome the morning tide and see the evening tide out hold her in their hearts. All those who return to the south, who live in the north, depend on her. Those who defend the borders and resist in the villages depend on her for their lives. Merchants do not concern themselves with food and goods: they only listen to her. (*Xianchun Lin'an* 73:16a)

Regional pride fuels these grand, even hyperbolic, assertions. A look at the distribution of temples to the Heavenly Consort suggests that the first claim to the support of people who make their living on the water is the most plausible: when not on the coastline of Fujian, her temples lay along the Grand Canal. It certainly makes sense that it was

---

15. At the same time that Chen Chun was making these criticisms, other Neo-Confucians were building shrines to founders of their movement regardless of their links to a particular place. In 1182 Zhu Xi wrote an inscription for a shrine in Huizhou to Zhou Dunyi and the Cheng brothers (Cheng Yi and Cheng Hao), but only after protesting that the three men had no connection with the county: "Wuyuan is not their native place, nor is it a place where they sojourned or served in office" (*Zhuzi daquan* 79:3a–4a). His criticism is, of course, in exactly the same vein as Chen Chun's of the Heavenly Consort. I am indebted to Ellen Neskar, who is doing a study of the development of Neo-Confucian shrines, for providing me with a translation of this text.

merchants—and not just those from Fujian—who supported this cult. They, after all, did have to contend with the dangers of ocean travel, and the Heavenly Consort could help them to do so.

Whereas the author of the Hangzhou inscription has, without even mentioning the problem of exceeding one's realm, asserted the Heavenly Consort's divinity on an all-China basis, an inscription dated 1251–1252 by another native of Putian, Li Choufu, addresses the issue head on: "Zhenjiang is three thousand li from Putian. 'The making of offerings should not transgress the boundaries of one's own fief.' " To refute his passage, Li paraphrases Mencius: " 'There are gentleman of one district or one county. There are also gentlemen of the world.'[16] Thus how can one harbor doubts [about the suitability of worshipping the goddess] on the basis of the distance between Fujian and here?" (*Zhishun Zhenjiang* 8:13a). Mencius was discussing people, not gods. But other Song observers[17] also cited this passage to challenge that from *Zuo Commentary* about the unsuitability of worshipping gods from other regions: the gods' very humanness makes it possible to quote Mencius on their behalf.

Having come up with a classical citation that can be stretched to support his position, Li musters a more practical argument. "It is suitable that the people of Zhejiang, Fujian, Guangdong, and further south, which all abut the great sea, and where the winds and waves push the boats, should depend on the Heavenly Consort" (*Zhishun Zhenjiang* 8:13a). Here is the crux of his position. As long as the Heavenly Consort can protect the seafaring people along the southern coast, nothing should prevent them from worshipping her. This inscription ends with a description of the new temple built to the Heavenly Consort in Zhenjiang, in which there are side altars to two Fujian heroes and to dragon gods. Li also explains how it is that he came to write the text: in 1238 the main donor, Weng Zaiyi, had dreamt that the Heavenly Consort asked for a temple in Zhenjiang. And thirteen years later, having raised the needed funds, it was natural for him to ask Li, for as Li explains, "both Weng and I are from the Heavenly Consort's district" (*Zhishun Zhenjiang* 8:13a–b).

As long as opponents of the regional cults cited the classics to condemn them, the supporters of those cults, who were often natives of the gods' home districts, dredged up and twisted other classical citations on behalf of these new cults. Although the propriety of worshipping gods from other regions could be debated endlessly, the propo-

16. *Mengzi, Wan Zhang xia* 10:2746.
17. For example, Liu Kezhuang, as cited below.

nents had actual religious practice on their side. People had most definitely begun to worship regional deities, and, as far as anybody could tell, the deities appeared to be responding.

King Zhang

Given the restricted nature of the sources, which do not provide attendance figures for popular temples, any assessment of a deity's popularity in the Song must be tentative. But several indicators suggest that King Zhang was very popular in the Song, possibly even more so than the Five Manifestations, Zitong, or the Heavenly Consort. My survey of local histories shows that King Zhang had forty-two temples throughout south China by 1275; this was a greater number than for any other formerly local god (see map 6). He performed an extraordinary number of miracles cutting across social strata. At the same time he brought rain for cultivators, he also enabled candidates to pass the civil service examinations. Finally, the government awarded titles not just to him but to many of his purported relatives. In assessing the reasons underlying the phenomenal growth of his cult, one can look to the many anecdotes culled from different sets of miscellaneous notes and inscriptions in local gazetteers that record his miracles; more helpful still is a history of the base temple in Guangde commandery (Anhui), originally dating to the Song, *A History of Temple Mountain*.[18]

Several biographies of King Zhang circulated in the Song. Whereas some accounts record that he was born in Wucheng county, Huzhou, others say he was born elsewhere but traveled to Huzhou; all agree that the major events of his life took place once he had settled in Huzhou. Throughout the Song, King Zhang was called either King Zhang of Huzhou or, more often, King Zhang of Guangde commandery, the district neighboring Huzhou in the west, where he died and where his main temple was located. An 1150 inscription from Ningbo relates

---

18. The edition used here of the *Cishan zhi* (*A History of Temple Mountain*) is dated 1886; it is a reprint of a Ming edition that incorporated entire sections of the 1295 text, which in turn was based on a 1239 book. This book belongs to a special genre of books in China: mountain gazetteers. It is a history of Temple Mountain, where King Zhang's base temple was located. The text is divided into ten topical chapters, including the genealogy of King Zhang and his family, his life, his miracles, his birthday festival and temples, methods of worship, "firsts" (e.g., the first miracle, the first title), subdeities, prayers and poems, and inscriptions. Because the sections from the 1295 edition are clearly marked off from later additions, the text is particularly valuable. It also, in some sense, skews the source base; because this text is extant, we know much more about King Zhang's cult than about those to the Five Manifestations, Zitong, or the Heavenly Consort.

that once King Zhang had reached Huzhou, "he wanted to bore a river from the Jing stream in Changxing county (Huzhou) to Guangde commandery to facilitate transportation by boat. Just as the work was half-completed, he suddenly turned into a strange animal who drove spirit soldiers to do the work" (*Qiandao siming* 10:4a).[19] Like General Zhu of New Market, Huzhou (whose miracles bear an uncanny resemblance to King Zhang's), the story of King Zhang's digging a canal suggests strong links with those merchants and traders who made their living on the water, but this inscription reveals that officials also played a key role in the dissemination of the cult to King Zhang. The man who introduced the cult in Ningbo had served as a low military official in Guangde commandery and, following his return home, appealed to King Zhang to keep away the pirates off the coast of Ningbo.

The early spread of his temples along waterways further suggests merchant support. The cult began with temples in Guangde commandery and the adjacent prefectures of Huzhou and Ningguo. The first temples farther away were located in Zhenjiang, where the Grand Canal intersected the Yangzi River (see map 3). A 1332 local history recounts a legend about the founding of the first temple at the end of the Tang dynasty:

> During the Tang, a man named Qin peddled goods between Changzhou [now Wujin county, Jiangsu] and Zhenjiang. He took the deity's image with him on every trip. One day he came here (Zhenjiang). His pack was so heavy that it weighed down on him, and his shoulders could not bear it. He prayed, asking, "Does the deity want to receive temple offerings here?" As soon as he finished speaking, the pack resumed its former weight. (*Zhishun Zhenjiang* 8:18a)

The construction of the temple right on the Grand Canal underlines the links between traders and King Zhang. By 1150 a temple to King Zhang had been built at the southern end of the Grand Canal, where it met the ocean, in Dinghai county (see map 3). In the thirteenth century, temples along the Grand Canal continued to proliferate, and there were also a few farther inland, but always on waterways, in Xianju county, in Chuzhou, and in Tingzhou (see map 6).

Several inscriptions and accounts of the founding of temples give other indications of merchant support for the cult. A 1078–1085 in-

---

19. For another version of King Zhang's life, in which King Zhang is transformed into a pig, see *Nenggai zhai manlu* 18:521 (I am indebted to Bob Hymes for this reference). The Qing scholar Zhao Yi says this motif derives from the *Huainan zi* account in which the Great Yu is transformed into a bear who digs a road (*Gaiyu congkao* 35:763).

scription from the base temple on Temple Mountain reports that in 862 "a merchant, Wang Ke, was selling tea. When he crossed the Li river[20] he encountered ferocious winds and waves. Of the five boats traveling with him, four had already overturned. Only Wang put up the king's image in the middle of the boat and began to pray." He was subsequently saved (*Cishan zhi* 3:14b–15a). Here again is hard evidence that the people traveling by water to trade took images of the deities they worshipped with them. Another inscription from the base temple, dated 1179, records that money for temple repairs came both from the government and from traveling merchants (*Cishan zhi* 10:25a). And the temple gazetteer contains yet one more anecdote linking King Zhang with those involved in commerce. At the end of the twelfth century a Jiangxi merchant delegated an agent to accompany a shipment of glutinous rice, an important ingredient in moonshine. The agent did not realize that the government had cracked down on the private production of wine. When the merchant heard that local officials had seized his cargo and had taken it to a tax station, he prayed to King Zhang for help. The agent managed to escape in the moonless night, and his guard was so humilated that he returned the shipment of rice to the merchant (*Cishan zhi* 4:17b–18a). Nothing is known about the authors of these inscriptions but their names; it is likely that they, like the authors of the inscriptions to the Heavenly Consort and Zitong, were also officials who had served in or were natives of King Zhang's home district.

Although the distribution of temples and these inscriptions suggest that merchants actively fostered the spread of the cult during their travels along the waterways of south China, especially the Grand Canal, the extraordinary diversity of King Zhang's miracles indicates more than mercantile support. His first major miracle was to bring rain in 506 in response to the emperor's prayers (*Cishan zhi* 4:1a). Throughout the Song he continued to bring rain, and officials regularly prayed to him to do so, suggesting he was popular also with people who lived off the land (*Shuixin wenji* 26:29b; *Longchuan wenji* 22:3a–5a). *The Record of the Listener* tells of many of his miracles in the late twelfth century: curing a sick magistrate of a painful carbuncle on his chest, accurately predicting exam results, and helping the stupid son of a bureaucratic family to pass the exams (*Yijian zhi* 16:1:23:1795; 9:10:2:1128; 7:10:3:958). Other collections of miscellaneous notes reveal that he continued to be as eclectically powerful in the thirteenth

20. There are several rivers of this name in Henan, but the context here suggests a river in the immediate vicinity of the base temple in Guangde commandery.

century: in 1260–1264 he transformed earthen tiles into glazed ones, and in 1268 he provided a prescription for aching bones (*Xinwen Yijianxu, houji* 2:215–16; *Qidong yeyu* 13:240). The list of miracles in *A History of Temple Mountain* reveals that followers of King Zhang used all available means of prognostication: moonblocks, divination sticks, and dreams (*Cishan zhi* 4:10b–15a). Here, to borrow an oft-used line from temple inscriptions, the list of miracles is so long that it cannot be given in full. Suffice it to say that King Zhang's miracles were so many and so frequent that, while defying categorization, they testify to his great popularity among all social strata.

The titles bestowed on him also testify to his popularity. Sometime between 742 and 755 he received his first title and was later promoted to a two-character king in the Five Dynasties period (910–960). In 1040 he was made a four-character king, in 1121 a six-character king, and in 1132 an eight-character king. Even though all the legends concerning King Zhang mention no other kin but his wife, in 1114 King Zhang's wife and sons were all granted titles (*Cishan zhi* 1:9a–10a). The government awarded titles to an ever increasing number of his relatives. By 1149 not only his wife, but also five sons, their wives, his parents, his grandparents, and his grandchildren had all received titles (*Cishan zhi* 1:11b–12a). In 1150 images of King Zhang, four sons, eleven grandsons, and nineteen wives graced the Ningbo temple (*Qiandao siming* 10:5a). Of course the family members of other deities also received titles, but not to such a great extent; far more common was the award of titles to only the god's spouse and children. The posthumous population explosion in King Zhang's family suggests that, barraged with requests for promotion, the central government had no choice but to continue giving King Zhang and his family longer and longer and higher and higher titles. Because his relatives had their own birthdays, each had a temple festival on a different day (*Cishan zhi* 5:1a–1b).

These festivals drew large crowds. A detailed description of Hangzhou from 1274 suggests how lavish the celebrations for King Zhang's birthday were. Groups of jewelers, shoemakers, and hatmakers joined in a procession to honor the god; actors and musicians performed on a stage in front of the temple. Wu Zimu reports, "From morning to night came onlookers in droves." They flocked to the pleasure boats on Western Lake and crowded the causeways across the lake to watch boatmen armed with poles who competed to throw each other in the water. Wu reveals that lower social strata also participated: "Even the poor borrow money to bring their wives and children to have fun for the whole day. No one goes home without getting drunk" (*Mengliang lu* 1:7–8; Gernet 1962:190–91). A late Southern Song observer, Zhou Mi (1232–1298), may be summarizing Wu's account when he comments, "there were many worshippers at the Huoshan branch temple; many performers competed to attend." Troupes of musicians, actors, puppeteers, and story-tellers made it a festive occasion (*Wulin jiushi* 3:5a–b).

The central government's attempts to associate itself with King Zhang did not stop with the granting of titles. The 1265–1274 gazetteer from Hangzhou reports that the first temple to King Zhang was built in 1170 slightly outside the city; in 1194 the emperor issued an edict ordering the renovation of a palace office to serve as a temple, explaining that he hoped that the proximity of the new temple would make it easier for people to pray. "But the people of the capital, both male and female, competed to go to Huoshan; no one was in the slightest way troubled" (*Xianchun Lin'an* 73:10a). This remark is important for it suggests that the residents of the capital believed the first site was more powerful than the second. More significant still, it shows that popular belief was not easily manipulated.

The high number of branch temples, the extraordinary multiplicity of miracles, and the titles for the entire extended family testify to King Zhang's appeal to lots of people in many places. But what of local loyalties and scruples about worshipping the deities of other places? Why did people so willingly embrace King Zhang when they had to overcome their doubts about other deities?

King Zhang's Subdeities:
The Spider Plant's New Leaves

The 1201 gazetteer of Huzhou mentions a local deity who, having confessed to a murder actually committed by his father, was executed in his stead. During the period following his death, when several miracles occurred, and before the receipt of his first temple plaque in the early 1120s, his image was housed in the Huzhou temple to King Zhang (*Jiatai Wuxing* 13:11a). Similarly, in 1205–1207, one of King Zhang's temples in Zhenjiang was flooded; rebuilt on a new site, this temple held images of both King Zhang and Ding Ren, a local deity about whom nothing else is known (*Zhishun Zhenjiang* 8:18b). The presence of images of deities other than the main deity was not in itself unusual; the temple to the Heavenly Consort in Zhenjiang also contained side halls for dragons and local gods (*Zhishun Zhenjiang* 8:13b). But King Zhang's relationships with these subdeities were more institutionalized, more structured, and more formal than those of other gods. It was these relationships that accounted for the phenomenal success of his cult: King Zhang was as popular as he was because people could continue to worship their own local gods at the same time—and in the same temples—that they worshipped King Zhang.

The structure, then, of the cult to King Zhang was much like a spider plant that begins as one tier of leaves supported by a central stalk, the cult to King Zhang. From this upper tier, stems sprouted that supported lower tiers of leaves—the cults to the subdeities and to King Zhang's family members. And from these tiers, yet another tier sprouted—the cults to the family members of the subdeities. At least one of these subdeities became a regional deity in his own right, with temples in his hometown of Huzhou as well as in Suzhou. The success of these subdeities reflected back on King Zhang, much as the lower whorls of leaves on a spider plant contribute to its overall beauty.

A temple grant dated 1209 gives the biography of one of these subdeities; it is from the base temple to Marquis Li (Li Hou) in Changxing county, Huzhou. A native of Changxing, Li Lu announced in 1121 he was going to Shandong to serve his country; on his return, he meditated and died. He subsequently protected his district from locusts and bad harvests (*Jiaqing Changxing* 26:20a–21b). Marquis Li died in 1121, his temple received its first plaque in 1209, and he received the title of marquis in 1226 (*Cishan zhi* 7:6b). The 1209 title grant does not mention King Zhang,[21] but, by at least 1227, he had become associated with King Zhang. An account of a 1227 miracle performed by one of these subdeities, Marquis Li, is given in the 1298 edition of *A History of Temple Mountain*. Xu Wenzhi, a devotee of King Zhang, who lived in Anji county (Huzhou), went to the main temple in Guangde commandery to perform a rite to give food to the hungry ghosts on land and water (*shuiluhui*). Before his return journey, he tossed moonblocks but failed to determine an auspicious time for his trip. He went anyway and was caught in a terrible storm.

Just as the ship he was in was about to capsize, he hurriedly prayed to Marquis Li to take charge of the boat. The boat suddenly landed on shore, where there were poplar trees. . . . They used a big rope to tie the boat to a tree. Suddenly the tree fell, and the rope snapped. The people in the boat fell into the water and clung to the boat. They had an instant left to live. Wenzhi rocked

21. The editor of the 1805 gazetteer containing this text describes the temple, however, saying that Marquis Li was subordinate to (*shu*) King Zhang for a long time; this unique way of characterizing the relationship between two deities suggests a special bond between them but gives no indication when such a bond first developed.

and prayed for a miracle and promised to sponsor a purification
ceremony (*jiao*). The boat then regained the stability of a rock.
(*Cishan zhi* 4:15b)

The narrator does not explain why he chose to pray to Marquis Li and
not to King Zhang; one can surmise only that Marquis Li was a local
deity he was familiar with. *A History of Temple Mountain* records that
Li's statue was seated in a side hall of King Zhang's main temple and
faced slightly north. Marquis Li's image was so efficacious that people
did not want to alter it in any way; instead they put the clothing and
hat of a marquis on it, presumably following his promotion to marquis. But the old image was not suited to the deity's new robes. In
1239, on the initiative of one devotee, a new image was put up (*Cishan
zhi* 8:4a–b). Marquis Li's association with King Zhang certainly dated
to 1227, when he saved Xu Wenzhi in the storm; the two gods may
have been linked even earlier.

As Marquis Li hung suspended on a stem that had sprouted from
the cult to King Zhang, so too did another tier hang down from Li's
own cult: that consisting of the Li family members. In the Song, his
parents, his paternal grandparents, his uncle and younger brother and
their wives, and his nephew, wife, and child all received titles (*Cishan
zhi* 8:5a). More interesting still, the cult to Marquis Li was not limited
to Changxing county. Sometime between 1260 and 1264 a branch temple was built in Changshu county, Suzhou, and between 1265 and 1274
in Suzhou proper. A 1346 inscription from Changshu explains that in
the reign of Emperor Lizong (1225–1265) two brothers in Huzhou
planned a rebellion; when the emperor discovered the plot he resolved
to massacre all of Huzhou.[22] But then Marquis Li appeared in a dream
to both the emperor and the prime minister, Shi Miyuan, saying it was
permissible to kill the two brothers, but not the entire city. Huzhou
was saved (*Qianlong Suzhou* 23:32b). This miracle suggests Marquis Li
had strong associations with the city of Huzhou. Devotees of King
Zhang from Huzhou, such as Xu Wenzhi, worshipped both King
Zhang, a regional deity, and Marquis Li, a local deity. It may have been
people from Huzhou who built the temples in Suzhou.

The chapter of the 1298 *A History of Temple Mountain* devoted to
these assistant deities recounts the miracles of another such deity as

22. The rebellion concerned a succession dispute between Zhao Hong and Zhao Yun
over who should succeed Emperor Ningzong. Ningzong died in 1224, and Shi Miyuan
supported Zhao Yun, who became Emperor Lizong. The disappointed Zhao Hong was
sent to Huzhou, where in the second month of 1225 a group of rebels rose up demanding
that he be named emperor. Their rebellion was suppressed in two weeks (R. Davis
1986:96–97).

recorded by the temple caretaker (*miaozhu*). Emissary Fang (Fang shizhe) came from Guangde commandery. In 1182 a family commissioned an iron incense burner for King Zhang's temple, but they had no way to transport it there. A man appeared and asked for a container made of willow and one stick of rattan; he came back three days later with thirty strings of cash. He said, "I will wait for you at the front of the temple." When the donor arrived, he saw a majestic statue of the very man who had spoken to him (*Cishan zhi* 8:6b–7a). Similar miracles involving the mysterious materialization of money followed this one. Following the construction of a separate temple to Fang in 1252, he was granted a title in 1258. The emperor's order read: "Because the Marquis was originally worshipped (*fu*) in the temple to King Zhang at Guangde, we do not grant a separate plaque. . . . We bestow a title on Emissary Fang, assistant deity (*zhushen*) to the temple of King Zhang on Temple Mountain" (*Cishan zhi* 8:8a). The Board of Rite's choice of words is startling: *fu* referred to the practice of performing sacrifices to someone's sons and grandsons at his own tomb, rather than at their own. Its use here indicates that these subdeities were quasi-family members, who bore roughly the same relationship to King Zhang as his ostensible blood kin. Whatever the exact relationship between King Zhang and his subdeities, it was acknowledged by the title-granting branch of the government, which deemed these deities "assistants."

The subdeities discussed above were all deities whose main temples were located in the vicinity of the temple at Temple Mountain. One inscription from Gutian county, Fujian, is especially interesting for the insights it provides into the spread of the cult to King Zhang in areas far from the base temple and also for the way it resolves the issue of local versus regional deities. In the early 1230s, Liu Kezhuang (1187–1269) wrote an inscription for a temple to King Zhang and a local Fujian deity (from Shaowu commandery), Ouyang Hu, a Sui dynasty official (*Bamin tongzhi* 60:7a; *Yinju tongyi* 30:5a–b). The original temple to Ouyang had dated to 1216, and King Zhang had been housed in a side altar. But in the reconstructed temple of 1229, the two gods had altars of equal size. Liu begins by quoting the passage from *Zuo Commentary* about the unsuitability of worshipping deities from other regions; and he too cites the passage from Mencius about men of a district, of a country, or of the world, saying that deities are the same. He then describes the extraordinary multiplicity of deities:

> There are those who can control good and bad fortune in one place. There are those whose accomplishments extend over the ocean and inland waters and flow to later generations. There are

those who like offerings of pig's feet, fish, and wine. Some eat ten thousand sheep annually. Some depend on grass and wood in order to trick men. Some wear the robes and ceremonial caps of high officials and receive titles from the nation.

Now, the worship of these two deities [King Zhang and Ouyang Hu] began in the Han and Sui dynasties. Today it extends from Jiangsu and Zhejiang to Fujian and Guangdong. It continues without end; their temples face each other everywhere. How can they not be those who are extremely brilliant and correct? How can they not be those whose accomplishments extend over the ocean and inland waters and flow to later generations? Thus worshipping them is not distorting[23] the way of the ancients. Even though Gutian is not in their realm, worshipping them here is not exceeding their domains. (*Houcun xiansheng quanji* 88:2b–3a)

Of course, worshipping the two gods in Gutian exceeded their domains. Liu has not resolved the issue of violating the prescriptions of the classics: he has merely asserted that because the cults to these two deities extend over large areas, they must be powerful deities. Most interesting here is his encomium in which he celebrates the wide diversity of deities in the early thirteenth century. Local or regional, carnivorous or devious, officially recognized or not, all deities deserve worship. Liu exhibits a tolerance that will not be matched by later generations of bureaucrats who will condemn those deities who consume pig's feet, fish, wine, or ten thousand sheep as well as those who trick people. For these conservatives, the only gods deserving recognition will be those who have government titles; for Liu, the titled deities are but one subgroup of all deities.

In the same century that Liu wrote his paean celebrating the diversity of popular deities, others began to protest that very diversity. The evidence suggests that although officials of both camps—those supporting and those criticizing popular cults—had always been present, the balance began to shift in the late thirteenth century. It has been shown that individual officials had proscribed popular cults even as early as the Tang, and also that the central government continued to grant titles to local deities through the last years of the Southern Song. Yet earlier in the twelfth century, the dominant political culture had favored the recognition of new deities and their incorporation into the register of sacrifices; by the end of the thirteenth, more officials, espe-

23. Emending *chan* (to mock) to *tao* (to confuse, to distort).

cially those associated with the Neo-Confucian philosophical school, called for both closer regulation of those cults listed in the register of sacrifices and suppression of all those outside it.

At the end of the Southern Song, in the 1260s, Huang Zhen, the prefect in Guangde commandery, the site of the base temple to King Zhang, wrote two memorials calling for the suppression of certain specific practices. To Huang, the annual sacrifice of thousands of cows is both extremely wasteful and infringes on the prerogative of the emperor to offer such sacrifices. The ritual implements carried in the processions on King Zhang's birthday resemble weapons and so foster unrest; similarly, the use of a prisoner's cap and a cangue encourage people to view incarceration lightly. One cannot help wishing Huang Zhen had been more curious about these processions and more specific in his descriptions: what did these iconographic details mean to people at the time? He protests as well the onerous burden placed on the leader of the organizing committee of the festival and the greed of temple officials, whom he calls "foxes and rats," who exact payment from merchants who have come a great distance to attend the festival (*Huangshi richao* 74:9a–10b).

His criticisms of the disorder stemming from the transformation of King Zhang into a regional cult are even more telling: "The people in all directions travel so much that no one any longer knows where he belongs." Gods are meant to be local, deities are supposed to rule over one village, and people are to stay home. The people coming from nearby Anji county in Huzhou as well as from the more distant Yixing county (Jiangsu) contribute to disorder, as demonstrated by a murder the previous year (*Huangshi richao* 74:10a). As Huang deplores the loss of control over this enormous number of people, so too does he bemoan the constant changes in popular religious practices:

> Moreover there is one who is linked with the god of Temple Mountain [King Zhang] whose relationship is extremely close. He is called the god of Mount Fang. I have heard that he serves the god of Temple Mountain. He is displayed in a hall of the temple. His many achievements have been recorded before. He has also received a title. Recently the title of the god of Temple Mountain has been changed to immortal (*zhenjun*) and the people think he is slacking off. They then built this temple as an alternate to receive offerings. Fang's miracles reverberate near and far. (*Huangshi richao* 74:10a)

The god of Mount Fang is Emissary Fang, the sub-deity of King Zhang who appeared to the man who donated an incense burner. The constant flux of popular religion, the incessant sprouting of new tiers on the spider plant, unsettles Huang: he cannot control this change, nor his uneasiness at a possible source of local disorder.

Huang is not alone in his fears: the pacification commissioner (*anfu*) to whom Huang addresses his petition accepts all his recommendations. Moreover, the commissioner writes that the judicial intendant (*tixing*) has recently forbidden the annual festival to the Five Manifestations in Wuyuan county and the festival to the God of the Eastern Peak in Xinzhou (Shangrao county, Jiangxi). The pacification commissioner too bans boat travel for the purpose of participating in the festivals to Emissary Fang or King Zhang (*Huangshi richao* 74:12a–13a). Unlike many of their twelfth-century predecessors and some of their contemporaries who sought to rule with the help of the deities, these thirteenth-century government officials have come to see popular religious worship as a threat to order.

In another memorial criticizing the cult to King Zhang, Huang applies an absolute standard: does the deity protect the district? Huang points out that even though the people of Guangde commandery had uninterruptedly continued to sacrifice cows, a famine occurred in 1247. And in 1266, when drought did not affect other districts, it did strike Guangde commandery. "It has yet to be seen that killing cows can prevent drought." The same goes for floods: why was the district inundated in 1261 when others were not? Huang answers his own query, saying that the topography of the region has much more to do with these disasters than the acts of the gods (*Huangshi richao* 74:14a–b). Huang is convinced that because the gods do not respond to prayers, one can safely stop making offerings.

Had Huang Zhen's reasoning been universally accepted, the worship of popular deities would have ceased at the end of the Song, for no deity could perform on command. But worship did not stop. Because the followers of these deities continued to use the kind of logic described in chapter 3 into the twentieth century, it is familiar even now. Even in the case of Guangde commandery in the 1260s, lay people may not have been persuaded by, or even have known of, Huang's argument. As was to become more and more common in the succeeding centuries, Huang Zhen does not report on the reaction of King Zhang's devotees. If they had used the standards of proof applied by Hong Mai and the authors of temple inscriptions, they surely would have found some way to account for the droughts and floods. They might have even said that King Zhang was angry because Huang Zhen had ordered the people not to sacrifice cows to him. Huang Zhen's ban on the annual festival must have been difficult, if not impossible, to implement. Very possibly it was not carried out at all. The temple to King Zhang at Guangde commmandery continued to flourish after the fall of China to the Mongols in the 1270s.

The critics of these cults were as strident as the devotees were fervent. Qualms about violating classical precedent, worries about keeping order, and attempts at suppression did nothing to check the dramatic rise of the deities. The continued strength of the regional cults underlines the extent to which these cults enjoyed popular and official support and resisted control. As long as the laity thought these gods could perform miracles, they flocked to their temples, participated in annual pilgrimages, and built branch temples in new places. Literati and bureaucrats were powerless to limit the scope of the popular pantheon in the face of such enthusiasm.

CHAPTER VII Conclusion

"Because lay people sought the help of the gods or religious specialists whenever they faced the unknown or the uncertain, popular religion cannot be separated out from the stuff of medieval life." So I claimed in the introduction. I then promised that each chapter would touch on people, money, and the government and so provide a new vantage point for viewing the social, economic, and political changes of the Song. The intervening pages have covered a variety of topics in Song popular religion: choices the laity had to make, contemporary understanding of reciprocity with the gods, the government's granting of titles, the pantheon in Huzhou, and the rise of regional cults. I now return to the broader issues raised in the introduction: what light does popular religious change cast on the developments of the medieval transformation? Information about the social context of popular religion provides some answers to this question; actual changes within the pantheon suggest others.

Responding to the increasing competition for places in the national civil service, Yuan Cai (c. 1140–1190) advised young men to pursue different careers—medicine, clergy, agriculture, trade, and crafts—rather than to concentrate exclusively on taking the civil service examinations. He seems not to have realized that becoming an ordained Buddhist or Daoist monk was also increasingly difficult.[1] The inflated cost of ordination certificates meant that many of the potential clergy could no longer afford to buy one. Why study Buddhist and Daoist doctrine for long years in preparation for certification if no examinations were held? Instead, more and more religious specialists concentrated on performing rites, Buddhist sutra-readings, or Daoist purification ceremonies, and they traveled from market to market peddling their services. By the second half of the twelfth century, as Hong Mai's account makes clear, lay people had the money to pay these unschooled practitioners, and they consulted them frequently.

At the same time, they consulted the gods as well. The major tenet of popular religion held that the more honors a god received, the more he or she would perform miracles. This belief in reciprocity gave peo-

1. Peter Bol, personal communication, January 1988.

160

ple enormous power over the gods; their acts of reverence shaped the gods' ability to control the elements, to prevent epidemics, to secure good harvests, and to protect local residents. Even the earth god who is the butt of so many jokes in *Zhang Xie Comes First in the Exams* needs offerings of food and wine from the local inhabitants. Because he has only eaten meat three times in the previous eight hundred years, he is weakened. His diet of rice cakes and bean paste dumplings grants him enough power to cause a fog to descend on the road but not enough to prevent Zhang from being robbed. Like the earth god of Five Chicken Hill, the deities' desire for recognition manifested itself in the most material of ways. What the gods wanted—rather, what they were thought to want—were beautiful images, new temples, spectacular plays, and adulatory inscriptions. This hunger for tangible forms of recognition meant that those individuals or groups who had the money to erect beautiful statues, to build new temples, to sponsor spectacular plays, and to carve adulatory inscriptions had a distinct advantage over those who did not (chapter 3).

A distinct advantage over the poor and unconnected they may have had, but this did not grant them hegemony over the popular religious pantheon. Recall the Zhu lineage of South Bank in Huzhou who were unable to launch a cult to their ancestor because they lacked popular support. Remember too the nephew of the dead official in Guangdong who claimed to have had a visit from his uncle but who was unable to secure a title for him. These examples indicate that members of a given descent group might try to organize on behalf of a deity, especially if he or she happened to have the same last name that they did, but they would not necessarily succeed in launching a popular cult. The list of activities a lineage could pursue in the twelfth and thirteenth centuries included composing genealogies, amassing communal lands, building an ancestral hall, observing the spring festival together, building temples, and seeking titles for a god they worshipped in common.

As the rich and well-organized could give the gods material recognition, so too were they able to secure government honors for them. Following the dramatic increase in title granting in the 1070s, temple inscriptions regularly credit the gods with a desire for titles from the central government. The first step was to get a petition filed on behalf of the deity; extant inscriptions reveal that usually county officials wrote petitions to promote local gods at the behest of the resident elders, holders of advanced degrees, or people with *lang* ranks. The long, complex canonization process with its requirements of miracles to be certified by official inspectors—from first a neighboring county and then one farther away—ensured that only a god who had already secured the support of all the local people would be included in the register of sacrifices.

To say "all the local people" is probably to exaggerate slightly; no doubt the government inspectors did not consult with the itinerant field workers in deciding whether or not a god was powerful. But the inscriptions cited in chapter 4 show that they did talk to many people from different social strata: to elders, to people with positions in the village service system, and to local clergy. Lists of donors confirm the tendency for different social strata to join together in worshipping popular gods: elders and village service personnel, holders of advanced degrees and bearers of *lang* titles, officials and those without office all appear in these documents. Evidently a wide social gulf did not separate those who held office from those who did not. Otherwise, they would hardly have joined together to worship popular gods.

While the effect of the title-granting system may have been to keep the central government responsive to local society, the primary intent of granting titles in the Southern Song—as stated over and over again—was to harness powerful deities to the yoke of governance. The central government recognized gods for the same reasons the common people did: to encourage them to bring good weather, to prevent famine and drought, to forestall enemy attacks, and, above all, to secure a good harvest—an item of great importance in the predominantly agricultural society of twelfth- and thirteenth-century China. In spite of the fact that the register of sacrifices had the potential to be employed in an exclusionary way, for most of the twelfth and thirteenth centuries it was not. Any god who performed miracles and passed the government inspections received a temple plaque. In the late thirteenth century, with the rise of Neo-Confucianism, the ranks of those calling for the denial of titles to the so-called licentious cults swelled, and in subsequent dynasties the government did indeed use, or at least tried to use, the system to suppress undesirable cults.

Change Within the Pantheon

What did popular pantheons look like before the tenth century? Because extant sources from the period preceding the development of woodblock printing are so much more limited in their coverage than those after it, to answer this question involves some slight of hand; for one, no local histories, with their listings of the popular temples in a given place, are available before the eleventh century. But it is possible that the local pantheons before the Song were like those in less developed areas during the Song—places like the highland areas of Huzhou.

There, the local gods included ancient heroes, original settlers, and some animal gods, like the Wukang dragon and the white monkey god (appendix table 3). Given that so many of their devotees grew their own foodstuffs, these gods probably performed primarily agricultural miracles—bringing rain or clear skies. In sum, it appears that before the Song, local people worshipped local gods.

In some respects, this sketch matches that of twelfth- and thirteenth-century conservatives, especially those like Chen Chun. These critics depicted popular gods of earlier times as having possessed all the qualifications they specified for gods in their own time: to be connected to the place where they were worshipped, to come from noble backgrounds, to have long histories, and to be included in the register of sacrifices. To be sure, this picture was more programmatic than accurate; these conservatives never mentioned animal gods, including the still-prevalent dragon deities. Nor did their view of the past allow for the birth of new gods. It was also anachronistic for them to envision a system in which all gods were in the register of sacrifices; such registers had existed under previous dynasties, but only in the late eleventh century did the awarding of titles to gods become widespread.

Few of the gods described in the preceding pages fit all aspects of this romanticized picture, but many of them, like Commander Fan and Wang 33, fulfilled one of Chen Chun's requirements: they had strong links to the places where they were worshipped. Born in the districts where they died, they performed miracles, underwent apotheosis, and became gods. But they fell short on another point: they were not ancient heroes of noble background, but commoners who had died within the recent past. By the thirteenth century, they had become an important presence in local pantheons throughout south China. In Huzhou, for example, these low-born gods constituted twelve of ninety-two gods whose temples date to the Song.

In many parts of China, like the lowlands of the Lower Yangzi valley, which had only just been or were in the process of being settled, the sole people who could become gods were the recently dead; the heroes of the past had not served as officials in or even visited these formerly remote areas. For their devotees, the gods' low station preceding their deaths was much less of an issue than their ability to perform miracles. The growth of the government system of granting titles fueled the rise of new, low-born gods. Chen Chun, in particular, objected to the collusion of local officials with "good-for-nothings" who wanted to get titles for the gods they backed. The officials sent to check on Wang 33's divinity did not concern themselves with his biography: they barely even mention the events of his lifetime in their final report to the emperor. They did concern themselves with miracles: had Wang really proved himself to be a powerful god? One other reason for the success of these commoner gods was that they embodied people's sense of place. Social historians have described a trend in the Southern Song of elites' turning away from national politics. Their children married the children of other local elites, they ran family estates and businesses, and they worshipped local gods like Wang 33 and Commander Fan. Their activities on behalf of such local deities enabled them to develop further bonds with their neighbors.

But not all new gods stayed local, and not all gods performed only the traditional miracles of curing illness, preventing illness, and bringing rain or clear skies. The people of New Embankment took images of their earth god, Lu Zai, with them on their trips to sell lotus pods and roots. Lu Zai remained a local god, worshipped only in New Embankment, but other gods' cults spread as their devotees traveled. The Heavenly Consort and the Five Manifestations began as gods like Commander Fan and Wang 33. The Heavenly Consort's success in the Song indicates how much the requirements for godhead had loosened; her being a poor fisherman's daughter (and a woman) before her death did not stand in the way of her becoming one of the most popular regional gods after her apotheosis. Unfortunately, title grants from the Imperial Secretariat offer much better information about the supporters of local gods like Wang 33 than do extant sources about those of the Five Manifestations, Zitong, the Heavenly Consort, and King Zhang. Information from inscriptions and contemporary anecdotes suggests that these regional gods derived their support from two major groups: traveling merchants and officials stationed away from home. In some cases officials took gods from their native places with them— as did the men from Putian who introduced the Heavenly Consort's cult to the capital. The opposite also occurred: officials who had served near the base temples of regional gods would bring the gods back with them once their terms were up, as did the official who asked King Zhang for help against the pirates off the coast of Ningbo.

As more and more people were drawn into the marketing system, so too were the gods they prayed to. Many gods possessing entrepreneurial skills have appeared in these pages: Zhao Bing of Taizhou (Zhejiang), who advised grain merchants to bring food to his starving devotees; the god from Ningbo who enabled fish and salt merchants to increase their profits tenfold; Lü Dongbin, who made a killing in the national mat market in Hangzhou; the god in Fuliang who knew how to make wine; the Purple Maiden, who advised her spirit-writing followers in Jianchang about tea and rice prices; King Zhang, who saved the Jiangxi merchant who smuggled glutinous rice; and the Five Manifestations, who predicted a peasant's losses and gains in Fuzhou (Jiangxi). Taizhou and Ningbo were major trading centers on the coast, Hangzhou was the capital, and the remaining cities in Jiangxi were in the economically advanced region of Lake Boyang. Each of these gods was active in the commercial centers of south China; the pantheons in more rural areas do not show this diversification of the gods. The extension of the gods' power into financial dealings did not occasion much notice at the time, possibly because it was so limited, more probably because the classics contained no restrictions on the type of miracles a god could perform.

Other changes in the Song pantheon, especially the rise of regional cults, excited much more comment and controversy. Many of those defending regional gods drew a parallel between the divine realm and the human empire: if people, especially merchants and officials, could travel across all of south China, how could the gods be restricted to just one village? When people went on journeys and took up their posts, they wanted to take their gods with them. They simply could not believe that the gods governed smaller realms than those they could traverse themselves. In supporting these cults to regional deities, their defenders had to ignore or twist the classical strictures against worshipping gods from other places. Of all the arguments they mustered on behalf of the new deities, that of efficacy was the most compelling. As long as the regional gods were able to perform miracles even away from their base temples, what was to prevent their worship? Temples to regional gods were located just where the merchants went, in the large cities along the waterways and coast of south China. As the Grand Canal attained higher and higher levels of urbanization, more and more regional temples clustered along its banks. Yet, as urbanization was limited to the major ports and waterways, so too was the spread of regional gods.

Of the many charges leveled against the new gods of the Southern Song, those against the regional gods were the most vituperative. Chen Chun objected to the temples to regional gods in his own district because the gods had not been born there and had never even visited the area in their lifetimes. How could the local people worship a god like the Heavenly Consort who had no ties to their native villages? He advocated a traditional interpretation of the classics that restricted worship to well-established, local deities. Of the reasons Huang Zhen, then prefect of Guangde commandery, presented for banning the annual festival to King Zhang in the 1260s, the most urgent was the disorder arising when thousands of people converged on the town for the deity's birthday celebrations. Such chaos would never have occurred if people had worshipped only the gods of their own villages.

It was hardly a coincidence that these critics of regional cults advocated the worship of only local gods at a time when many formerly powerful bureaucratic lineages, repelled by the factional conflicts in the capital, had already shifted their gaze to their home counties. Such people figured among the supporters of such local deities as Grand Guardian Wang 33, Zhou Chu, and General Zhu. This rejection of a regional identity, however much it appealed to these power-weary elites, simply did not satisfy those merchants who made their living plying the waterways of the Lower Yangzi or those officials stationed far from home. Traveling from post to post, or from marketplace to marketplace, they were the ones who propagated the regional cults with increasing enthusiasm. Protest as their opponents might, the regional cults were there to stay.

APPENDIX I   Comparison of *The Record of the Listener* and a Temple Inscription Recording the Same Miracle

The Record of the Listener (1:10:15:88)

GUANYIN HEALS AN ARM

An old village woman of Huzhou suffered an aching arm for a long time with no respite. During the night she dreamt that a white-clothed woman came and said: "I am also like this. If you can cure my arm, I can cure yours."

The old woman said: "Where do you live?"

She replied: "I stay in the west corridor of Revering Peace (Chongning) Monastery."

The woman then awoke. She went into town, to Revering Peace Monastery, and told what she had dreamt to monk Zhongdao of the Western Hall. He pondered and then said, "It must have been Guanyin [the Buddhist goddess of mercy]. Our hall has a white-robed image. Because of a gap in the thatch, her shoulder is hurt."

He led her to the room to perform her obeisance, and indeed one arm was missing. The elderly woman then ordered workmen to repair it.

When the image was complete, the woman's disease was cured.

This story was told by Wu Jie of Huzhou.

Tiaoxi ji 22:7a–10b; *Wuxing jinshi* 8:20b–22b[1]

THE CONSTRUCTION OF A NEW GUANYIN

The Repaying Imperial Kindness and Bright Filial Piety (Bao'en guangxiao) Monastery of Wuxing [Huzhou] lies in the northeast of the prefectural seat. The natural setting is very refreshing, and the buildings are very impressive.

---

1. Liu Yizhi (1078–1160) was a native of Gui'an county, Huzhou, who received his advanced degree in 1121 and served in the central government. The Siku quanshu edition of his collected papers, *Tiaoxi ji*, preserves this text as it has been transmitted; the *Wuxing jinshi ji* version was transcribed from a stele excavated at the end of the nineteenth century. Because a corner of the stele was missing, the editor, Lu Xinyuan, has supplemented the text, presumably on the basis of the Siku quanshu version. Lu comments that other epigraphical collections covering Huzhou do not include this text (*Wuxing jinshi* 8:27a–b). A comparison of the two versions illuminates the differences between these two types of sources. There are some textual variations: in some cases the transmitted version gives a better reading; in some, the transcribed rubbing does. The character count in the transcribed rubbing is not always accurate: some characters are missing. Unlike the transmitted version, however, the rubbing gives the date for the completion of the new hall and, most importantly, a full list of donors and their contributions. I am grateful to Dan Getz and Liu Xinru for their help in interpreting this often abstruse text.

The gates, the halls, the feasting palaces, and the rest huts are extremely orderly. No other monastery is like this. It was probably in the middle of the Yongding reign period (557–559) of the Chen dynasty that the empress's family donated their dwelling, and the monastery was built.[2] At first it was called Awakening Dragon (Longxing), and afterward Filial Righteousness (Xiaoyi). In the Tang dynasty it was again called Awakening Dragon. During the Wuyue kingdom, the Qians[3] changed the named to Great Peace (Daning). Because their daughter became a nun, it was subsequently a nunnery for all of one hundred years.

In the second year of the Revering Peace (Chongning) reign period of this dynasty (1103), it again became a monastery at which succession was not limited to the disciples of the abbot. It was called Revering Peace and Ten Thousand Longevities (Chongning wanshou). Afterward, its name was changed from Revering Peace to Heavenly Peace (Tianning). In 1137 it received its current plaque (jin'e) and was respectfully designated a site where rites for the deceased emperor were to be conducted.[4]

For a long time there was a statue of the bodhisattva Guanyin in between two pillars on the western side of the monastery. Zhang of the prefecture[5] had been paralyzed for three years.

One night Zhang dreamt of a white-robed woman who said: "You cannot lift your arm. I also suffer from this. If you can heal my arm, I will also cure your shoulder and give you long life."

Zhang asked her where she lived, and she said, "I live in the west corridor of Heavenly Peace Monastery."

The next day Zhang was carried to the monastery to the statue of the bodhisattva, and it was just as Zhang had dreamt. Zhang looked at the statue with reverence and was moved to tears. Zhang examined the right arm of the bodhisattva and noticed that it had been damaged by a piece of falling wood. Zhang ordered it repaired, and Zhang's illness was subsequently cured.

From this time on, the people of the prefecture believed in Guanyin. No less

2. The 1201 local history for Huzhou says that the legendary settlers of Huzhou, the Fangfengs, were said to have donated their residence (Jiatai Wuxing 13:12b).

3. The Qians were the ruling family during this period.

4. Liu Yizhi is actually simplifying the history of the monastery. In 1103, the prime minister Cai Jing petitioned that a Chongning monastery be designated in each prefecture to pray for the longevity of the reigning emperor Huizong. New monasteries were not built; instead, as in this case, already existing monasteries were renamed. These monasteries received tax benefits and land grants so that they could conduct services on the emperor's behalf. In the following year, the two characters Wanshou were added to the name of these monasteries. In 1111, Chongning was changed to Tianning, in further praise of Huizong's rule. In 1126, when the north fell to the Jurchen invaders, Huizong was taken prisoner, and he died in 1135. In 1137 the name of these monasteries was changed from Tianning wanshou to Bao'en guangxiao (Repaying Imperial Kindness and Broadening Filial Piety) and later to Bao'en guangxiao (Repaying Imperial Kindness and Bright Filial Piety). Their function was to burn incense for Huizong and to conduct prayers for his welfare in the underworld (Chikusa 1982b:95–96; Song huiyao, Li 5:15–16).

5. Zhang's sex is not clear from the text, which says only "a person of the prefecture, named Zhang" (junren Zhangshi).

than several tens of people a day came seeking relief from illness and pain, suffering and danger. The number of miracles cannot be told. The place Guanyin's image was located was dark and decrepit, narrow and cramped. It did not fulfill people's expectations.

Then teacher (*daoshi*) Jujiu and his disciple Huizhi gathered the crowd to raise money. They planned to build another hall to house the exquisite image suitably, but they were concerned that it would take a long time to have such large beams and pillars cut from the hill forests. Someone said: "In a nearby area called Treasure Stream (Baoxi) is an old estate, whose occupant has left and no longer lives there. Why don't you go take a look?"

Huizhi went there in a hurry. A relative of the owner had already had a dream, when Huizhi made his request to the master, who happily granted permission [to donate the wood to the monastery]. Thus, on the left, in front of the existing hall, they built four rows of houses. In front was another hallway. On the sides were two more side rooms. The building was deep, bright, and splendid. Everything was extremely beautiful and impressive. It was probably just as the previous head of the monastery had planned for years but had been unable to achieve. The monks and lay people were happy and respectfully sang hymns of praise. They all felt as if they had a refuge.

Jujiu asked me to write an inscription about this matter to celebrate their accomplishment. I said, "I have heard that the bodhisattva Guanyin's nature and appearance are empty. There is no monastery in which she is not present. Her form and her radiance are interrelated. If there is faith in her (*gan*), she will certainly respond. She is compassionate and abandons no sentient beings. For this reason her body has thirty-two manifestations.[6] She is able to change shape as befits the situation. Her blessings can be seen and heard. Furthermore, my body and your body—one a monk and one a lay person—are both among her thirty-two transformations. This is the ultimate principle (*zhenyuan*) and the projection of herself as a phenomenon (*shiji*). We see that this bodhisattva is both two [the ultimate principle and her projection] and one. They [the ultimate principle and her projection] are the same, and they are different. With this in mind, we recognize her as a bodhisattva.

"The sentient beings are the essence of things (*tiben*) and the fulfillment of enlightenment (*yuancheng*). So we and the bodhisattva are the same, and there is no difference between us and her. Because of this nonduality (*wu'er*) and nondifferentiation (*wubie*), the faith in the hearts of the sentient beings extends everywhere without physical trace. The bodhisattva not only has no fixed identity but also has no fixed dwelling. Yet, you put up a statue in a designated place for them to seek refuge. Are you not creating a false distinction?"

Jiu replied, "Not so. The goddess's manifestations are limitless. Because she has no one place of her own, but is worshiped in the hearts of believers, she

---

6. The *Wuxing jinshi ji* text gives thirty-two, the number of her manifestations in the *Surangama Sutra*; the Siku quanshu edition gives thirty-three, the number of her manifestations in the *Lotus Sutra*. The characters for two (*er*) and three (*san*) differ only by a stroke and are easily confused. Because the *Surangama Sutra* was an important Chan text, Liu really may have meant thirty-two, but since both of these texts are corrupt, it is impossible to decide conclusively.

thus has a place. I see that monks and lay people go in front of the statue, gather their robes and bow, burn incense and pray on their knees, and tell her of all their illnesses and troubles and ask her for help. Full of sincere emotion, sweat dripping down their faces, they tell her their inner thoughts. The bodhisattva responded to their faith by appearing in a dream.

"Ultimately they [the bodhisattva and sentient beings] are as one. I admire the place she is worshipped and make it imposing in order to augment their faith. If they believe, in one instant they view matter, and they understand emptiness. Then they will attain enlightenment. They will know that the bodhisattva does not arise from her image. She is everywhere, in all directions. Every place is her place of worship. And this place of worship is nowhere specific.

"If she blesses the sentient beings, and no one receives the benefits [because they are all bodhisattvas], does what I have said constitute creating a false distinction? or does it not? For you to ask questions and me to respond like this may also have no real meaning."

I responded: "This is called real meaning. This is called the bodhisattva who is compassionate and saves all things. These qualities are not dual and not differentiated. What you say is similar. I used this information to write this record."

Construction of the new hall began on [gap in the text]. It was completed on the *gengxu* day of the fourth month of the twenty-seventh year (in 1157). After some days, Taijian householder Liu Yizhi wrote this and appended a hymn.

(The text of the hymn praising Guanyin follows. On the back of the stele is a list of donors and their contributions.)

APPENDIX II   Selected Translations from
The Record of the Listener

The Office of the Record Keeper in Xiuzhou

There were many strange apparitions in the office of the record keeper (*silu*) in Xiuzhou (Jiaxing county, Zhejiang). One always wore a green kerchief and cloth robe, had a short and broad shape, and walked with slow and heavy steps. A woman also went out every night and bewitched and beat the runners.

At the time my father occupied this post, my older brother the future grand councillor was just nine.[1] In broad daylight he opened his eyes and stared just as if he had seen something and said, "Water, water." Only when we moved him did he regain consciousness.

Two days later, my father came home late from the office. A concubine grabbed his robe from behind, suddenly called out, and fell to the ground. My father had heard that ghosts feared leather belts, so he took one to bind the concubine and carried her to bed. After a long while, [the ghost speaking through her] said, "This person has previously insulted ghosts and gods. Just now he is carrying something in his right hand that is frightening [the belt]. I do not dare to come close. Furthermore he does not know I come from the left, I was just captured, and that I have been detained by an official who uses the Zhong Kui [a famous demon queller] method. I will go now without causing mutual inconvenience."

He was asked, "Who are you?"

He did not want to answer.

After several repetitions he said, "I am farmer Stem Nine (Zhi Jiu) from Jiaxing. With my fellow canton resident Water Three (Shui San), we had nine mouths in our two households. During the flood two years ago we all began to wander begging for food. We died just before the officials began famine relief. Now I live on top of the big tree behind your house. Several days ago, the one the little official [your son] saw was Water Three.

My father said, "I worship Zhenwu[2] [a star divinity] because he is very effi-

---

1. Hong Mai's father, Hong Hao (1088–1155), served as a record keeper in Jiaxing sometime between 1119 and 1125 (see his biography in *Songshi* 373:11557–62). Hong Mai's brother, Hong Gua (1117–1184), was grand councillor (*zhongshu menxia pingzhang shi jian shumi shi*) (see his biography in *Songshi* 373:11562–65). By Chinese reckoning, he would have been nine in 1124. Hong Mai was only one year old at the time.

2. Zhenwu is often depicted with his hair unbound. In a transformation text from Dunhuang, Wu Zixu smoothes his hair because disheveled hair symbolizes a deranged state of mind (Mair 1983:291). For an interesting study of the history of Zhenwu, his appearance in Ming novels, and iconography in pre-1949 China, see Grootaers (1952).

171

cacious, and I also have images of the Buddha, and of the earth (*tudi*) and stove god (*zaoshen*). How is it that you come here?"

The ghost said, "The Buddha is a benevolent deity who does not concern himself with such trivial matters; every night Zhenwu unbinds his hair, grasps his sword, and flies from the roof. I carefully avoid him, that's all. The earth god behind your house is not easily aroused. Only at the small temple in front of your house [to the stove god] am I reprimanded every time I'm seen. I just entered the kitchen, and His Lordship asked, 'Where are you going?'

"I answered, 'I'm just looking around.'

"He upbraided me, 'You're not allowed here.'

"I said, 'I do not dare,' and came here."

My father said, "What are the two things that always come out?"

The ghost said, "The one with the kerchief is Shi Jing, who's called Gentleman Shi. He's just under the hedge outside the study window, about three *chi* [90 cm]³ under the ground. The woman is Qin Erniang. She's lived here a long time."

My father said, "I give paper money to the earth god on the first and fifteenth day of every month. How can he allow ghosts from outside to come in? You go and ask him for me. Tomorrow I shall destroy his shrine."

The ghost said, "Do you mean to say you don't understand? Even though he has money, how can he go without food? When I enter your house, if I get something, I must give him a share to keep him quiet, and that is why he has always permitted me to come." He ate for a while and then spoke again, "Were I to proceed as you admonish and tell the earth god, he'll be angry that I'm so loquacious, and will use a stick to drive me out."

My father said, "Have you seen my family's ancestors or not?"

He said, "Every time there is a holiday and you make offerings, I definitely come to observe. I smell the fragrant food and want to eat it but do not get any. Among the places are a few empty places, but if a yellow-clothed woman sees me, she gets angry."

After looking around, the ghost gasped and became pale. Eventually he spoke, saying, "Just as I reached the door, I was chased by a woman carrying a stick. I quickly ran in the other direction and barely escaped."

The woman he spoke of was my great-grandmother Jiguo.

My father had asked all that he wanted and said, "You're consumed by suffering and hunger. Would you like a meal? Some wine and a fat chicken? I will offer them to everyone. It won't be like usual when I give a skinny chicken."

When my father had finished speaking, the ghost cocked his ear as if someone had called him and said, "The earth god is very angry and has expelled our two households. Now we'll briefly go to the top of the city wall. We have nowhere to return to. Please free me quickly. I don't dare to come again."

My father undid his belt. The concubine slept in a daze for several days and then woke up. (*Yijian zhi* 2:8:8:250)

3. A *chi* is a unit of measure equaling 30.72 centimeters (Ogawa 1968:1225).

Righteous Husband, Virtuous Wife[4]

There was also Commander Fan Wang of Shunchang county (now Nanbei county, Fujian). At the time of Fan Ru's uprising, Yu Sheng and other bandits in the district rebelled.[5] Chen Wangsu of the local militia was a trouble-maker, and he wanted to take the bandit's lair to retaliate. Fan Wang scolded the crowd, saying, "Our parents, wives, and children obtain their livelihood from the country. Today we're not strong enough to attack the bandits. If we do so, it will help them to be even more terrible. How can you not be ashamed to view heaven and earth?" Angered by his cutting words, the leader of the bullies [Chen Wangsu] killed him.

One son, called Fosheng, was twenty and famed for his courage. The bandits falsely used his father's name to summon him and killed him when he arrived. When Fan's wife, née Ma, heard that her husband and son were both dead, she sobbed in the road. The bandits wanted to rape her, but she resisted. They dismembered her with a piece of wood and divided her into sections. After several months the bandits were subdued.

The bricks where Commander Fan had been killed retained obscure outlines of his corpse, which were very faint. The people of the district gathered the bricks and joined together to build a shrine to him. They also painted his likeness on the wall of the temple to the god of walls and moats. In 1136 the vice-prefect, Wu Kui from Jian'an [now Jian'ou county, Fujian], petitioned the court about the deity. An edict awarded him the posthumous title of chengxin gentleman and granted permission to build a temple to him.

Then Su Hao, the Shunchang sheriff directing the corvée laborers [building the temple], dreamt that Commander Fan, clothed in the garb of a high official, came to visit him and thanked him for overseeing the work. He said, "At the time I was hurt, my left eye was gouged out by the bandits." He led Su to the place to see it; there was his corpse, clothed in a short white shirt, as well. Commander Fan pointed again to the southeast corner of the temple and said, "The leftover traces are still here. I already have sent a message to the magistrate and hope you will remind him."

The next day Su entered the temple and asked how Wang had died. Everyone said Wang's story was true, but no one had been aware that his eye had been gouged out. The southeast corner was the original site of the shrine. Accordingly he asked and received five bricks, which he brought to the temple.[6]

The district magistrate Huang Liang heard about this and asked his wife, née Cai. She answered, very surprised, "Last night I also dreamt that a purple-clad person visited you in your chambers. You bowed to him to enter the room, and climbed the steps. He then refused and left. His name was Fan Wang. Could that be what the sheriff refers to as leaving a message?"

---

4. This entry actually contains two anecdotes. I translate the second.

5. Fan Ru organized a rebellion in Fujian in 1131, Yu Sheng in this particular district (*Jian-yan yilai xinian yaolu* 41:759, 761).

6. This is not clear. It may mean that people had taken some of the bricks to their homes and brought them back once the sheriff asked for them.

Commander Fan died as a loyal martyr, and his wife died unmolested. They died but are not forgotten. How can one not believe this? (*Yijian zhi* 1:20:9:182–183)

The Bandit of Xincheng County

Chen Changyan was the sheriff of Xincheng county, Lin'an [Hangzhou, Zhejiang]. An evil youth killed one person, wounded one person within his district, and fled without being caught, causing more than ten people in his mutual responsibility group (*baowu*) to be taken into custody. Chen prayed to the God of the Pine Stream (Songxi shen) and petitioned heaven,[7] saying, "I would usually not dare to pray on my own behalf. Only if my parents were ill would I cut my thigh or cauterize my shoulder; there is no avenue that I would not exhaust in my selfishness. Barring this, even when my plight involved my wife or me, I have never dared to bother the gods. Now evil bandits have knifed two people, wounding one and killing the other, implicating those of the district and their kin. Concerned with the well-being and peace of the people within 100 li,[8] I ask that you above take notice."

Not long after, when a bowman who had tried to capture the bandit died, Chen said to his wife, "A bow-carrying soldier has died on the road. How can I sleep peacefully?" He dressed simply and went to the suburbs, where he spent the night in the open at a Daoist monastery. He observed that there was a guest who could summon the immortal, the Purple Maiden (Zigu).[9] Chen went and respectfully kowtowed and asked, "According to the law, if a sheriff does not capture five major criminals, then he is only fined one month's salary. This is not much. I am asking on behalf of the people."

The goddess wrote, saying, "In Ganpu township, Haiyan county, Xiu prefecture [Jiaxing, Zhejiang]." Chen immediately dispatched soldiers. After ten days, he again asked, and the immortal [the Purple Maiden] said, "The original evil-doer has already been caught. But as my own strength is insufficient to deal with this matter for you, I could not avoid petitioning a higher god. Now, capturing the bandit is the accomplishment of the God of the Pine Stream, who has recently brought him to the border of Fuyang county [Hangzhou]!" She also wrote the character *zi* ["catalpa"]. She said, "Your lordship should send a boat. You will see the delegated spirit soldiers guarding him; they await your going to pick him up."

After several days, someone from Ganpu returned to report, "At first, on the day we arrived at the township, the criminal had already boarded a sea-going vessel. Just as we sighed angrily several times, we heard the sound of human cries. People said Doctor Xu from East Catalpa, Fuyang county, had a placard to arrest the criminals. After following a sandbar all night, he reached and captured him."

7. I take this to mean he directly addressed the skies.

8. The li was a unit of length, equaling 552.96 meters in the Song (Ogawa 1968:1224–25).

9. The Purple Maiden was one of the major goddesses of spirit writing in the Song. See chapter 3.

On another day, someone asked the prisoner what had happened, and he said, "At first, I was in Ganpu, and we knew of the arrival of a clerk who was pursuing us. I desperately wanted to go to sea. Because I thought of my parents, wife, and children, I went back to the East Catalpa Gate, and entered the temple to King Yu. I then fell into a daze so I could not leave, and I saw many black-clothed figures guarding the door. The next day I was caught."

Chen then returned, reported the criminal's confession to the magistrate, released all the hostages, and sent the prisoner in a cangue to the prefectural office. (*Yijian zhi* 15:12:15:1668)

APPENDIX III   Tables

TABLE I

Titles Granted Popular Deities Year by Year:
A Tabulation of the Lists in Chapters 20 and 21
of the *Li* (Rites) Section of the *Song huiyao*[a]

Year	No.	Year	No.	Year	No.	Year	No.
960	0	987	0	1014	4	1041	0
961	0	988	0	1015	1	1042	2
962	0	989	0	1016	0	1043	0
963	0	990	0	1017	0	1044	1
964	0	991	0	1018	2	1045	1
965	1	992	0	1019	0	1046	0
966	0	993	0	1020	0	1047	0
967	0	994	0	1021	0	1048	0
968	0	995	0	1022	0	1049	0
969	0	996	1	1023	0	1050	0
970	1	997	0	1024	0	1051	1
971	0	998	1	1025	0	1052	1
972	1	999	0	1026	1	1053	0
973	1	1000	2	1027	0	1054	0
974	1	1001	1	1028	1	1055	2
975	0	1002	0	1029	0	1056	0
976	0	1003	0	1030	0	1057	0
977	7	1004	1	1031	0	1058	0
978	0	1005	0	1032	0	1059	1
979	0	1006	0	1033	0	1060	0
980	0	1007	1	1034	0	1061	0
981	0	1008	3	1035	1	1062	1
982	0	1009	3	1036	1	1063	2
983	0	1010	3	1037	0	1063	0
984	0	1011	2	1038	0	1064	0
985	0	1012	2	1039	0	1065	0
986	0	1013	4	1040	5	1066	0

[a]Figure 1 is a graph of the information contained in this table. In most instances the *Song huiyao* gives the exact year in which a title was awarded. In the few (less than ten) cases where only the reign period is given, I have placed the listing in the middle year of the reign period.

176

Year	No.	Year	No.	Year	No.	Year	No.
1067	1	1107	58	1147	21	1187	9
1068	2	1108	46	1148	16	1188	10
1069	1	1109	15	1149	23	1189	20
1070	0	1110	29	1150	13	1190	1
1071	1	1111	24	1151	14	1191	1
1072	1	1112	33	1152	8	1192	1
1073	2	1113	30	1153	16	1193	5
1074	1	1114	33	1154	11	1194	0
1075	37	1115	39	1155	5	1195	12
1076	11	1116	12	1156	28	1196	3
1077	16	1117	8	1157	11	1197	15
1078	17	1118	10	1158	15	1198	7
1079	7	1119	1	1159	24	1199	1
1080	16	1120	5	1160	33	1200	5
1081	7	1121	24	1161	19	1201	3
1082	10	1122	11	1162	25	1202	2
1083	5	1123	23	1163	24	1203	2
1084	10	1124	11	1164	33	1204	0
1085	7	1125	5	1165	12	1205	5
1086	1	1126	1	1166	37	1206	14
1087	3	1127	1	1167	35	1207	8
1088	2	1128	8	1168	33	1208	20
1089	4	1129	6	1169	14	1209	12
1090	2	1130	18	1170	7	1210	9
1091	2	1131	27	1171	5	1211	13
1092	5	1132	21	1172	26	1212	6
1093	3	1133	10	1173	10	1213	8
1094	2	1134	10	1174	9	1214	5
1095	3	1135	24	1175	5	1215	7
1096	3	1136	23	1176	0	1216	3
1097	3	1137	27	1177	1	1217	4
1098	4	1138	19	1178	1	1218	1
1099	12	1139	16	1179	0	1219	2
1100	9	1140	33	1180	0	1220	11
1101	8	1141	24	1181	1	1221	20
1102	28	1142	10	1182	2	1222	4
1103	59	1143	9	1183	22	1223	0
1104	87	1144	12	1184	19	1224	4
1105	88	1145	19	1185	7	1225	0
1106	33	1146	10	1186	12		

TABLE 2
Population Data from Huzhou

Year	Households (hu)	Residents (kou)[a]	Percentage of change[b]
HUZHOU: ENTIRE PREFECTURE			
1008–1016	129,540	436,372	
1068–1077	145,121		
1130–1162	159,885		
1182	204,594	571,812	
1290	236,570		+ 83%
LOWLAND AREAS BY COUNTY			
Wucheng county			
1008–1016	26,357	90,373	
1290	68,437		+160%
Gui'an county			
1008–1016	26,913	121,119	
1290	49,894		+ 68%
Deqing county			
1008–1016	10,434	33,200	
1131–1162	33,749	78,655	
1237–1240	36,831	67,533	
1290	31,465		+202%
HIGHLAND AREAS BY COUNTY			
Changxing county			
1008–1016	34,103	104,292	
1174–1189	49,811	54,838	
1208–1224	62,300	273,000	
1290	54,151	70,882	+ 59%
Anji county			
1008–1016	22,285	71,612	
1174–1189	25,298	65,860	
1290	25,298		+ 5%
Wukang county			
1007	4,619		
1290	17,261		+273%

SOURCE: Compiled on the basis of population figures from different local histories (*Yongle dadian* 2277:3b; *Chenghua Huzhou* 8:8b–16a; *Jiaqing Deqing* 3:2a; *Shunzhi Changxing* 3:1b; *Jiaqing Anji* 5:25a).

[a]Because the government counted households and not residents, figures for the number of residents are often not available.

[b]The percentage of change is calculated on the basis of the number of households.

TABLE 3 : Reconstructing the Huzhou
Pantheon

On the basis of a survey of extant local histories from the six counties and
county seat of Huzhou, I have compiled a list of popular religious temples
founded before or during the Song.[1] The sections about buildings and monu-
ments in gazetteers usually list Buddhist monasteries and nunneries, Daoist
monasteries, and popular religious temples separately. The Chinese term for
Buddhist monastery is *si* and for Daoist monastery, *guan*. Two terms appear
for popular temples, *ci* and *miao*. As with so many terms from the Song, there
is no hard line between the two. *Ci* implies shrine, in the sense of a building
to someone who is alive or once lived—hence the term *shengci* (living shrine),
which denotes shrines built to living people, often to virtuous officials upon
their leaving a given district. When the recipient of a living shrine died, the
same building then became a *ci*. The term *miao* seems to be less identified with
actual people and more with deities. But to say even this much is perhaps to
overstate the difference, because, after all, most deities had once been people.
The terms for branch temples, *xingci*, *xinggong*, and *xingmiao*, seem to have
been used interchangeably.[2]

Local histories usually give a brief history of all the temples in the area including the dates of construction, major repairs, and receipt of titles from the
central government. They also often excerpt temple inscriptions or print them
in their entirety. Especially in the case of Yuan and later local histories, the
authors may list only those temples receiving official government patronage
(those in the register of sacrifices [*sidian*]). Even in those cases where the com-
piler aspired to total coverage he may not have conducted exhaustive surveys
of standing temples. In some cases the listings seem to be only slight rework-
ings of those in earlier histories. Obviously, local histories provide better coverage of temples that enjoyed some success; a temple standing for only a short
time had little chance of being included in these lists, which were compiled
roughly every hundred years. And because they listed only temples, household altars and subshrines within temples were omitted. Later local histories
usually list a few Song temples not included in earlier sources. I have included
these temples in my study, both because so few temples claim a Song founding
date that there is no reason to suspect the sources of systematically exaggerating their age and because it is very possible that the original temple surveys
were not thorough.

The gazetteers refer to temples in several different ways: taking the name of
the god directly; using his latest title from the central government; or giving
the name by which a temple is known in other places. So, for example, temples
to the same deity could be listed under three different names: temple to King

---

1. Local histories date back to predynastic China, although the earliest surviving fragments
date to the Qin (221–207 B.C.) and the Han (206 B.C.–A.D. 220) (Lu Tao et al. 1984:194).
2. See also Chikusa 1982c:142, note 26.

Zhang (Zhangwang miao); Efficacious Salvation temple (Lingji miao); or Temple Mountain branch temple (Cishan xingmiao). Temples named directly for a god are the most easily identified. Yet, because the central government frequently awarded the same titles to different gods—and different titles to the same god—knowing just the god's title is not enough to make a definite identification. Fortunately most of the temple lists also give some information about the deity so it is possible to classify the temples. When sufficient information is not provided, I have listed the temples as unclassifiable.

Unlike the listings in most local histories, which lump all the popular religious temples into one section, I have divided the temples into eight different categories: traditional, commoner, Buddhist, Confucian, Daoist, generic, nature, and regional.[3] Doing so has many pitfalls, not least that many Huzhou residents may have drawn no such distinctions, choosing instead to visit whichever temples was closest or most efficacious. Yet without some categorization it is impossible to characterize changes in the popular religious pantheon.

Traditional and Commoner Gods

Both traditional and commoner gods were those who had been people identified with specific places before their deaths: the main differences had to do with their origins. Traditional gods, usually officials, generals, or emperors, had a higher social status and had received recognition under earlier dynasties. Many of the temples to traditional gods in Huzhou predated the Song, but some new temples were also built in the Song. Also appearing in the Song were commoner gods who had not served as officials or generals, whose lives had been cut off, and who came to be worshipped for their power to perform miracles.

Buddhist, Daoist, and Confucian Gods

Different from both traditional and commoner gods are the various figures originally from the Buddhist and Daoist pantheons like Guanyin, Zhenwu, and the God of the Eastern Peak. In contrast to the vast majority of deities, these gods were not the spirits of historical or legendary people linked with their native place. The inscriptions I cite in chapter 2 indicate strong Buddhist support for the Guanyin cult: her temples often stood on monastery grounds, and monks were major fund-raisers. Yet unlike a regional deity, no one Guanyin temple was acknowledged as the base temple. Similarly, Lü Dongbin and

3. Only one contemporary source divides the gods in the pantheon into subgroups. In 1270, Qian Yueyou compiled a local history of Hangzhou, the *Xianchun Lin'an zhi* (A history of Hangzhou compiled in the Xianchun [1265–1274] reign period), famed among historians for its detail. He lists temples according to seven groups: local deities, hill and river deities, martyrs, nobles, ancient gods, temples formerly in Kaifeng, and regional temples of gods based in other places. Qian's breakdown is most significant for its inclusion of regional temples, which by 1270 had become so numerous as to merit their own category. Because the distinction among nobles, martyrs, and heroes is often arbitrary, I have collapsed them all into one category: traditional gods.

Zhenwu seem to have been worshipped in their own right as popular deities. Although Guanyin, Lü Dongbin, and Zhenwu had temples in different places, their temples do not seem to have been linked organizationally. No records describe annual pilgrimages to any one temple.

Characterizing the cult to the God of the Eastern Peak is especially difficult. This cult began in the Han dynasty, if not earlier, as a cult to the mountain in Shandong, and the god of the mountain, who had no known pre-apotheosis identity, was thought to be the judge presiding over Hell (Sakai 1937). Originally the temples to the God of the Eastern Peak were viewed as branch temples of the temple at Mount Tai; after the fall of North China in 1127, his devotees were no longer able to go to Shandong. Here too the central government's extensive patronage, especially during the reigns of Zhenzong (998–1022) and Huizong (1101–1125), resulted in the construction of many temples to the God of the Eastern Peak. Further study drawing on Daoist sources, data about patronage, and popular conceptions of hell will be necessary before all the dimensions of this cult—Daoist, popular, and governmental—can be understood fully.

I have included the Confucian temple in Deqing county in this list even though it is unlikely that many residents prayed to Confucius for miracles. In an 1133 inscription describing the reconstruction of the temple, Shen Yuqiu says that the temple, founded in the period 1008–1017, when a local man came first in the exams, was designed to encourage scholarship in the district. The 1133 repairs were financed by the literati of the district (*Guixi ji* 11:1a). At no point does he mention popular participation, but it is possible that local literati prayed at the temple before sitting for the civil service examinations.

Generic Gods

Certain deities within the pantheon were referred to by type more frequently than by their own individual names; these I call generic. The clearest example of such a class of deity is city gods (*chenghuang shen*). David Johnson argues persuasively that the concept of a city god dates to the sixth century and caught on only in the eighth. He explains:

> The first, most fundamental point to make about these city gods is that they all have different names: they are the spirits of different persons. They share a label, not an identity. Thus we are dealing here not with belief in a specific deity like Maitreya or Mazu [the Heavenly Consort], but with the idea that there was *a class of divine beings* who were especially concerned with cities. (1985:388, emphasis added)

The gazetteers list city god temples only in Huzhou county seat and in Deqing. Tan Yue, the author of the earliest extant local history from Huzhou, the *Jiatai Wuxing zhi* (A history of Huzhou compiled in the Jiatai [1201–1204] reign period), does not even identify the deity who serves as the city god of Huzhou. Like Tan, Zhao Yushi (1175–1231), the author of an essay about city gods, does not give the deity's pre-apotheosis biography, but he notes that Huzhou residents referred to the city god as King of Peace Wall (Ancheng wang). As is oft-remarked, in some ways city gods can be thought of as holding bureau-cratic posts. Different figures served as the city gods of different prefectures and even of different counties. Zhao cites one example of a virtuous official who, after leaving the county of Longshu (Lujiang county, Anhui), died and became the city god (*Bintui lu* 8:103–105). The bureaucratic comparison is clearest here: in life the official had been the district magistrate, in death the city god.

Dragons, almost the only nonhumans in the Song pantheon, are similar. Often associated with mountain pools, many localities had dragon temples dating to long before the Song; in Huzhou, they were located in the prefectural seat of Huzhou and in Wukang and Anji counties. The local histories often identify the resident dragon deity either as white or black, or by the name of the mountain or stream he dwelled in—but people probably thought of the god nearest to them as the local dragon, to whom one prayed especially in times of drought. In much the same way they did not call city gods by their own names but just the city god.[4]

Earth gods (*tudi shen*) were also generic deities.[5] In some cases the local peo-ple referred to them as earth god, in others by name. Because the appellation was quite flexible, any local god may have been called an earth god: many of the deities I class as traditional and commoner deities may have served as earth gods, but the sources do not identify them as such. One 1187 inscription makes it very clear that the local people have no idea who their earth god is, and they are reduced to arguing that he must be the same deity as housed in a nearby temple with a similar, but not identical name (*Qianlong Wuqing* 6:1a). By the twelfth and thirteenth centuries most of the villages of Huzhou must have had earth gods, but their temples were so small that they are not listed in the sources.

City gods, dragons, and earth gods in different places were called by the same label, yet no organization bound these temples together. Supporters of one temple did not go on pilgrimage to another; no one city god temple was regarded as the home temple. So too for the dragon and earth god temples. Of all popular deities these generic gods leave the faintest traces; their very ubiquity makes it difficult to identify their supporters.

Animal and Nature Gods

By the Song, with the exception of dragon temples, cults to animals were almost nonexistent. Tan Yue lists just one in Huzhou: a temple to the White Monkey in Anji county (*Jiatai Wuxing* 13: 20a). He explains that during the Tang dynasty, a monkey swallowed some elixir that a Daoist had mixed, went

4. See David Johnson's (1985:379–88) discussion of a case where categories overlap: a dragon also serves as the city god of Taizhou (Linhai county, Zhejiang).

5. As were guardian deities of Buddhist monasteries (*qielan shen*). No such deities are listed in Huzhou, but they were common in south China. Inoue Ichii (1941) discusses a ninth-cen-tury temple inscription from a monastery in Shanxi where Guan Yu serves as the guardian deity and argues that he is the guardian deity of all Buddhist monasteries. Not so. Such deities, like city gods, were different in different places. The monastery in question is located very close to the site of Guan Yu's tomb, hence his association with it.

crazy, plunged into water, and drowned. "Afterward there were many strange miracles and thus I do not record them."[6] In a similar development, cults to streams and mountains were also dying out. In Huzhou, there was only the cult to Lake Tai, which is personified as a king who can keep the waters still.

Regional Gods

Regional cults differ from all the above cults because these branch temples were explicitly identified with the home temples of deities in other places. Followers did sometimes go on pilgrimages to the base temples; the branch temples were always named for the home temples. In Huzhou were temples to King Zhang of Temple Mountain in Guangde Commandery, to the Five Manifestations of Huizhou, and to Zitong, a Sichuanese god. The presence of this type of temple embodies the most obvious change in popular religion during the Southern Song: the spread of cults from one region to another. This development is the topic of chapter 6.

TABLE 3
A Reconstruction of the Huzhou Pantheon in the Song

Deity	Name of temple[b]	Nature of entry[c]	Source
	Huzhou Prefectural Seat		
TRADITIONAL			
項羽 Xiang Yu *Qin dynasty*[a]	西楚霸王 Xichu bawang	472 torn down 588 rebuilt 668 miracle	*Jiatai Wuxing* 13:12a–13a
吳文皇帝 Wu Wen huangdi [Emperor Wen] *Six dynasties*		c.618 rebuilt 834 rebuilt	*Jiatai Wuxing* 13:9b–10b
銅官山 Tongguan shan Zhao	通靈王 Tongling wang	923 title 934 promoted	*Jiatai Wuxing* 13:13a–b

6. See Wu Hung (1987) for more about this cult.

[a] The dates of pre-apotheosis lifetime are given when known.

[b] The name of the temple is given only in cases where it differs from the name of the god.

[c] When the gazetteer gives the date when the temple was founded or repaired, or when the god was awarded a plaque, given a title, promoted, or performed a miracle, that information is given. If the gazetteer merely lists the temple, I list it as "standing" in the year the gazetteer was compiled.

TABLE 3: (*cont.*)

Deity	Name of temple[b]	Nature of entry[c]	Source
Jian 趙監 [Supervisor Zhao of Tongguan Mountain] *Han dynasty*			
郭尙書 Guo shangshu [Secretary Guo] *Six dynasties*		988 rebuilt	*Jiatai Wuxing* 13:10b
沈約 Shen Yue *441–513*	德貺 Dekuang	1098 rebuilt 1101 title	*Jiatai Wuxing* 13:12a
防風氏 Fangfeng shi [The Fang-feng family] *Legendary settlers of Huzhou*		1201 standing	*Jiatai Wuxing* 13:14a
顏真卿 Yan Zhenqing *708–784*	忠烈 Zhonglie	1056–1063 built 1133 temple plaque	*Jiatai Wuxing* 13:10b
COMMONERS			
曹清 Cao Qing *dead c. 1100*	靈祐 Lingyou	1119 title	*Jiatai Wuxing* 13:11a
BUDDHIST			
觀音 Guanyin		1157 inscription	*Wuxing jinshi* 8:21a; *Yijian zhi* 1:10: 15:88; *Tiaoxi ji* 22:7b–10b
DAOIST			
東岳 Dongyue [God of the Eastern Peak]		1125 built	*Chenghua Huzhou* 11:6a

TABLE 3: (*cont.*)

Deity	Name of temple[b]	Nature of entry[e]	Source
GENERIC			
Dragon	祥應 Xiangying	916 miracle 1073 built 1080 title 1165 rebuilt	*Tongzhi Huzhou* 6:1a
城隍 Chenghuang [City god]		1148 rebuilt	*Jiatai Wuxing* 13:9b
REGIONAL			
廣德祠山 Guangde Cishan Zhangwang 張王 [King Zhang of Temple Mountain, Guangde commandery] *Han dynasty*	靈濟 Lingji	894 built 1101 rebuilt	*Jiatai Wuxing* 13:11b
梓童 Zitong	文昌 Wenchang	1261 built	*Yongle dadian* 2281:9b
UNCLASSIFIABLE			
保仁王 Baoren wang		1098 rebuilt	*Jiatai Wuxing* 13:13b

WUCHENG COUNTY

TRADITIONAL			
沈僕射 Shen puye [Chief Administrator Shen] *Six dynasties*		502 built	*Qianlong Wuqing* 6:4a
沈將軍 Shen jiangjun [General Shen Qing] 沈清 *Tang dynasty*		776–779 built	*Jiatai Wuxing* 13:14a–b

TABLE 3: (cont.)

Deity	Name of temple[b]	Nature of entry[c]	Source
蘇將軍 Su jiangjun [General Su] *Six dynasties*		1201 standing	*Jiatai Wuxing* 13:13b–14a
張循王 Zhang Xun wang [King Zhang Xun] *Song dynasty*		1130s built	*Qianlong* *Wuqing* 6:4a
胡進思 Hu Jinsi *Five dynasties*	靈昌 Lingchang	910–960 built 1119–1125 title 1174–1189 promoted	*Guangxu* *Wucheng* 6:10a–b
李靖 Li Jing *Tang dynasty*		618–910 inscription	*Jiatai Wuxing* 13:14a
項羽 Xiang Yu *Qin dynasty*	項王 Xiang wang	907 built	*Jiatai Wuxing* 13:14a
宋太祖 Emperor Song Taizu *Song dynasty*	廣惠 Guanghui	1175 built	*Wuqing* *wenxian,* siguan 7a
徐孺子 Xu Ruzi *Han dynasty*		1152 inscription	*Jiatai Wuxing* 13:14a; *Chenghua* *Huzhou* 11:7b
顏真卿 Yan Zhenqing *708–784*	東平王 Dong ping wang	1127–1130 built	*Qianlong* *Wuqing* 6:3a
COMMONERS 曹孝子 Cao Xiaozi [Filial Cao] *dead c. 1100*	靈祐 Lingyou	1201 standing	*Jiatai Wuxing* 13:14a

TABLE 3: *(cont.)*

Deity	Name of temple[b]	Nature of entry[c]	Source
李崔承事 Li Cui chengshi [Gentlemen Li and Cui] *dead c. 1140*	嘉應 Jiaying	1270 plaque	*Wuxing jinshi* 12:20a–23b
BUDDHIST			
觀音 Guanyin		c.1117 inscription	*Danyang ji* 9:2a–3a
DAOIST			
東嶽 Dongyue [God of the Eastern Peak]		1174–1189 built	*Chongzhen Wucheng* 8:11b
GENERIC			
索度明王 Suodu mingwang [Enlightened King of Suodu]	Green Mound Earth God	1119–1125 built 1176 inscription 1211 inscription	*Qianlong Wuqing* 6:1a
吳將軍 Wu jiangjun [General Wu] *Tang dynasty*	Crow Earth God	1201 standing	*Jiatai Wuxing* 13:14b–15a
NATURE GOD			
太湖神 Taihu shen also called Pingshui da wang 平水大王 [God of Lake Tai, the king who calms the waters]		960–1275 built	*Guangxu Wucheng* 6:5a–b
REGIONAL TEMPLES			
張王 Zhang wang [King Zhang]	廣惠宮 Guanghui gong	1064 built	*Chongzhen Wucheng* 8:11b

TABLE 3: (*cont.*)

Deity	Name of temple[b]	Nature of entry[e]	Source

DEQING COUNTY

TRADITIONAL

吳大帝 Wu dadi [Great Emperor Wu] *Six dynasties*		1127 built	*Deqing xian xuzhi* 2:5a
孔愉 Kong Yu *Six dynasties*	孔侯 Kong hou [Marquis Kong]	1201 standing	*Jiatai Wuxing* 13:19a
藺相如 Lin Xiangru *Warring states*		1201 standing	*Jiatai Wuxing* 13:19a
魏霸 Wei Ba *Han dynasty*	惠應 Huiying	1203 plaque	*Wuxing beizhi* 14:28b
陸載 Lu Zai *Six dynasties*	孚應 Fuying	1163–1164 plaque	*Wuxing jinshi* 9:16b–20a
朱泗將 Zhu Si jiang [General Zhu] *Han dynasty*	永靈 Yongling	953 title 1135 plaque	*Liangzhe jinshi* 8:36a– 42a, 11:18b– 19b; *Huzhou Tongzhi* 53:8b, 27a– 28a
沈麟士 Shen Linshi *Six dynasties*		1201 standing	*Jiatai Wuxing* 13:19a
孫皓 Sun Hao *Six dynasties*	孫王 Sun wang [King Sun]	1201 standing	*Jiatai Wuxing* 13:19a

COMMONERS

| 宣教劉侯
Xuanjiao Liu
hou [Marquis
Liu]
d. 1055 | | 1055 built | *Deqing xian
xuzhi* 2:5a |

TABLE 3 : (cont.)

Deity	Name of temple[b]	Nature of entry[c]	Source
曹孝子 Cao Xiaozi [Filial Cao] *dead c. 1100*	昭應侯 Zhaoying hou	1120–1275 built	*Qianlong Huzhou* 40:24a
載繼元 Zai Jiyuan *dead c. 1250*	顯祐侯 Xianyou hou	1260–1264 plaque	*Yongle dadian* 2281:15b
蔡欽 Cai Qin *dead c. 1119–1125*	靈應蔡侯 Lingying Cai hou	1119–1126 built	*Deqing xian xuzhi* 2:5a

CONFUCIAN

| 孔子
Confucius | | 1153 rebuilt | *Guixi ji* 11:1a |

DAOIST

東嶽 Dongyue [God of the Eastern Peak]			
in Deqing county seat		1201 standing	*Jiatai Wuxing* 6:3b
in New Market		1134 inscription	*Jiatai Wuxing* 6:3b

GENERIC

| 城隍
Chenghuang
[City god] | | 1131–1163 rebuilt | *Yongle dadian* 2281:15a |

GUI'AN COUNTY

TRADITIONAL

| 項羽
Xiang Yu
Qin dynasty | 項王
Xiang wang
[King Xiang] | 987 inscription | *Kangxi Gui'an xianzhi* 2:10a |
| 季札
Ji Zha
Spring and autumn period | 西吳季子
Xi Wu Jizi | 1241–1252 land purchased | *Wuxing beizhi* 14:27b |

TABLE 3 : *(cont.)*

Deity	Name of temple[b]	Nature of entry[c]	Source
COMMONERS			
陸圭 Lu Gui *dead c. 1119–1125*	石冢廣靈侯 Shizhong guangling hou	1241 plaque	*Wuxing jinshi* 12 : 10b–14a; *Jiatai Wuxing* 13 : 15b–16a
GENERIC			
東林土地 Donglin tudi [Donglin Earth God]		1127–1230 miracles 1133 plaque 1146 inscription	*Jiatai Wuxing* 13 : 15b
DAOIST			
東嶽 Dongyue [God of the Eastern Peak]			
in She village		1201 standing	*Jiatai Wuxing* 13 : 15a
in Lian market		1201 standing	*Jiatai Wuxing* 13 : 15a
呂洞賓 Lü Dongbin	回仙人 Huixian ren [returning immortal]	1102–1106 built	*Donglin shanzhi* 12 : 1a–4b
真武 Zhenwu		1238 built	*Linghu zhenzhi* 7 : 1a
UNCLASSIFIABLE			
廣明王 Guangming wang		1234–1236 plaque	*Linghu zhenzhi* 7 : 1a
白廟 Bai miao		1127–1275 built	*Shuanglin zhen zhi* 9 : 2b

ANJI COUNTY

TRADITIONAL			
施明侯 Shi Ming hou [Marquis Shi Ming] *Six dynasties*		849 rebuilt	*Jiatai Wuxing* 13 : 19b

TABLE 3 : (cont.)

Deity	Name of temple[b]	Nature of entry[c]	Source
李靖 Li Jing *Tang dynasty*	仁濟 Renji	1104 plaque	*Jiatai Wuxing* 13:19b
朱紀 Zhu Ji *Six dynasties*	朱明府君 Zhu Ming fujun	1201 standing	*Jiatai Wuxing* 13:19b
DAOIST			
東嶽 Dongyue [God of the Eastern Peak]		1112 built	*Jiatai Wuxing* 6:12a
GENERIC			
天目山龍王 Tianmu shan longwang [Dragon King of Tianmu Mountain]		1201 standing	*Jiatai Wuxing* 13:20a
黑龍潭 Heilong tan [Black Dragon Pool]		1247 plaque	*Chenghua Huzhou* 11:9a
NATURE			
白猨神 Bai yuan shen [White Monkey god]		1201 standing	*Jiatai Wuxing* 13:20a
REGIONAL TEMPLES			
張王 Zhang wang [King Zhang]	靈濟 Lingji	1135 built 1201 in ruins	*Jiatai Wuxing* 13:19a

WUKANG COUNTY

TRADITIONAL			
防風氏 Fangfeng shi [The Fangfeng family] *Legendary settlers of Huzhou*		291 built 910–960 plaque	*Jiatai Wuxing* 13:17a

TABLE 3: (cont.)

Deity	Name of temple[b]	Nature of entry[c]	Source
蔣靈帝 Jiang ling di [Efficacious emperor Jiang] *Six dynasties*		220–280 built	*Jiatai Wuxing* 13:17b
銅官趙監 Tongguan Zhao Jian [Supervisor Zhao of Tongguan Mountain] *Han dynasty*		923 title 935 promotion	*Jiatai Wuxing* 13:17b
樊將軍 Fan jiangjun [General Fan] *Han dynasty*		1201 standing	*Jiatai Wuxing* 13:18a
九沈 Jiu Shen [Nine Shens] *Legendary original settlers*		1201 standing	*Jiatai Wuxing* 13:18b
沈伯儀 Shen Boyi *Tang dynasty*	沈尚書 Shen shangshu [Minister Shen]	1201 standing	*Jiatai Wuxing* 13:18a
楊存中 Yang Cunzhong *Song dynasty*	旌忠 Zuzhong	1165 plaque	*Jiatai Wuxing* 13:18b
COMMONERS			
徐天祐 Xu Tianyou *dead c. 1127*	靈應 Lingying	1227 plaque	*Yongle dadian* 2281:14a
曾雪之 Zeng Zhazhi *dead 1253–1258*	靈祐照應 Lingyou zhaoying	1253–1258 built	*Kangxi* *Wukang* 4:25a

TABLE 3 : (cont.)

Deity	Name of temple[b]	Nature of entry[c]	Source
DAOIST			
東岳 Dongyue [God of the Eastern Peak]		1008 built	*Jiatai Wuxing* 6 : 11a
嶽帝 Yue di [God of the Eastern Peak (?)]		1100 built	*Jiatai Wuxing* 13 : 18a
GENERIC			
Dragon	淵德 Yuande	815 entered in the register of sacrifices 1101 built 1167 rebuilt	*Jiatai Wuxing* 13 : 17b
REGIONAL			
張王 Zhangwang [King Zhang]	靈濟 Lingji	1185 built	*Jiatai Wuxing* 13 : 18b
UNCLASSIFIABLE			
陳許二侯 Chen Xu er hou [Marquises Chen and Xu]		910–960 built	*Jiatai Wuxing* 13 : 18a
梓華 Zihua		1201 standing	*Jiatai Wuxing* 13 : 18a

CHANGXING COUNTY

Deity	Name of temple[b]	Nature of entry[c]	Source
TRADITIONAL			
錢卿 Qian Qing *Han dynasty*		63 built 627 rebuilt 1040 built 1067 rebuilt	*Jiatai Wuxing* 13 : 16a

TABLE 3: *(cont.)*

Deity	Name of temple[b]	Nature of entry[c]	Source
吳夫槩王 Wu Fuchai wang [King Fuchai of Wu] *Spring and autumn period*		1201 standing	*Jiatai Wuxing* 13:16a
吳夫槩 Wu Fuchai	漁陂王 Yupi wang [Fish pond king]	1201 standing	*Jiatai Wuxing* 13:17a
季札 Ji Zha *Spring and autumn period*	吳西季王 Wu xi Ji wang [King Ji of Western Wu]	1131–1162 inscription	*Jiatai Wuxing* 13:17a
謝太傅 Xie taifu [Grand Mentor Xie] *Six dynasties*		1040 built 1067 rebuilt	*Jiatai Wuxing* 13:16b
COMMONERS			
李侯 Li hou [Marquis Li] *dead 1121*		1209 plaque	*Cishan zhi* 7:6b; *Jiaqing Changxing* 26:20a–21b
DAOIST			
東嶽 Dongyue [God of the Eastern Peak]		1138 built	*Yongle dadian* 2281:12b
GENERIC			
Earth God	雲鶴仙人 Yun he xianren [Cloud Crane Immortal]	1230 rebuilt	*Kangxi Changxing* 2:64a
REGIONAL			
五顯靈官 Wuxian lingguan [Five Manifestations]		1084 built	*Qianlong Changxing* 4:19a

TABLE 3 : (cont.)

Deity	Name of temple[b]	Nature of entry[c]	Source
UNCLASSIFIABLE			
斫射神 Zhuo she shen		787 built 841–846 rebuilt	Jiatai Wuxing 13 : 16b
堯氏 Yao shi [Yao family]		1201 standing	Jiatai Wuxing 13 : 16b
羿后 Yi hou [Empress Yi]		1201 standing	Jiatai Wuxing 13 : 16b

TABLE 4
Breakdown of Huzhou Pantheon by Type of Deity

	Huzhou	Wucheng	Deqing	Gui'an	Anji	Wukang	Changxing	Total
Traditional	7	10	8	2	3	7	5	42
Commoner	1	2	4	1	0	2	1	11
Buddhist	1	1	0	0	0	0	0	2
Confucian	0	0	1	0	0	0	0	1
Daoist	1	1	2	2	1	2	1	10
Generic	2	2	1	1	2	1	1	10
Nature	0	1	0	0	0	0	0	1
Animal	0	0	0	0	1	0	0	1
Regional	2	1	0	0	1	1	1	6
Unclassifiable	1	0	0	2	0	2	3	8
TOTAL	15	18	16	8	8	15	12	92

TABLE 5
Distribution of Regional Temples by Circuit and Prefecture

Prefecture and County Name of Deity	Year	Source

WEST LIANGZHE CIRCUIT

Prefecture and County Name of Deity	Year	Source
SUZHOU		
Five Manifestations	1008–1016	1379 *Hongwu Suzhou* 15:24a
King Zhang	1197	1642 *Chongzhen Wuxian* 21:3b
Heavenly Consort	1275	1379 *Hongwu Suzhou* 15:22a
Changshu county		
King Zhang	1133	1506 *Zhengde Gusu* 28:12b
Kunshan county		
Five Manifestations	1251	1251 *Chunyou Yufeng* 3:20a
Zitong	1251	1251 *Chunyou Yufeng* 3:21a
CHANGZHOU		
Five Manifestations	906	1484 *Chenghua chongxiu Piling* 27:6a
King Zhang	1241–1252	1484 *Chenghua chongxiu Piling* 27:5b
Zitong	1268	1268 *Xianchun Piling* 14:6a
Wujin county		
King Zhang	1268	1268 *Xianchun Piling* 14:10b
Wuxi county		
King Zhang	1268	1268 *Xianchun Piling* 14:12a
Yixing county		
King Zhang	1268	1268 *Xianchun Piling* 14:14b
ZHENJIANG		
Five Manifestations	1040	1332 *Zhishun Zhenjiang* 8:8b–9a
	1241–1252	1332 *Zhishun Zhenjiang* 8:8b–9a
King Zhang	910	1332 *Zhishun Zhenjiang* 8:18a
	1205–1207	1332 *Zhishun Zhenjiang* 8:18a
	1237–1240	1332 *Zhishun Zhenjiang* 8:18a
Dantu county		
King Zhang	1008–1016	1332 *Zhishun Zhenjiang* 8:15b–16a
	1101	1332 *Zhishun Zhenjiang* 8:15b–16a

Note: After surveying the thirty local histories surviving from the Song and the Yuan, I determined which cults occurred most frequently. Because the local histories are all from the south, I did not examine the region north of the Yangzi river, much of which was under Jin rule during the Southern Song. Once I had narrowed the field, I surveyed later local histories from the five modern provinces: Jiangsu, Zhejiang, Jiangxi, Anhui, and Fujian. The use of these Ming and Qing sources means that these maps show temples founded in—or at least claimed to date to—the Song that were still standing at the time of compilation. Any temples built in the Song that had subsequently disappeared are of course not listed. Some of these founding dates may be dubious, but because very few temples do claim to have been founded in the Song, and many more admit to having been founded in the Ming or Qing, I have included these in my lists.

This chart is divided by Song circuit: it gives the prefecture or county, the name of the god, the date that a temple is first mentioned, and then the date and name of the source. If a temple was located in the prefectural seat, then it directly follows the name of the prefecture; otherwise it follows the name of the county.

TABLE 5 (*cont.*)

Prefecture and County Name of Deity	Year	Source
Heavenly Consort	1241–1252	1332 *Zhishun Zhenjiang* 8:13a–14b
Danyang county		
King Zhang	910	1332 *Zhishun Zhenjiang* 8:18a–b
	1205–1207	1332 *Zhishun Zhenjiang* 8:18a–b
	1237–1240	1332 *Zhishun Zhenjiang* 8:18a–b
Zitong	1253–1258	1332 *Zhishun Zhenjiang* 8:18b
Five Manifestations	1275	1569 *Longqing Danyang* 8:3b
Jintan county		
King Zhang	1133	1332 *Zhishun Zhenjiang* 8:24a
YANZHOU		
King Zhang	1241	1262 *Jingding Yanzhou* 4:3b–4a
Zitong	1260	1262 *Jingding Yanzhou* 4:4a–5a
JIAXING		
King Zhang	1275	1288 *Zhiyuan Jiahe* 12:5b
HANGZHOU		
King Zhang	1170	1265–1274 *Xianchun Lin'an* 73:9a–11a
	1194	1265–1274 *Xianchun Lin'an* 73:9a–11a
	1274	1265–1274 *Xianchun Lin'an* 73:9a–11a
Five Manifestations	1131–1162	1265–1274 *Xianchun Lin'an* 73:14a–b
	1213	1265–1274 *Xianchun Lin'an* 73:14a–b
	1236	1265–1274 *Xianchun Lin'an* 73:14a–b
	1237	1265–1274 *Xianchun Lin'an* 73:14a–b
	1249	1265–1274 *Xianchun Lin'an* 73:14a–b
	1260–1264	1265–1274 *Xianchun Lin'an* 73:14a–b
	1274	1265–1274 *Xianchun Lin'an* 73:14a–b
Zitong	1236	1265–1274 *Xianchun Lin'an* 73:17a
Heavenly Consort	1205–1207	1265–1274 *Xianchun Lin'an* 73:14b–16b
Xincheng county		
Five Manifestations	1274	1265–1274 *Xianchun Lin'an* 74:13a
Changhua county		
King Zhang	1191	1265–1274 *Xianchun Lin'an* 74:18a
Five Manifestations	1274	1265–1274 *Xianchun Lin'an* 74:18b
HUZHOU		
King Zhang	894	1204 *Jiatai Wuxing* 13:11b
Zitong	1261	(undated) *Wuxing xuzhi*, as cited in 1408 *Yongle dadian* 2281:9b
Wucheng county		
King Zhang	1064	1638 *Chongzhen Wucheng* 8:15b
Changxing county		
Five Manifestations	1084	1749 *Qianlong Changxing* 4:19a
King Zhang	984	1886 *Cishan zhi* 10:9b

TABLE 5 (*cont.*)

Prefecture and County Name of Deity	Year	Source
Si'an township		
King Zhang	1102	1886 *Cishan zhi* 10:6b

EAST LIANGZHE CIRCUIT

CHUZHOU		
King Zhang	1184	1690 *Kangxi Chuzhou* 8:28a
WENZHOU		
Five Manifestations	1119–1125	1756 *Qianlong Wenzhou* 9:21a
TAIZHOU		
King Zhang	1186	1223 *Jiading Chicheng* 31:7b
Five Manifestations	1221	1223 *Jiading Chicheng* 31:7b
Xianju county		
Five Manifestations	1184	1680 *Kangxi Xianju* 30:8a
MINGZHOU (NINGBO)		
Heavenly Consort	1132	1560 *Jiaqing Ningbo* 15:24a
Five Manifestations	1205–1207	1320 *Yanyou siming* 15:12b
King Zhang	1246	1320 *Yanyou siming* 15:12a
Zitong	1271	1320 *Yanyou siming* 18:30b
Dinghai county		
Ding Zhang	1150	1298 *Dade Changgouzhou* 7:17a
Zitong	1269	1298 *Dade Changgouzhou* 7:14b
Yin county		
Heavenly Consort	1191	1937 *Yinxian tongzhi* 727a
Five Manifestations	1275	1937 *Yinxian tongzhi* 735a
Cixi county		
King Zhang	1205	1320 *Yanyou siming* 15:21b
Fenghua county		
Zitong	1261	1320 *Yanyou siming* 18:35a
SHAOXING		
Sheng county		
King Zhang	1201	1201 *Jiatai Guiji* 6:17a
Zhuji county		
Five Manifestations	1201	1201 *Jiatai Guiji* 6:19a
Yuyao county		
King Zhang	1198	1201 *Jiatai Guiji* 6:23b
Shangyu county		
King Zhang	1201	1201 *Jiatai Guiji* 6:25b

TABLE 5 *(cont.)*

Prefecture and County Name of Deity	Year	Source
FUJIAN CIRCUIT		
FUZHOU		
Five Manifestations	1004–1008	1182 *Sanshan zhi* 7702
Ningde county		
Five Manifestations	1103	1538 *Jiaqing Ningde* 2:24b
Gutian county		
King Zhang	1216	c.1270 *Houcun xiansheng quanji* 88:2a–3a
QUANZHOU		
Heavenly Consort	1195–1200	1612 *Wanli Quanzhou* 24:2b
Yongchun county		
King Zhang	1210	1526 *Jiaqing Yongchun* 9, unpaginated
SHAOWU		
Five Manifestations	1270	1619 *Wanli Shaowu* 15:15b
TINGZHOU		
Five Manifestations	1131–1162	1637 *Chongzhen Tingzhou* 6:2a
	1241–1252	1497 *Hongzhi Tingzhou* 9:2a
King Zhang	1253–1258	1497 *Hongzhi Tingzhou* 9:4a
Changting county		
Five Manifestations	1131–1162	1258 *Linting zhi*, as cited in 1408 *Yongle dadian* 7892:2b[a]
Five Manifestations	1253–1258	1258 *Linting zhi*, as cited in 1408 *Yongle dadian* 7892:2b
Shanghang county		
Five Manifestations	1208–1224	1497 *Hongzhi Tingzhou* 9:8a–b
Liancheng county		
Five Manifestations	1208–1224	1258 *Linting zhi*, as cited in 1408 *Yongle dadian* 7892:5b
King Zhang	1258	1258 *Linting zhi*, as cited in 1408 *Yongle dadian* 7892:5b
Qingliu county		
Five Manifestations	1131–1162	1637 *Chongzhen Tingzhou* 6:37a
Wuping county		
Five Manifestations	1241–1252	1637 *Chongzhen Tingzhou* 6:61a
XINGHUA		
Heavenly Consort	1119–1125	1602 *Wanli Xinghua* 2:54a
Putian county		
Heavenly Consort	1157	1491 *Bamin tongzhi* 60:12b–13b

TABLE 5 (*cont.*)

Prefecture and County Name of Deity	Year	Source
Heavenly Consort	1160	1491 *Bamin tongzhi* 60:12b–13b
	1275	1491 *Bamin tongzhi* 60:12b–13b
Xianyou county		
Heavenly Consort	1178	1491 *Bamin tongzhi* 60:19a

EAST JIANGNAN CIRCUIT

RAOZHOU
Zitong	1275	1683 *Kangxi Raozhou* 12:11b

NINGGUO
King Zhang	424–453	1577 *Wanli Ningguo* 10:8a

HUIZHOU
Wuyuan county
Five Manifestations	1109	1175 *Chunxi Xin'an* 5:12a

GUANGDEJUN
King Zhang	220	1881 *Guangxu Guangde* 55:1b

JIANKANG (NANJING)
King Zhang	1174–1189	1261 *Jingding Jiankang* 44:28a–b
Zitong	1235	1344 *Zhizheng Jinling* 11:15b
Five Manifestations	1275	1569 *Jinling shiji* 4:11b

Jurong county
King Zhang	984	1886 *Cishan zhi* 10:6b

WEST JIANGNAN CIRCUIT

FUZHOU
Five Manifestations	1264	1260–1264 *Jingding Linchuan zhi*, as cited in 1408 *Yongle dadian* 10950:8a[b]
Zitong	1253	1260–1264 *Jingding Linchuan zhi*, as cited in 1408 *Yongle dadian* 10950:8a

JIANGZHOU
King Zhang	1222	1241–1253 *Chunyou Jiangzhou zhi*, as cited in 1408 *Yongle dadian* 6700:5b[c]

[a]See Zhang Guogan 1974:430–31.
[b]See Zhang Guogan 1974:564–65.
[c]See Zhang Guogan 1974:559.

GLOSSARY

An (name of mountain) 庵
Ancheng wang (King of Peace Wall) 安城王
anfu (pacification commissioner) 安撫
Anji 安吉
Bai Yuchan 白玉蟾
Baihua dawang (Hundred Flowers Great King) 百花大王
bao (mutual surveillance group) 保
Bao'en guangxiao (Repaying Imperial Kindness and Bright Filial Piety)
    報恩光孝
Bao'en guangxiao (Repaying Imperial Kindness and Broadening Filial Piety)
    報恩廣孝
baohu (mutual surveillance household) 保戶
Baoning jiangjun (Keeping-the-Peace General) 保寧將軍
baowu (mutual responsibility group) 保伍
Baoxi (Treasure Stream) 寶溪
baoyi lang (gentleman of military rank 8a) 保義郎
baozhang (guard chief) 保長
baozheng (guard leader) 保正
bei (moonblocks) 盃, 杯
beijiao (moonblocks) 盃珓
benmiao (base temple) 本廟
Bianxiu ju (Bureau of Compilation) 編修局
biji (miscellaneous notes) 筆記
bing (section 3 of *The Record of the Listener*) 丙
bingma dujian (supervisor of soldiers and horses) 兵馬都監
bishu jian (director of the palace library) 秘書監
Bo Yi 伯益
boshi (staff member) 博士
bu (diviner) 卜
bu (section 15 of *The Record of the Listener*) 補
bu　xuesheng (some type of student) 補　學生
Cai 蔡
Cai Jing 蔡京

cesi (toilet death) 廁死

chan (to flatter) 諂

Changshu 常熟

Changxing 長興

Changzhou (now Wujin county, Jiangsu) 常州

Changzhou (Suzhou, Jiangsu) 長洲

Chen 陳

chen (one of twelve celestial branches) 辰

Chen Changyan 陳昌言

Chen Jian 陳戩

Chen Nan 陳楠

Chen Wangsu 陳望素

Chen Xiu 陳修

Cheng Hao 程顥

Cheng Yi 程頤

cheng (assistant magistrate) 丞

Chengdu 城都

chengshi lang (gentleman of civil rank 9a) 承事郎

chengxin lang (gentleman of military rank 8b) 承信郎

chi (unit of measure equaling 30.72 centimeters) 尺

Chong'an 崇安

Chongde 崇德

Chongning (Revering Peace) 崇寧

Chongning wanshou (Revering Peace and Ten Thousand Longevities) 崇寧萬壽

Chongren 崇仁

Chu 楚

chu (place) 處

Chuzhou 處州

ci (shrine, temple) 祠

Cishan xingmiao (Temple Mountain branch temple) 祠山行廟

cishi (prefect) 刺史

daibu jinshi (self-styled advanced degree holder) 待補進士

dan (unit of volume equaling 94.88 liters) 石

Daning (Great Peace) 大寧

Danyang 丹陽

dao (way) 道

daojia (Daoist) 道家

daomin (people of the way) 道民

daoren (people of the way) 道人

daoshi (ordained Daoist) 道士

daoshi (teacher) 道師

daosu (monks and lay people) 道俗

daozhe (people of the way) 道者

Datong 大同

daxing jia (great families) 大姓家

Dazu 大足

dengshi lang (gentleman of executory rank 9a) 登仕郎

Deqing 德清

Dexing 德興

di (emperor) 帝

Di Renjie 狄仁傑

dian (ritual, register) 典

dianyu (hall) 殿宇

difang zhi (local history, gazetteer) 地方志

difen baozhang (superior guard leader) 地分保長

digong lang (gentleman of executory rank 9b) 廸功郎

Ding Bogui 丁伯圭

Ding Ren 丁壬

ding (section 4 of *The Record of the Listener*) 丁

Dinghai 定海

Donghai wang (King of the Eastern Sea) 東海王

Dongting (name of a lake) 洞庭

dou (unit of volume equaling 9.488 liters) 斗

du (sector) 都

dubao hu (superior guard household head) 都保戶

dubao zheng (superior guard leader) 都保正

dudie (ordination certificate) 度牒

e (plaques) 額

er (two) 二

Erlang 二郎

Ezhou 鄂州

fa (methods) 法

Fan (name of mountain) 范

Fan Ru 范汝

Fan Wang 范旺

Fang shizhe (Emissary Fang) 方使者

fangzhi (local history, gazetteer) 方志

fashi (master of rites) 法師

fei (consort) 妃

feng (to enfeoff, fief) 封

fenghao (title) 封號

Fenghua 奉化

fengjue (titles) 封爵

fengshan (imperial ceremony worshipping heaven and earth) 封禪

fenmiao (branch temple) 分廟

Fosheng 佛勝

Fu (name of mountain) 福

fu (prefecture) 府

fu (to perform sacrifices to someone's sons and grandsons at his tomb) 祔

fu dubao zheng (assistant superior guard leader) 副都保正

fujun (lord of the prefecture) 府君

fulao (elder) 父老

Fuliang 浮梁

fumin (rich people) 福民

furen (lady) 夫人

fuwei (assistant sheriff) 副尉

Fuyang 富陽

Fuzhou (Fujian) 福州

Fuzhou (Jiangxi) 撫州

Fuzhou (Sichuan) 涪州

gan (faith) 感

ganban gongshi (subofficial functionary) 幹辦公事

Ganpu 澉浦

Ganzhou 贛州

ge (tower) 閣

geng (one of ten celestial stems) 庚

gengxu (one of sixty days in a cycle) 庚戌

gong (lord) 公

gong (work) 工

gongde (merit) 功德

gonglie (merit) 功烈

gongtian fa (public field system) 公田法

Gongzhou 恭州

Gu Duanming 顧端明

guan (Daoist monastery) 觀

guan (string of money) 貫

guan zhishi congshi (supervisor of a Daoist monastery) 觀知事從士
Guancheng 管城
Guangde 廣德
Guangling (Broadly Efficacious) 廣靈
guanhu (official household) 官戶
Guanyin 觀音
guanyuan (officials) 官員
gui (ghost) 鬼
Gui'an 歸安
Gutian 古田
Haiyan 海鹽
Hangzhou 杭州
Hanyang 漢陽
He Dedai 何德待
He Zhitong 何志同
Henan 河南
Hezhou 和州
Hong Gua 洪适
Hong Hao 洪皓
Hongzhou 洪州
hou (marquis) 侯
hu (household) 戶
Huai Nanzi 淮南子
Huang Chang 黃裳
Huang Liang 黃亮
huanglu (yellow register) 黃錄
Huating 華亭
Huizhi 慧智
Huizhou 徽州
Huizong 徽宗
Huolu 獲鹿
Huoshan 霍山
Huzhou 湖州
Ji 計
ji (commemorative text) 記
ji (salvation) 濟
ji (winnowing basket) 箕
jia (section I of *The Record of the Listener*) 甲
Jian'an 建安

Jianchang 建昌

Jiangnan 江南

jiangshi lang (gentleman of executory rank 9b) 將仕郎

Jiangyin 江陰

Jiangzhou 江州

Jianyang 建陽

jiao (dragon) 蛟

jiao (moonblocks) 珓, 校, 教, 筊, 筶

jiao (purification ceremony) 醮

Jiaxing 嘉興

Jiaying (Auspicious Response) 嘉應

Jiguo 紀國

jin (gold) 金

jin'e (current plaque) 今額

Jinci (Jin shrine) 晉祠

Jing 涇

Jing (name of stream) 荊

jingchao guan (administrative officials) 京朝官

jinshi (advanced degree) 進士

Jiu 久

Jizhou 吉州

juan (division in a book, chapter) 卷

juehao (noble rank) 爵號

Jujiu 居久

jun (commandery) 郡

junren Zhangshi (a person of the prefecture, named Zhang) 郡人張氏

junshou (prefect) 郡守

Kaifeng 開封

Kaiyuan 開元

kou (resident) 口

kun (mythical fish) 鯤

lang (gentleman) 郎

langwu (hallway) 廊屋

Langzhou 閬州

leifa (thunder rites) 雷法

Leizhou 雷州

Leping 樂平

Li 李

Li (name of river) 澧

Li choufu 李丑父
Li hou (Marquis Li) 李侯
Li Lu 李祿
Li Shun 李順
Li Xinchuan 李心傳
Li Zhongyong 李仲永
li (a unit of length equaling 552.96 meters) 里
li (rites) 禮
Liang Wan Fu (Liangshan, Wanzhou, and Fuzhou prefectures in Sichuan)
    梁萬涪
Liangshan 梁山
Licheng 歷城
lie (martyr) 烈
liezhuang (testify orally) 列狀
Lin Lingsu 林靈素
Lin'an 臨安
ling (power or efficacy) 靈
lingguai (mysterious and strange) 靈怪
Lingji miao (Efficacious Salvation temple) 靈濟廟
Lingkang (Efficacious Abundance) 靈康
lingyan (evidence of efficacy, power) 靈驗
lingyi (anomaly associated with power) 靈異
Liu 劉
Liu Daochang 劉道昌
Liyang 溧陽
Lizong 理宗
Longxing (Awakening Dragon) 龍興
louyu (two-story building) 樓宇
Lu 魯
Lu Jiuxu 陸九敍
Lu Jiuyuan 陸九淵
Lu Xiu (scribal error for Chen Xiu) 陸修
Lu Zao 陸藻
lu (circuit) 路
lushi canjun (administrative supervisor) 錄事參軍
Luzhou 瀘州
Lü Dongbin 呂洞賓
Ma 馬
Ma Jin 馬進

Ma Xianmin 馬先民

mianjie jinshi (exempted advanced degree holders) 免解進士

miao (temple) 廟

miaoji (temple inscriptions) 廟記

miaozhu (temple caretaker) 廟祝

Mou Zicai 牟子才

Mu Bing 木胥

mu (a unit of area equaling 5.66 are) 畝

muyuan fenxiu daoshi (donation-solicitor devout practitioner) 募緣焚修
道士

Nankang 南康

nanxi (Southern drama) 南戲

Nanxun (South Bank) 南潯

neidan (inner alchemy) 內丹

Nie 聶

nifeng (provisional title) 擬封

Ningbo 寧波

Ningde 寧德

Ningdu 寧都

Ningguo 寧國

Ningzong 寧宗

Ouyang Dachun 歐陽大春

Ouyang Hu 歐陽祜

pai'an jian chuanchang (official in charge of maintaining embankments and
boat yards) 排岸兼船場

Peng Xiu 彭修

peng (mythical bird) 鵬

Pichang 皮場

Pingjiang 平江

Pinnü (Poor Girl) 貧女

Poyang 鄱陽

Putian 莆田

Qian 錢

qian (divination sticks) 籤

qian (money) 錢

qian (thousand) 千

Qianfu ci (Repeated Fortune temple) 薦福祠

qiao (skillful) 巧

qielan shen (monastic guardian deity) 伽藍神

qilao (elder) 耆老

Qin 欽

Qin Erniang 秦二娘

Qin Gui 秦檜

Qingdun (Green Mound) 青墩

Qingyuan zhenjun 清元真君

Raozhou 饒州

ren (one of twelve celestial branches) 壬

Ruijin 瑞金

san (three) 三

sanbu (section 17 of *The Record of the Listener*) 三補

sanguan dadi (gods of heaven, earth, and water) 三官大帝

sanren (section 14 of *The Record of the Listener*) 三壬

Santang shen (God of Three Chambers) 三堂神

sanxin (section 13 of *The Record of the Listener*) 三辛

sanyi (section 12 of *The Record of the Listener*) 三己

shanxiao (hill spirit) 山魈

Shangshu sheng die (grant from the Imperial Secretariat) 尚書省牒

Shaoxing 紹興

Shehong 射洪

Shen Chun 沈春

shen (deity) 神

shenbing (spirit soldier) 神兵

sheng (unit of volume equaling .9488 liters) 升

shengci (living shrine) 生祠

Shengmu dian (Goddess Mother Hall) 聖母殿

shengyuan (licentiate) 生員

shenjiang (spirit general) 神將

shenyi (divine anomaly) 神異

Shi Jing 石精

Shi Miyuan 史彌遠

shi zhe qiu shen yi (causing type of person to seek the god's
      intention) 使 者求神意

shihu (market householders) 市戶

shihuan (official) 仕宦

shiji (phenomenal projection) 實際

shiren (literati) 士人

shouci sheng (student with a stipend) 守祠生

shu (technique) 術

shu (to be subordinate to) 屬

shuai (commander) 帥

Shuangdian 雙店

Shui San (Water Three) 水三

shuiluhui (a Buddhist rite to give food to the hungry ghosts on the land and water) 水陸會

Shunchang 順昌

Shunji longwang (Dragon King of Opportune Aid) 順濟龍王

Shunji wang (King of Opportune Aid) 順濟王

Shunying hou (Rapid Response Duke) 順應侯

Shuzhou 舒州

si (Buddhist monastery) 寺

si (to perform a sacrifice) 祀

si zhishi seng (supervisor of Buddhist monastery) 寺知事僧

sidian (register of sacrifices) 祀典

silu (record keeper) 司錄

silu canjun (administrator of public order) 司錄參軍

Sima Qian 司馬遷

siyong (city walls, city god) 四墉

Songxi shen (God of the Pine Stream) 松溪神

Su Hao 蘇灝

Sun 孫

Sun Yujin 孫與進

Suzhou 蘇州

Tai'an 泰安

taibao (Grand Guardian) 太保

Taichang si (Court of Imperial Sacrifices) 太常寺

Taijian (title) 太簡

Taishi Zhang 太史章

taixue sheng (student at the imperial university) 太學生

Taizhou (Jiangsu) 泰州

Taizhou (Zhejiang) 台州

Tang Zhongyou 唐仲友

tanyue (donor) 檀越

Tanzhou 潭州

tao (to confuse) 謟

te xiangcun (special village) 特鄉村

tezou ming jinshi (facilitated degrees) 特奏名進士

tianchai zhenshui (temporarily appointed tax official) 添差鎮稅

Tianfei (Heavenly Consort) 天妃

Tianhou (Heavenly Consort) 天后

Tianning (Heavenly Peace) 天寧

tianxin fa (Celestial Heart method) 天心法

tiben (essence of things) 體本

Tingzhou 汀州

tixing (judicial intendant) 提刑

tong (to transmit) 通

Tongxiang 桐鄉

tudi (earth god) 土地

tudie (local history) 圖牒

waidan (outer alchemy) 外丹

wan (ten thousand) 萬

Wang 王

Wang Anshi 王安石

Wang Gu 王古

Wang Huan 汪渙

Wang Ke 王穀

Wang Wenqing 王文卿

wang (king) 王

Wanzhou 萬州

Wei 魏

wei (sheriff) 尉

wen (civil) 文

Wenchang 文昌

wenji (collected papers) 文集

Wenxuan wang (Culture-Propagating King) 文宣王

wenxue (professor) 文學

Wenzhou 溫州

wo (I) 我

Wu 吳

Wu (Crow) 烏

Wu Jie 吳价

Wu Kui 吳逵

Wu Zixu 伍子胥

wu (five) 五

wu (I) 吾

wu (military) 武

wu'er (nonduality) 無二

wubie (nondifferentiation) 無別

Wucheng 烏程

Wuji shan (Five Chicken Hill) 五雞山
Wukang 武康
Wutong (Five Transmitters) 五通
Wuxian (Five Manifestations) 五顯
Wuyue 吳越
Wuzhou 婺州
xi (to play) 戲
xian (county) 縣
xian (immortal) 仙
xian (to manifest) 顯
xianggong jinshi (tribute scholars) 鄉貢進士
Xiangtan 湘潭
Xiangyang 襄陽
Xianju 仙居
xianling (county magistrate) 縣令
Xiaoyi (Filial Righteousness) 孝義
Xiazhou 峽州
Xincheng 新城
xingci (branch temple) 行祠
xinggong (branch temple) 行宮
Xingguo 興國
xingmiao (branch temple) 行廟
xingzai (temporary capital) 行在
Xinshi (New Market) 新市
Xintang (New Embankment) 新塘
Xinzhou 信州
Xiong 熊
xiuwu lang (gentleman of military rank 7a) 修武郎
Xiuzhou 秀州
xiyi (lizard) 蜥蜴
Xizhu ganfa (Indian drought method) 西竺乾法
Xu 徐
Xu Wenzhi 徐文之
xuanren (executory officials) 選人
Xuanwu 玄武
Xue 薛
Yang 楊
Yang Wei 楊緯
Yangzi 揚子

yanhuo gongshi (fire-fighting) 煙火公事

Yanluo tianzi (King of Hell) 閻羅天子

Yanyu 演嶼

Yanzhou 嚴州

Yao Xide 姚希得

Yao Yi 姚毅

Ye 鄴

Yi Jian 夷堅

yi (anomaly) 異

yi (heal) 醫

yi (section 2 of *The Record of the Listener*) 乙

yin (one of ten celestial stems) 寅

yin (shadow, right of protection) 蔭

yin (unofficial, unauthorized, even licentious) 淫

yinci (unofficial, unauthorized, even licentious, cults) 淫祠

Yinglie (Heroic Martyr) 英烈

Yingzong 英宗

yinsi (unofficial, unauthorized, even licentious, cults) 淫祀

yiren (local man) 邑人

yishi (local man) 邑士

Yixing 宜興

Yongding 永定

Yongfeng 永豐

Yongle 永樂

Yongling (Eternally Efficacious) 永靈

Yu 禹

Yu Sheng 余勝

yu (govern) 馭

yu (reside) 寓

yuancheng (fulfillment of enlightenment) 圓成

Yuande (Deep Virtue) 淵德

Yuanying (Deep Response) 淵應

yuejiang (transgressing upon another god's territory) 越疆

yuqian tiju suo shichen (emissary of the imperial intendant) 御前提舉所使臣

yushi zhongcheng (vice-censor-in-chief) 御史中丞

Yuzhang 豫章

zaibu (section 16 of *The Record of the Listener*) 再補

zaoshen (stove god) 竈神

Zhang 張

Zhang Kan 張侃

Zhang wang (King Zhang) 張王

Zhang Xiaosan (Zhang Little-three) 張小三

Zhang Xie 張協

Zhang Yazi (Mute Zhang) 張啞子

zhang (a unit of measure equaling 3.072 m.) 丈

Zhangwang miao (temple to King Zhang) 張王廟

zhangwu bao (village service elder) 長屋保

Zhao 趙

Zhao Bing 趙炳

Zhao Hong 趙竑

Zhao Yun 趙昀

zhen (township) 鎮

zheng (heal) 拯

Zhenjiang 鎮江

zhenjun (immortal) 真君

zhenren (people of the township) 鎮人

Zhenwu 真武

zhenyuan (ultimate principle) 真源

Zhenzhou 真州

Zhenzong 真宗

Zhi Jiu (Stem Nine) 支九

zhiding (section 8 of *The Record of the Listener*) 支丁

zhigeng (section 10 of *The Record of the Listener*) 支庚

zhiguai (recording anomalies) 志怪

zhigui (section 11 of *The Record of the Listener*) 支癸

zhijia (section 5 of *The Record of the Listener*) 支甲

zhijing (section 7 of *The Record of the Listener*) 支景

zhiqian (paper money, spirit money) 紙錢

zhiwu (section 9 of *The Record of the Listener*) 支戊

zhiyi (section 6 of *The Record of the Listener*) 支乙

zhizhou (prefect) 知州

Zhong Kui 鍾馗

Zhongdao 忠道

Zhongshu sheng (Secretariat Chancellery) 中書省

zhongshu menxia pingzhang shi jian shumi shi (grand councillor) 中書門下
    平章事兼樞密使

Zhou Chu 周處

Zhou Dunyi 周敦頤

Zhou Rong 周容

zhou (prefecture) 州

Zhu Fei 朱芾

Zhu Fu 朱復

Zhu Lin 朱林

Zhu Ran 朱冉

Zhu Ren 朱仁

Zhu Renfu 朱仁福

Zhu Si 朱泗

Zhu Zao 朱藻

zhubu (registrar) 主簿

zhujiao (assistant instructor) 助教

zhushen (assistant deity) 助神

zi (catalpa) 梓

Zigu (Purple Maiden) 紫姑

Zitong 梓童

zu (lineage) 族

zuren (members of a lineage) 族人

BIBLIOGRAPHY

Primary Sources

Because methods of citing classical Chinese sources vary, depending on the available information and the type of book, I have adopted a flexible format, which reads as follows:

Abbreviated name of book as cited in the text. Original publication date when available. Author's name in romanization. In characters. (His dates). *Full name of book in romanization.* Characters for book title. (English translation of title). Then, one of the following: 1. city: name of publisher, date of publication; 2. name of edition and/or publisher, date when known; 3. name of reprinted series; or 4. especially in the case of local histories, the number of *juan* (originally separately bound chapters).

Bamin tongzhi. 1491. Chen Dao 陳道. *[Hongzhi] Bamin tongzhi* 弘治八閩通志 (A complete history of the eight provinces of Fujian compiled in the Hongzhi [1488–1505] reign period). 87 *juan*.

Baoqing Siming. 1227. Luo Jun 羅濬 and Fang Wanli 方萬里. *[Baoqing] Siming zhi* 寶慶四明志 (A history of Ningbo compiled in the Baoqing [1125–1227] reign period). Song Yuan difang zhi congshu edition.

Baqiong shi jinshi. Lu Zengxiang 陸增祥 (1816–1882). *Baqiong shi jinshi buzheng* 八瓊室金石補正 (Supplement to inscriptions from the Eight Treasure room). Shike shiliao congshu edition.

Beishi. Li Yanshou 李延壽 (Tang dynasty). *Beishi* 北史 (A history of the Northern dynasties). Beijing: Zhonghua shuju, 1974.

Beixi xiansheng daquan wenji. Chen Chun 陳淳 (1159–1223). *Beixi xiansheng daquan wenji* 北溪先生大全文集 (The complete writings of Chen Chun). Seikadō edition, 51 *juan*.

Beixi ziyi. 1241–1252. Chen Chun 陳淳 (1153–1223). *Beixi ziyi* 北溪字義 (The meaning of terms). 1882 Jinhe guangren edition.

Bintui lu. 1224. Zhao Yushi 趙與時 (1175–1231). *Bintui lu* 賓退錄 (Records written after the guest has left). Shanghai: Shanghai guji, 1983.

Changshan zhenshi. Shen Tao 沈濤 (1789–1861). *Changshan zhenshi zhi* 常山 貞石志 (Collected inscriptions from Changshan). Shike shiliao congshu edition.

Chenghua chongxiu Piling. 1469. Zhuo Tianxi 卓天錫. *[Chenghua] chongxiu Piling zhi* 成化重修毗陵志 (A revised history of Chuzhou compiled in the Chenghua [1465–1487] reign period). 40 *juan.*

Chenghua Huzhou. 1475. Wang Xun 王珣. *[Chenghua] Huzhou fuzhi* 成化 湖州府志 (A history of Huzhou prefecture compiled in the Chenghua [1465–1487] reign period). 25 *juan* (missing *juan* 14–16, 23–24).

Chongzhen Tingzhou. 1637. Tang Shihan 唐世涵. *[Chongzhen] Tingzhou fuzhi* 崇禎汀州府志 (A history of Tingzhou prefecture compiled in the Chongzhen [1628–1644] reign period). 24 *juan.*

Chongzhen Wucheng. 1638. Liu Yichun 劉沂春. *[Chongzhen] Wucheng xian-zhi* 崇禎烏程縣志 (A history of Wucheng county compiled in the Chongzhen [1628–1644] reign period). 12 *juan.*

Chongzhen Wuxian. 1642. Niu Ruolin 牛若麟. *[Chongzhen] Wuxian zhi* 崇禎吳縣志 (A history of Suzhou compiled in the Chongzhen [1628–1644] reign period). 54 *juan.*

Chunqiu Zuozhuan. Chunqiu Zuozhuan zhengyi 春秋左傳正義 (The Spring and Autumn annals, the commentary of Zuo), in *Shisan jing zhushu* 十三經注疏 (An annotated edition of the thirteen classics). Edited and punctuated by Ruan Yuan. 阮元 Beijing: Zhonghua shuju, 1980.

Chunxi Xin'an. 1175. Luo Yuan 羅源. *[Chunxi] Xin'an zhi* 淳熙新安志 (A history of Huizhou compiled in the Chunxi [1174–1189] reign period). 11 *juan.* Song Yuan difang zhi congshu edition.

Chunyou Yufeng. 1251. Ling Wanqing 凌萬頃. *[Chunyou] Yufeng zhi* 淳祐 玉峯志 (A history of Kunshan county compiled in the Chunyou [1241–1252] reign period). 3 *juan.* Song Yuan difangzhi congshu edition.

Chunzhu jiwen. He Wei 何薳 (1077–1145). *Chunzhu jiwen* 春渚紀聞 (Record of hearsay at a spring waterside). Beijing: Zhonghua shuju, 1983.

Cishan zhi. 1298. Originally edited by Zhou Bingxiu 周秉秀. Revised by Zhou Xianjing 周憲敬 (Ming). *Cishan zhi* 祠山志 (A history of Temple Mountain). 1886 edition.

Dade Changguozhou. 1298. Guo Jian 郭薦. *[Dade] Changguozhou tuzhi* 大德 昌國州圖志 (A history of Changguo county compiled in the Dade [1297–1307] reign period). Song Yuan difang zhi congshu edition.

Danyang ji. Ge Shengzhong 葛膭仲 (1072–1144). *Danyang ji* 丹陽集 (Collected writings from Danyang). Congshu jinghua edition.

Deqing xian xuzhi. 1808. Zhou Shaolian 周紹濂. *[Jiaqing] Deqing xian xuzhi*

嘉慶德清縣續志 (A continuation of the history of Deqing county compiled in the Jiaqing (1796–1820] reign period). 10 *juan*.

Donglin shanzhi. Originally 1813. Reprinted 1922. Wu Yushu 吳玉樹. *Donglin shanzhi* 東林山志 (A history of Donglin Mountain [Gui'an County, Huzhou]). *24 juan*.

Dongpo quanji. Su Shi 蘇軾 (1036–1101). *Dongpo quanji* 東坡全集 (The complete writings of Su Shi). Meizhou san Suci edition, 1832.

Dongtang ji. Mao Pang 毛滂 (fl. 1086–1093). *Dongtang ji* 東堂集 (Writings of the eastern hall). Siku quanshu edition.

Gaiyu congkao. Zhao Yi 趙翼 (1727–1814). *Gaiyu congkao* 陔餘叢考 (Accumulated layers of investigations). Shanghai: Commercial Press, 1957.

Guangxu Guangde. 1881. Hu Youcheng 胡有誠. *[Guangxu] Guangde zhouzhi* 光緒廣德州志 (A history of Guangde county compiled in the Guangxu [1875–1908] reign period). *62 juan*.

Guangxu Wucheng. 1879. Pan Yuxuan 潘玉璿. *Guangxu Wucheng xianzhi* 光緒烏程縣志 (A history of Wucheng County compiled in the Guangxu [1875–1908] reign period). *36 juan*.

Guixi ji. Shen Yuqiu 沈與求 (1086–1137). *Shen Zhongmin gong guixi ji* 沈忠敏公龜谿集 (The collected writings of Shen Yuqiu). *12 juan*. Wuxing congshu edition.

Gujin kao. Wei Liaoweng 魏了翁 (1178–1257) and Fang Hui 方回 (1227–1307). One *juan* by Wei, thirty-seven *juan* by Fang. *Gujin kao* 古今考 (An examination of ancient and modern times). Taibei: Xuesheng shuju, 1971.

Hanshu. Ban Gu 班固 (Han dynasty). *Hanshu* 漢書 (A history of the Han dynasty). Beijing: Zhonghua shuju, 1962.

Han Yu wenji. Han Yu 韓愈 (768–824). *Zhu Wengong jiao Changli xiansheng quanwenji* 朱文公校昌黎先生全文集 (The collected papers of Han Yu, annotated by Zhu Xi). Sibu congkan edition.

Hongwu Suzhou. 1379. Lu Xiong 盧熊. *[Hongwu] Suzhou fuzhi* 洪武蘇州府志 (A history of Suzhou Prefecture compiled in the Hongwu [1368–1398] reign period). *51 juan*.

Hongzhi Tingzhou. 1497. Wu Wendu 吳文度. *[Hongzhi] Tingzhou fuzhi* 弘治汀州府志 (A history of Tingzhou compiled in the Hongzhi [1488–1505] reign period). *18 juan*.

Houcun xiansheng quanji. Liu Kezhuang 劉克莊 (1187–1269). *Houcun xiansheng quanji* 後村先生全集 (The complete writings of Liu Kezhuang). Sibu congkan edition.

Huangshi richao. Huang Zhen 黃震 (1213–1280). *Huangshi richao* 黃氏日鈔 (The daily writings of Mr. Huang). Gengyou lou edition.

Jiading Chicheng. Chen Qiqing 陳耆卿 (ca. 1180–1236). *Jiading Chicheng zhi* 嘉定赤城志 (A history of Taizhou compiled in the Jiading [1208–1224] reign period). Song Yuan difang zhi congshu edition.

Jiading Zhenjiang. 1213. Lu Xian 盧憲. *[Jiading] Zhenjiang zhi* 嘉定鎮江志 (A history of Zhenjiang compiled in the Jiading [1208–1224] reign period). Song Yuan difang zhi congshu edition.

Jiajing Anji. 1534. Wu Yufu 伍餘福. *[Jiajing] Anji zhouzhi* 嘉靖安吉州志 (A history of Anji prefecture compiled in the Jiajing [1522–1566] reign period). 16 *juan.*

Jiajing Deqing. 1525. Hao Chengxing 郝成性. *[Jiajing] Deqing xianzhi* 嘉靖德清縣志 (A history of Deqing county compiled in the Jiajing [1522–1566] reign period). 10 *juan.*

Jiajing Ningbo. 1560. Zhou Xizhe 周希哲. *[Jiajing] Ningbo fuzhi* 嘉靖寧波府志 (A history of Ningbo compiled in the Jiajing [1522–1566] reign period). 42 *juan.*

Jiajing Ningde. 1538. Min Wenzhen 閔文振. *[Jiajing] Ningde zhouzhi* 嘉靖寧德州志 (A history of Ningde prefecture compiled in the Jiajing [1522–1566] reign period). 4 *juan.*

Jiajing Yongchun. 1526. Zi Biao 紫鑣. *[Jiajing] Yongchun xianzhi* 嘉靖永春縣志 (A history of Yongchun County compiled in the Jiajing [1522–1566] reign period). 9 *juan.*

Jiangsu jinshi. 1927. Compiled by Jiangsu Tongzhi ju 江蘇同治局. *Jiangsu jinshi zhi* 江蘇金石志 (A collection of inscriptions from Jiangsu). Shike shiliao congshu edition.

Jiannan shigao. Lu You 陸游 (1125–1210). *Jiannan shigao* 劍南詩稿 (The draft poems from Qiannan [Sichuan]) in *Lu Fangweng ji* 陸放翁集 (The collected works of Lu You). Guoxue jiben congshu edition.

Jianyan yilai xinian yaolu. Li Xinchuan 李心傳 (1166–1243). *Jianyan yilai xinian yaolu* 建炎以來繫年要錄 (A digest of important affairs since the beginning of the Jianyan [1127–1130] reign period). Shanghai: Zhonghua shuju, 1956.

Jiaqing Changxing. 1805. Xing Shu 邢澍. *[Jiaqing] Changxing xianzhi* 嘉慶長興縣志 (A history of Changxing county compiled in the Jiaqing [1796–1820] reign period). 29 *juan.*

Jiatai Guiji. 1201. Shen Zuobin 沈作賓. *[Jiatai] Guiji zhi* 嘉泰會稽志 (A history of Shaoxing compiled in the Jiatai [1201–1204] reign period). 20 *juan.* Song-Yuan difang zhi congshu edition.

Jiatai Wuxing. 1201. Tan Yue 談鑰 (c. 1150–1220). *Jiatai Wuxing zhi* 嘉泰 吳興志 (A history of Wuxing compiled in the Jiatai [1201–1204] reign period). Song Yuan difang zhi congshu edition.

Jile ji. Preface dated 1094. Chao Buzhi 晁補之 (1053–1110). *Jile ji* 雞肋集 (Collected chicken scrap writings). Sibu congkan edition.

Jingding Jiankang. 1261. Ma Guangzu 馬光祖. *[Jingding] Jiankang zhi* 景定 建康志 (A history of Nanjing compiled in the Jingding [1260–1264] reign period). Song Yuan difang zhi congshu edition.

Jingding Yanzhou. 1262. Qian Keze 錢可則. *[Jingding] Yanzhou xuzhi* 景定 嚴州續志 (A continuation of the history of Yanzhou compiled in the Jingding [1260–1264] period). Song Yuan difang zhi congshu edition.

Jinling shiji. 1569. Chen Yi 陳沂. *Jinling shiji* 金陵世紀 (A record of generations in Nanjing). 4 *juan.*

Jinshi cuibian. Wang Chang 王昶 (1725–1807). *Jinshi cuibian* 金石萃編 (Collected inscriptions). Shike shiliao congshu edition.

Jinshu. Fang Xuanling 房玄齡 (578–648). *Jinshu* 晉書 (A history of the Jin dynasty). Beijing: Zhonghua shuju, 1974.

Kangxi Changxing. 1673. Han Yingheng 韓應恒. *[Kangxi] Changxing xianzhi* 康熙長興縣志 (A history of Changxing county compiled in the Kangxi [1662–1722] reign period). 8 *juan.*

Kangxi Chuzhou. 1690. Liu Tingji 劉廷璣. *[Kangxi] Chuzhou fuzhi* 康熙 處州府志 (A history of Chuzhou compiled in the Kangxi [1662–1722] reign period). 12 *juan.*

Kangxi Gui'an. 1673. Yao Shiliang 姚時亮. *[Kangxi] Gui'an xianzhi* 康熙歸安 縣志 (A history of Gui'an county compiled in the Kangxi [1662–1722] reign period). 10 *juan.*

Kangxi Raozhou. 1683. Wang Zehong 王澤洪. *[Kangxi] Raozhou fuzhi* 康熙 饒州府志 (A history of Raozhou prefecture compiled in the Kangxi [1662–1722] reign period). 41 *juan.*

Kangxi Wucheng. 1679. Gao Biteng 高必騰. *[Kangxi] Wucheng xianzhi* 康熙 烏程縣志 (A history of Wucheng county compiled in the Kangxi [1662–1722] reign period). 12 *juan.*

Kangxi Wukang. 1672. Feng Shengze 馮聖澤. *[Kangxi] Wukang xianzhi* 康熙 武康縣志 (A history of Wukang county compiled in the Kangxi [1662–1722] reign period). 8 *juan.*

Kangxi Xianju. 1680. Zheng Luxun 鄭錄勳. *[Kangxi] Xianju xianzhi* 康熙 仙居縣志 (A history of Xianju county compiled in the Kangxi [1662–1722] reign period). 30 *juan.*

Kuocang buyi. Zou Baisen 鄒柏森. *Kuocang jinshi zhi buyi* 括蒼金石志補遺 (A supplement to the collection of inscriptions from Lishui, Zhejiang). Shike shiliao congshu edition.

Kuocang jinshi. Li Yusun 李遇孫. *Kuocang jinshi zhi* 括蒼金石志 (A collection of inscriptions from Lishui, Zhejiang). Shike shiliao congshu edition.

Langyu ji. Xue Jixuan 薛季宣 (1134–1173). *Langyu ji* 浪語集 (Collected unorganized musings). Siku quanshu edition.

Liangzhe jinshi. Ruan Yuan 阮元 (1764–1849). *Liangzhe jinshi zhi* 兩浙金石志 (A collection of inscriptions from Jiangsu and Zhejiang). Shike shiliao congshu edition.

Liezi. Lie Yukou 列禦寇. *Liezi* 列子 (The writings of Liezi). Sibu beiyao edition.

Liji. *Liji* 禮記 (The book of rites), in *Shisan jing zhushu* 十三經注疏 (An annotated edition of the thirteen classics). Edited and punctuated by Ruan Yuan. Beijing: Zhonghua shuju, 1980.

Linghu zhenzhi. 1893. Sun Zhixiong 孫志熊. *Linghu zhenzhi* 菱湖鎮志 (A history of Linghu Township [Gui'an county]). 45 *juan.*

Longchuan wenji. Chen Liang 陳亮 (1143–1194). *Longchuan wenji* 龍川文集 (The writings of Chen Liang). Yongkang ying edition, 1869.

Longqing Danyang. 1569. Ma Zhi 馬豸. *[Longqing] Danyang xianzhi* 隆慶丹陽縣志 (A history of Danyang county compiled in the Longqing [1567–1572] reign period). 12 *juan.*

Lunyu. Kongzi 孔子. *Lunyu* (The Analects) in *Shisan jing zhushu* 十三經注疏 (An annotated edition of the thirteen classics). Edited and punctuated by Ruan Yuan. Beijing: Zhonghua shuju, 1980.

Mengliang lu. 1274. Wu Zimu 吳自牧. *Mengliang lu* 夢梁錄 (A record of dreams of happiness.) Hangzhou: Zhejiang renmin chubanshe, 1984.

Mengxi bitan. Shen Gua 沈括 (1030–1095). *Mengxi bitan jiaozheng* 夢溪筆談校證 (An annotated and corrected edition of dream brook notes). Edited by Hu Daojing 胡道靜. Shanghai: Shanghai chuban gongsi, 1956.

Mengzi. Meng Ke 孟軻. *Mengzi* 孟子 (Mencius), in *Shisan jing zhushu* 十三經注疏 (An annotated edition of the thirteen classics). Edited and punctuated by Ruan Yuan. Beijing: Zhonghua shuju, 1980.

Mozi. Mo Di 墨翟. *Mozi* 墨子 (The writings of Mozi). Sibu congkan edition.

Nanxun zhenzhi. 1859. Wang Rizhen 王日楨. *Nanxun zhenzhi* 南潯鎮志 (A record of South Bank township). 41 *juan.*

Nanxun zhi. 1922. Zhou Qingyun 周慶雲. *Nanxun zhi* 南潯志 (A record of South Bank). 61 *juan.*

Nenggai zhai manlu. 1157. Wu Zeng 吳曾. *Nenggai zhai manlu* 能改齋漫錄 (Free recollections from the can-change studio). Shanghai: Shanghai guji chubanshe, 1960.

Nongshu. 1154. Chen Fu 陳旉. *Nongshu* 農書 (Treatise on agriculture). Beijing: Zhonghua shuji, 1956.

Pingzhou ketan. 1118–1119. Zhu Yu 朱彧 (1048–after 1102). *Pingzhou ketan* 萍州可談 (Talk of Pingzhou [Huangzhou, Guangdong]). Siku quanshu edition.

Qiandao Siming. 1169. Zhang Jin 張津. *[Qiandao] Siming tujing* 乾道四明圖經 (A history of Ningbo compiled in the Qiandao [1165–1173] reign period).

Qianlong Changxing. 1749. Tan Zhaoji 譚肇基. *[Qianlong] Changxing xianzhi* 乾隆長興縣志 (A history of Changxing county compiled in the Qianlong [1736–1795] reign period). 21 *juan.*

Qianlong Huzhou. 1758. Li Tang 李堂. *[Qianlong] Huzhou fuzhi* 乾隆湖州府志 (A history of Huzhou compiled in the Qianlong [1736–1795] reign period). 49 *juan.*

Qianlong Suzhou. 1748. Yaer Hashan 牙爾哈善. *[Qianlong] Suzhou fuzhi* 乾隆蘇州府志 (A history of Suzhou compiled in the Qianlong [1736–1795] reign period). 81 *juan.*

Qianlong Wenzhou. 1756. Li Wan 李琬. *[Qianlong] Wenzhou fuzhi* 乾隆溫州府志 (A history of Wenzhou prefecture compiled in the Qianlong [1736–1795] reign period). 31 *juan.*

Qianlong Wuqing. 1760. Dong Shining 董世寧. *[Qianlong] Wuqing zhenzhi* 乾隆烏青鎮志 (A history of Wu and Qing townships compiled in the Qianlong [1736–1795] reign period). 12 *juan.*

Qidong yeyu. Zhou Mi 周密 (1232–1298). *Qidong yeyu* 齊東野語 (Scattered talk from east of Qi). Beijing: Zhonghua shuju, 1983.

Qinchuan zhi. 1365. Lu Zhen 盧鎮. *Chongxiu Qinchuan zhi* 重修琴川志 (A revised history of Qinchuan [Changshu county, Jiangsu]). Song Yuan difang zhi congshu edition.

Qingming ji. 1240–1275. Anon. *Minggong shupan qingming ji* 名公書判清明集 (A collection of lucid decisions written by famous gentlemen.) Beijing: Zhonghua shuju, 1987.

Quesao bian. c. 1130. Xu Du 徐度 (?–c. 1156). *Quesao bian* 却掃編 (Notes compiled in seclusion). Baibu congshu jicheng edition.

Rongzhai suibi. 1162–1202. Hong Mai 洪邁. *Rongzhai suibi* 容齋隨筆 (Notes from my studio). Shanghai: Shanghai guji chubanshe, 1979.

Sanshan zhi. 1182. Liang Kejia 梁克家. *[Chunxi] Sanshan zhi* 淳熙三山志 (A history of Fuzhou compiled in the Chunxi [1174–1189] reign period). 42 *juan.* Song Yuan difang zhi congshu edition.

Shijing. Shijing 詩經 (The book of poetry), in *Shisan jing zhushu* 十三經注疏

(An annotated edition of the thirteen classics). Edited and punctuated by Ruan Yuan. Beijing: Zhonghua shuju, 1980.

Shuixin wenji. Ye Shi 葉適 (1150–1223). *Shuixin wenji* 水心文集 (The writings of Ye Shi). 1755. Wenzhou fuxue edition.

Shuanglin zhen zhi. 1870. Revised 1917. Cai Rongsheng 蔡蓉升. *Shuanglin zhen zhi* 雙林鎮志 (A history of Shuanglin township [Gui'an county, Huzhou]). 33 *juan.*

Shunzhi Changxing. 1649. Zhang Shenwei 張慎為. *[Shunzhi] Changxing xianzhi* 順治長興縣志 (A history of Changxing county in the Shunzhi [1644–1661] reign period). 11 *juan.*

Song huiyao. Edited by Xu Song 徐松 (1781–1848). *Songhui ya jigao* 宋會要輯稿 (A draft version of the important documents of the Song). Taibei: Xinwenfeng chubanshe, 1962.

Songshi. Tuo Tuo 脫脫 (1313–1355) et al. *Songshi* 宋史 (A history of the Song). Beijing: Zhonghua shuju, 1977.

Soushen ji. Gan Bao 干寶. *Soushen ji* 搜神記 (Investigations into the divine). Beijing: Zhonghua shuju, 1979.

Taizhou jinshi. Huang Rui 黃瑞 (Qing dynasty). *Taizhou jinshi lu* 台州金石錄 (A record of inscriptions from Taizhou). Shike shiliao congshu edition.

Tang huiyao. Wang Pu 王溥 (922–982). *Tang huiyao* 唐會要 (The important documents of the Tang). Beijing: Zhonghua shuju, 1955.

Tiaoxi ji. Liu Yizhi 劉一止 (1078–1160). *Tiaoxi ji* 苕溪集 (Records of Tiao Stream). Siku quanshu edition.

Tongzhi Anji. 1874. Wang Rong 汪榮 and Liu Lanmin 劉蘭民. *[Tongzhi] Anji xianzhi* 同治安吉縣志 (A history of Anji county compiled in the Tongzhi [1862–1874] reign period). 17 *juan.*

Tongzhi Huzhou. 1874. (Compilers) Zong Yuanhan 宗源瀚 and Guo Shichang 郭式昌. *[Tongzhi] Huzhou fuzhi* 同治湖州府志 (A history of Huzhou prefecture compiled in the Tongzhi [1862–1874] reign period). 97 *juan.*

Wang Shipeng wenji. Wang Shipeng 王十朋 (1112–1171). *Song Wang Zhongwen gong wenji* 宋王忠文公文集 (The collected papers of Wang Shipeng). 1728. Yanjiu tang edition.

Wanli Ningguo. 1577. Chen Jun 陳俊. *[Wanli] Ningguo fuzhi* 萬曆寧國府志 (A history of Ningguo prefecture compiled in the Wanli [1573–1619] reign period). 20 *juan.*

Wanli Quanzhou. 1612. Yang Siqian 陽思謙. *[Wanli] Quanzhou fuzhi* 萬曆

泉州府志 (A history of Quanzhou prefecture compiled in the Wanli [1573–1619] reign period). 24 *juan.*

Wanli Shaowu. 1619. Han Guofan 韓國藩. *[Wanli] Shaowu fuzhi* 萬曆邵武府志 (A history of Shaowu prefecture compiled in the Wanli [1573–1619] reign period). 64 *juan.*

Wanli Xinghua. 1602. Ma Mengji 馬夢吉. *[Wanli] Xinghua fuzhi* 萬曆興化府志 (A history of Xinghua prefecture compiled in the Wanli [1573–1619] reign period). 59 *juan.*

Wenxian tongkao. 1224. Ma Duanlin 馬端臨. *Wenxian Tongkao* 文獻通考 (General history of institutions and critical examination of documents). Shanghai: Tushu jicheng ju edition, 1901.

Wudai huiyao. Wang Pu 王溥 (922–982). *Wudai huiyao* 五代會要 (The important documents of the Five Dynasties). Shanghai: Shanghai guji chubanshe, 1978.

Wulin jiushi. c. 1280. Zhou Mi 周密 (1232–1298). *Wulin jiushi* 武林舊事 (Old times in Hangzhou). Siku quanshu edition.

Wuqing wenxian. 1688. Zhang Yuanzhen 張園真. *Wuqing wenxian* 烏青文獻 (Documents from Wu and Qing townships). 10 *juan.*

Wuxing beizhi. 1624. Dong Sizhang 董斯張. *Wuxing beizhi* 吳興備志 (Preparatory history of Huzhou). 32 *juan.*

Wuxing jinshi. Lu Xinyuan 陸心源 (1834–1894). *Wuxing jinshi ji* 吳興金石記 (A collection of inscriptions from Wuxing [Huzhou]). Shike shiliao congshu edition.

Xianchun Lin'an. 1265–1274. Qian Yueyou 潛說友. *[Xianchun] Lin'an zhi* 咸淳臨安志 (A history of Hangzhou compiled in the Xianchun [1265–1274] reign period). Song Yuan difang zhi congshu edition.

Xianchun Piling. 1268. Shi Nengzhi 史能之. *[Xianchun] chongxiu Piling zhi* 咸淳重修毗陵志 (A revised history of Changzhou compiled in the Xianchun (1265–1274) reign period). 30 *juan.* Song Yuan difang shi congshu edition.

Xinshi zhenzhi. Originally 1516. Reprinted 1811. Chen Ting 陳霆. *Xinshi zhenzhi* 新市鎮志 (A history of New Market township). 8 *juan.*

Xinshi zhen xuzhi. 1812. Shen Chiran 沈赤然. *Xinshi zhen xuzhi* 新市鎮續志 (A continuation of the history of New Market township). 9 *juan.*

Xinwen Yijianxu. Anon. (Yuan). *Huhai xinwen yijian xuzhi* 湖海新聞夷堅續志 (A continuation of the newly heard record of the listener from Huhai). Edited and punctuated by Jin Xin 金心. Beijing: Zhonghua shuju, 1986.

Xiwen sanzhong. 1408. *Yongle dadian xiwen sanzhong jiaozhu* 永樂大典戲文

三種校注. Edited by Qian Nanyang 錢南揚. (A punctuated, annotated edition of three plays from the Yongle encyclopedia.) Beijing: Zhonghua shuju, 1979.

Xiwu liyu. Preface dated 1547. Song Lei 宋雷. *Xiwu liyu* 西吳里語 (Talk of the villages of the western Wu region). Congshu jinghua edition.

Xuanhe fengshi. 1124. Xu Jing 徐兢 (1091–1153). *Xuanhe fengshi Gaoli tujing* 宣和奉使高麗圖經 (Illustrated description of the Chinese embassy to Korea in the Xuanhe [1119–1125] reign period). Edited by Imanishi Ryû 今西龍. Seoul: Chikazawa shoten, 1932.

Xu zizhi tongjian changbian. Li Tao 李燾 (1115–1184). *Xu zizhi tongjian changbian* 續資治通鑑長編 (A continuation of the comprehensive mirror for aid in government). Taibei: Shijie shuju, 1961.

Yanfan lu. Cheng Dachang 程大昌 (1123–1195). *Yanfan lu* 演繁露 (Extended commentaries). Xuejin taoyuan edition.

Yanyi yimou. Wang Yong 王栐 (?–after 1227). *Yanyi yimou lu* 燕翼詒謀錄 (Secret writings on the politics of monarchs). Siku quanshu edition.

Yanyou siming. 1320. Ma Ze 馬澤. *Yanyou siming zhi* 延祐四明志 (A history of Ningbo compiled in the Yanyou [1314–1320] reign period). Song Yuan difang zhi congshu edition.

Yijian zhi. 1157–1202. Hong Mai 洪邁 (1123–1202). *Yijian zhi* 夷堅志 (The record of the listener). Edited and punctuated by He Zhuo 何卓. Beijing: Zhonghua shuju, 1981.

Yinju tongyi. Liu Xun 劉壎 (1240–1319). *Yinju tongyi* 隱居通議 (Collected opinions while in seclusion). Siku quanshu edition.

Yinxian tongzhi. 1933. Zhang Chuanbao 張傳保. *Yinxian tongzhi* 鄞縣通志 (A history of Yin county). 51 *juan.*

Yiyuan. Liu Jingshu 劉敬叔 (d. c. A.D. 470). *Yiyuan* 異苑 (Collection of essays on strange things). Xuejin taoyuan edition.

Yongle dadian. 1408. *Yongle dadian ben difang zhi huikan* 永樂大典本地方志彙刊 (The local histories from the Yongle Encyclopedia). Taibei: Zhongwen chubanshe, 1981.

Yuanshi shifan. Yuan Cai 袁采 (1140–1190). *Yuanshi shifan* 袁氏世範 (Mr. Yuan's principles of family behavior). Baoyantang miji edition.

Yuezhong jinshi. Du Chunsheng 杜春生. *Yuezhong jinshi ji* 越中金石記 (A collection of inscriptions from Yue [Shaoxing, Zhejiang]). Shike shiliao congshu edition.

Zhengde gusu. 1506. Wang Ao 王鏊. *[Zhengde] gusu zhi* 正德姑蘇志 (A history of Suzhou compiled in the Zhengde [1506–1521] reign period). 60 *juan.*

Zhishun Zhenjiang. 1332. Tuo Yin 脫困. *[Zhishun] Zhenjiang zhi* 至順鎮江志 (A history of Zhenjiang compiled in the Zhishun [1330–1332] reign period). Song Yuan difang zhi congshu edition.

Zhiyuan Jiahe zhi. 1288. Shan Qing 單慶. *[Zhiyuan] Jiahe zhi* 至元嘉禾志 (A history of Jiaxing compiled in the Zhiyuan [1264–1294] reign period). Song Yuan difang shi congshu edition.

Zhizheng Jinling. 1344. Zhang Xuan 張鉉. *[Zhizheng] Jinling xinzhi* 至正 金陵新志 (A revised history of Nanjing compiled in the Zhizheng [1341–1367] reign period). 15 *juan.*

Zhou Bida wenji. Zhou Bida 周必大 (1126–1204). *Yiguo Zhou Wenzhong gongji* 益國周文忠公集 (The collected papers of Zhou Bida). 1848. Luling Ouyang edition.

Zhuzi daquan. Zhu Xi 朱熹 (1130–1200). *Zhuzi daquan* 朱子大全 (The collected writings of Zhu Xi). Sibu beiyao edition.

Zhuzi quanshu. 1713. Zhu Xi 朱熹 (1130–1200). *Zhuzi quanshu* 朱子全書 (The complete works of Zhu Xi). Edited by Li Guangdi 李光地 (1642–1718). Neifu edition.

Zhuzi yulei. Zhu Xi 朱熹 (1130–1200). *Zhuzi yulei* 朱子語類 (The collected sayings of Zhu Xi). Edited by Li Jingde 黎靖德. Taibei: Zhengzhong shuju, 1962.

Zuoyi zizhen. 1117. Li Yuanbi 李元弼. *Zuoyi zizhen* 作邑自箴 (Self-admonitions for local administrators). Sibu congkan xuzhi edition.

Secondary Sources

Adachi Keiji 足立啓二 1985. "Sōdai Ryōsetsu ni okeru suitō saku no sei-sanryoku suijun 宋代兩浙における水稲作の生產力水準" (The level of productive power of irrigated rice cultivation in Liangzhe Circuit during the Song). *Bungaku ronsō* (Kumamoto University) 17:80–100.

Akizuki Kan'ei 秋月觀暎 1978. *Chūgoku kinsei dōkyō no keisei* 中国近世道教 の形成 (The formation of Daoism in the history of China). Tokyo: Sōbunsha.

Baity, Philip C. 1975. *Religion in a Chinese Town.* Taibei: Oriental Cultural Service.

Baldrian-Hussein, Farzeen 1984. *Procédés du joyau magique: traité d'alchemie Taoïste du XIe siècle.* Paris: Les Deux Océans.

——— 1986. "Lü Tung-pin in Northern Sung Literature." *Cahiers d'Extrême-Asie* 2:133–70.

Bokenkamp, Stephen R. 1983. "Sources of the Ling-pao Scriptures." In Michel Strickmann, ed., *Tantric and Taoist Studies in Honour of R. A. Stein*. Volume 2. Brussels: Institut Belge des Hautes Etudes Chinoises.

Bol, Peter K. 1986. Review of John Chaffee's *The Thorny Gates of Learning in Sung China*. Unpublished manuscript.

Brooke, Rosalind and Christopher 1984. *Popular Religion in the Middle Ages: Western Europe 1000–1300*. New York: Thames and Hudson.

Carter, Thomas 1925. *The Invention of Printing and Its Spread Westward*. New York: Columbia University Press.

Cedzich, Ursula-Angelika 1985. "Wu-t'ung: Zur bewegten Geschichte eines Kultes." In *Religion und Philosophie in Ostasien: Festschrift für Hans Steininger zum 65. Geburtstag*. Würzburg: Königshausen & Neumann.

Chaffee, John 1985. *The Thorny Gates of Learning in Sung China: A Social History of Examinations*. New York: Cambridge University Press.

Chai Degeng 柴德賡 1982. *Shiji juyao* 史籍舉要 (A concise guide to historical sources). Beijing: Beijing chubanshe.

Chan Wing-tsit 1980. "Chu Hsi's Religious Life." In *International Symposium on Chinese-Western Cultural Interchanges in Commemoration of the Four Hundredth Anniversary of the Arrival of Matteo Ricci*. Taibei.

———— 1986. *Neo-Confucian Terms Explained* (A translation of Chen Chun's *Beixi ziyi*). New York: Columbia University Press.

Chao Wei-pang 1942. "The origin and growth of the *fu-chi*." *Folklore Studies* 1:9–27.

Chen Bing 陈兵 1985. "Jindan pai nanzong qiantan 金丹派南宗浅探" (An exploration of the southern line of the *Jindan* faction). *Shijie zongjiao yanjiu* 22:35–49.

Ch'en, Kenneth 1964. *Buddhism in China: A Historical Survey*. Princeton: Princeton University Press.

Chikusa Masaaki 竺沙雅章 1982a (orig. 1979). "Sōdai baichō kō 宋代賣牒考" (A study of the sale of ordination certificates in the Song). In *Chūgoku bukkyō shakaishi kenkyū* 中國佛教社會史研究 (Studies in the social history of Chinese Buddhism). Kyoto: Dōhōsha.

———— 1982b (orig. 1980). "Jikan no shigaku ni tsuite 寺觀の賜額について" (Concerning the bestowal of plaques on Buddhist and Daoist monasteries). In *Chūgoku bukkyō shakaishi kenkyū*.

———— 1982c (orig. 1979). "Sōdai funji kō 宋代墳寺考" (A study of grave monasteries in the Song). In *Chūgoku bukkyō shakaishi kenkyū*.

———— 1982d (orig. 1956, 1958). "Fukken no jiin to shakai 福建の寺院と社會" (Fujian's monasteries and society). In *Chūgoku bukkyō shakaishi kenkyū*.

———— 1982e (orig. 1974). "Kissai jima ni tsuite 喫茶事魔について" (Concerning vegetarianism and demon worship). In *Chūgoku bukkyō shakaishi kenkyū*.

———— 1982f (orig. 1977). "Sessei no dōmin ni tsuite 浙西の道民について" (Concerning the *daomin* of Zhexi circuit). In *Chūgoku bukkyō shakaishi kenkyū*.

Chu Ron-Guey 1984. "Chu Hsi and Public Instruction." Unpublished paper given at the Conference on Neo-Confucian Education: the Formative Stage, Princeton University.

Davis, Edward L. 1985. "Arms and the Tao: Hero Cult and Empire in Traditional China." In *Sōdai no shakai to shūkyō* 宋代の社会と宗教 (Society and religion in the Sung). *Sōdaishi kenkyūkai kenkyū hōkoku* 2:1–56.

Davis, Richard L. 1986. *Court and Family in Sung China, 960–1279: Bureaucratic Success and Kinship Fortunes for the Shih of Ming-chou*. Durham: Duke University Press.

de Bary, Wm. Theodore 1960. *Sources of Chinese Tradition*. New York: Columbia University Press.

————, ed. 1985. *The Rise of Neo-Confucianism in Korea*. New York: Columbia University Press.

Des Rotours, Robert 1966. "Le culte des cinq dragons sous la dynastie des T'ang." In *Mélanges de Sinologie offert à Monsieur Paul Demieville*. Volume 1. Paris: Presses Universitaires de France.

DeWoskin, Kenneth J. 1977. "The Six Dynasties Chih-kuai and the Birth of Fiction." In Andrew H. Plaks, ed. *Chinese Narrative: Critical and Theoretical Essays*. Princeton: Princeton University Press.

Dolby, William 1976. *A History of Chinese Drama*. New York: Harper & Row.

Ebrey, Patricia 1981. "Women in the Kinship System of the Southern Sung Upper Class." *Historical Reflections* 8:113–28.

———— 1984. *Family and Property in Sung China: Yüan Ts'ai's Precepts for Social Life*. Princeton: Princeton University Press.

———— 1986. "The Early Stages in the Development of Descent Group Organization." In Patricia Ebrey and James Watson, eds., *Kinship Organization in Late Imperial China 1000–1940*. Berkeley: University of California Press.

Elvin, Mark 1973. *The Pattern of the Chinese Past: A Social and Economic Interpretation*. Stanford: Stanford University Press.

Fogel, Joshua A. 1984. *Politics and Sinology: The Case of Naitō Kōnan (1866–1934)*. Cambridge: Harvard University Press.

Franke, Herbert 1961. "Some Aspects of Private Historiography in the Thirteenth and Fourteenth Centuries." In W. G. Beasley and E. G. Pulleyblank, eds., *Historians of China and Japan*. London: School of Oriental and African Studies.

———— 1972. "Einege Drucke und Handschriften der frühen Ming-Zeit," *Oriens Extremus* 19:55–64.

————, ed. 1976. *Sung Biographies*. Wiesbaden: Franz Steiner.

———— 1977. "Bemerkungen zum volkstümlichen Taoismus der Ming-Zeit." *Oriens Extremus* 24:205–15.

———— 1984. "Zu einem apokryphen Dharani-sutra aus China." *Zeitschrift der Deutschen Morgenländischen Gesellschaft* 134.2:318–36.

Gernet, Jacques 1962 (orig. 1959). *Daily Life in China on the Eve of the Mongol Invasion 1250–1276*. Trans. H. M. Wright. Stanford: Stanford University Press.

Goody, Jack 1968. "Restricted Literacy in Northern Ghana." In J. Goody, ed., *Literacy in Traditional Societies*. New York: Cambridge University Press.

Granet, Marcel 1959 (orig. 1926). *Danses et légendes de la Chine ancienne*. Paris: Presses Universitaires de France.

———— 1975 (orig. 1922). *The Religion of the Chinese People (La religion des Chinois)*. Edited and translated by Maurice Freedman. Oxford: Basil Blackwell.

Grootaers, Willem A. 1952. "The Hagiography of the Chinese God Chen-wu: The Transmission of Rural Traditions in Chahar." *Folklore Studies* 11:139–82.

Haeger, John 1972. "The Intellectual Context of Neo-Confucianism." *Journal of Asian Studies* 31:499–515.

Hansen, Valerie 1987a. "Popular Deities and Social Change in the Southern Song Period (1127–1276)." Ph.D. dissertation, University of Pennsylvania.

———— 1987b. "Inscriptions: Historical Sources for the Song." *Sung–Yüan Bulletin* 19:17–25.

Harper, Donald 1985. "Chinese Demonography of the Third Century B.C." *Harvard Journal of Asiatic Studies* 45:459–98.

Harrell, C. Stevan 1974. "When A Ghost Becomes a God." In Arthur Wolf, ed., *Religion and Ritual in Chinese Society*. Stanford: Stanford University Press.

Hartwell, Robert M. 1966. "Markets, Technology, and the Structure of Enterprise in the Development of the Eleventh-Century Chinese Iron and Steel Industry." *The Journal of Economic History* 26:29–58.

———— 1967. "The Evolution of the Early Northern Sung Monetary System A.D. 960–1025." *Journal of the American Oriental Society* 87:280–89.

———— 1971. "Financial Expertise, Examinations, and the Formulation of Economic Policy in Northern Sung China." *Journal of Asian Studies* 30:281–314.

———— 1978. "Regional Economic Development and the Transformation of Chinese Society, 750–1250 A.D." Unpublished paper, presented at SORCE Conference on Regionalism and Economic Development in China, Philadelphia.

———— 1982. "Demographic, Political, and Social Transformations of China." *Harvard Journal of Asiatic Studies* 42.2:365–442.

Hayashi Kazuo 林和生 1984. "Chūgoku kinsei ni okeru chihō toshi no hattatsu—Taiko heigen U Sei chin no baai 中国近世における地方都市の發達太湖平原烏青鎮の場合" (The development of regional cities in early modern China—the case of Wu and Qing townships in the Lake Tai plains). In Umehara Kaoru 梅原郁, ed., *Chūgoku kinsei no toshi to bunka* 中国近世の都市と文化 (Cities and culture in early modern China). Kyoto: Kyoto University Institute for Humanistic Studies.

Hayes, James 1985. "Specialists and Written Materials in the Village World." In David Johnson et al., ed., *Popular Culture in Late Imperial China.* Berkeley: University of California Press.

Hervouet, Yves, ed. 1978. *A Sung Bibliography.* Hong Kong: The Chinese University Press.

Ho Ping-ti 1956. "Early Ripening Rice in Chinese History." *Economic History Review* 9:200–17.

Hucker, Charles O. 1985. *A Dictionary of Official Titles in Imperial China.* Stanford: Stanford University Press.

Hymes, Robert 1979. "Prominence and Power: The Local Elite of Fu-chou, Chiang-hsi." Ph.D. dissertation, University of Pennsylvania.

———— 1986a. *Statesmen and Gentlemen: The Elite of Fu-Chou, Chiang-Hsi, in Northern and Southern Sung.* New York: Cambridge University Press.

———— 1986b. "Marriage, Descent Groups, and the Localist Strategy in Sung and Yuan Fu-chou." In Patricia Ebrey and James Watson, eds., *Kinship Organization in Late Imperial China 1000–1940.* Berkeley: University of California Press.

———— 1987a. "Not Quite Gentlemen? Doctors in Sung and in Yuan." *Chinese Science* 8:9–76.

———— 1987b. "Way and Byway: Taoist Saints' Cults and Exorcist Masters in Sung and Yuan China." Unpublished paper.

Idema, Wilt, and Stephen H. West 1982. *Chinese Theater 1100–1450*. Wiesbaden: Franz Steiner.

Inoue Ichii 井上以智為 1941. "Kanu shibyō no yūrai narabi ni hensen 關羽祠廟の由来並に變遷" (The origin and development of temples dedicated to Guan Yu) (parts 1 and 2). *Shirin* 26: 41–51, 242–83.

Iwaki Hideo 岩城秀夫 1963. "Sōdai engeki kanki 宋代演劇管窺" (Speculations on the drama of the Sung period). *Chūgoku bungakuhō* 19: 102–107.

Johnson, David 1985. "The City-God Cults of T'ang and Sung China." *Harvard Journal of Asiatic Studies* 45: 363–457.

Jordan, David K. 1982. "Taiwanese poe divinations: Statistical awareness and religious belief." *Journal for the Scientific Study of Religion* 21: 114–18.

Jordan, David K., and Daniel L. Overmyer 1986. *The Flying Phoenix: Aspects of Chinese Sectarianism in Taiwan*. Princeton: Princeton University Press.

Kanai Noriyuki 金井德幸 1977. "NanSō saishi shakai no tenkai 南宋祭祀社会の展開" (The development of worshipping societies in the Southern Song). In [Risei Daigaku] *Shūkyō shakaishi kenkyū*.

———— 1979. "Sōdai no sonsha to shajin 宋代の村社と社神" (Worshipping groups and their objects of worship in the Sung rural communities). *Tōyōshi kenkyū* 38: 61–87.

———— 1983. "Shajin to Dōkyō 社神と道教" (Earth gods and Daoism). In *Dōkyō 2: Dōkyō no tenkai* 道教2:道教の展開 (Daoism 2: The development of Daoism). Tokyo: Heiga shuppan sha.

Kanaoka Shōkō 金岡照光 1977. "Tonkō bunken ni mirareru shoshin shobosatsu shinkō no ichi yōsō 敦煌文献に見られる諸神諸菩薩信仰の一様相" (Some problems concerning belief in bodhisattvas and devatas at Tun-huang). In *Yoshioka hakase kanreki kinen dōkyō kenkyū ronshū—dōkyō no shisō to bunka* 吉岡博士還暦記念道教研究論集—道教の思想と文化 (Collected essays on Taoist thought and culture: A festschrift honoring Dr. Yoshitoyo Yoshioka). Tokyo: Kokushokan gyōkai.

Kane, Virginia 1982–83. "Aspects of Western Chou Apppointment Inscriptions: The Charge, the Gifts, and the Response." *Early China* 8: 14–28.

Kani Hiroaki 可児弘明 1972. "Furan zakki 扶鸞雑記" (*Fu-luan* or Chinese automatic writing: Its history and present practices). *Shigaku* 45: 57–88.

Kao, Yu-kung 1963. "A Study of the Fang La Rebellion." *Harvard Journal of Asiatic Studies* 24: 17–63.

Katkov, Neil 1986. "Records of Yijian: Playing with Strangers." Unpublished paper.

Katō Shigeshi 加藤繁 1962. *TōSō jidai ni okeru kingin no kenkyū* 唐宋時代にお

ける金銀の研究 (A study of the incidence of silver and gold in the Tang and Song dynasties). Tokyo: Tōyō bunko.

Kinugawa Tsuyoshi 衣川強 1970. "Sōdai no hōkyū ni tsuite 宋代の俸給について" (Concerning Song dynasty salaries). *Tōhō gakuhō* 41:414–66.

Kracke, Edward A., Jr. 1957. "Region, Family, and Individual in the Chinese Examination System." In John Fairbank, ed., *Chinese Thought and Institutions*. Chicago: University of Chicago Press.

——— 1963. *The Civil Service in Early Sung China, 960–1067*. Cambridge: Harvard University Press.

Langlois, John D. 1981. "Introduction." In J. Langlois, ed., *China under Mongol Rule*. Princeton: Princeton University Press.

Legge, James, trans. 1885. *The Sacred Books of China: The Texts of Confucianism. Part IV: The Li Ki XI–XLVI*. Oxford: Clarendon Press.

Lévi, Jean 1986. "Les fonctionnaires et le divin: luttes de pouvoirs entre divinités et administrateurs dans les contes des Six Dynasties et des Tang." *Cahiers d'Extrême-Asie* 2:81–108.

——— 1987. "Les fonctions religieuses de la bureaucratie céleste." *L'Homme* (101) 27:35–57.

Li Hsien-chang 李獻璋 1979. *Masso shinkō no kenkyū* 媽祖信仰の研究 (Studies on the belief in Ma-tsu). Tokyo: Taizan bunbutsusha.

Liu Xinru 1982. "Buddhist Institutions in the Lower Yangtse Region—Sung Dynasty." Unpublished paper.

——— 1985. "Early Commercial and Cultural Exchanges Between India and China First-Sixth Centuries A.D." Ph.D. dissertation, University of Pennsylvania.

Lo, Winston W. 1974. *The Life and Thought of Yeh Shih*. Gainesville: University Presses of Florida.

——— 1974–75. "Circuits and Circuit Intendants in the Territorial Administration of Sung China." *Monumenta Serica* 31:39–104.

——— 1983. "A New Perspective on the Sung Civil Service." *Journal of Asian History* 17:121–35.

Long, Charles H. 1987. "Popular Religion." In Mircea Eliade, ed., *The Encyclopedia of Religion*. Volume 11. New York: Macmillan.

Lu Tao 呂涛 et al. 1984. *Shiji qianshuo* 史籍浅説 (A brief discussion of historical materials). Guangdong: Guangdong renmin chubanshe.

Ludden, David 1985. *Peasant History in South India*. Princeton: Princeton University Press.

Mair, Victor 1983. *Tun-huang Popular Narratives*. New York: Cambridge University Press.

Makita Tairyō 牧田諦亮 1981. *Chūgoku Bukkyōshi kenkyū daiichi* 中国佛教
　史研究第一 (Studies in the history of Chinese Buddhism, volume 1).
　Tokyo: Daitō shuppansha.

———— 1984. *Chūgoku Bukkyōshi kenkyū daini* 中国佛教史研究第二 (Studies
　in the history of Chinese Buddhism, volume 2). Tokyo: Daitō
　shuppansha.

Maspero, Henri 1981. *Taoism and Chinese Religion.* Translated by Frank A.
　Kierman, Jr. Amherst: University of Massachusetts Press.

Matsubara Saburō 松原三郎 1966. *Chūgoku bukkyō chōkokushi kenkyū* 中国
　仏教彫刻史研究 (Chinese Buddhist sculpture). Tokyo: Yoshikawa
　kōbunkan.

Matsumoto Kōichi 松本浩一 1979. "Sōdai no raihō 宋代の雷法" (Song
　thunder rites). *Shakai bunkashigaku* 17:45–65.

———— 1982. "Chō Tenshi to NanSō no Dōkyō 張天師と南宋の道教"
　(Zhang Tianshi and Southern Song Daoism). In *Rekishi ni okeru minshū
　to bunka—Sakai Tadao sensei koki shukuga kinen* 歴史における民衆と
　文化—酒井忠夫先生古稀祝賀記念 (Peoples and cultures in Asiatic his-
　tory: Collected essays in honour of Professor Tadao Sakai on his seven-
　tieth birthday). Tokyo: Kokusho kankōkai.

———— 1983a. "Dōkyō to shūkyō girei 道教と宗教儀礼." In *Dōkyō 1: Dōkyō
　wa nani ka* 道教1:道教は何か (Daoism 1: What is Daoism?). Tokyo:
　Heika shuppansha.

———— 1983b. "Sōrei·sairei ni miru Sōdai shūkyōshi no ichi keikō 葬礼·
　祭礼にみる宋代宗教史の一傾向" (A trend in the history of Song reli-
　gion in funerary and sacrificial rites). In *Sōdai no shakai to bunka* 宋代の
　社会と文化 (Society and culture in the Song). *Sōdaishi kenkyūkai hōkoku*
　1:169–94.

———— 1986. "Sōdai no shigaku/shigo ni tsuite—shu toshite *Sōkaiyō shūkō*
　ni mieru shiryō kara 宋化の賜額·賜号について—主として宋会要輯
　稿に見える史料から" (Concerning the granting of plaques and titles in
　the Song dynasty—primarily on the basis of materials contained in the
　Song huiyao). In *Chūgoku ni okeru chūō seiji to chihō shakai* 中国における
　中央政治と地方社会 (The central government and local society in
　China). Tokyo: Monbushō.

McKnight, Brian 1971. *Village and Bureaucracy in Southern Sung China.*
　Chicago: University of Chicago Press.

Michihata Ryōshū 道端良秀 1980. *Chūgoku Bukkyō to shakai to no kōshō*
　中国仏教と社会との交渉 (The interaction between Chinese Buddhism
　and society). Kyoto: Heirakuji shoten.

Miura Kunio 三浦國雄 1985. "Shushi kishin ronbo 朱子鬼神論補" (A supplement to Zhu Xi's religious philosophy). *Jimbun kenkyū* (Ōsaka Shiritsu Daigaku, bungakubu kiyō) 37:73–91.

Miyakawa Hisayuki 宮川尚志 1973. "Dōkyō shijō yori mitaru godai 道教史上より見たる五代" (Daoist trends in the Five Dynasties period). *Tōhō shūkyō* 42:13–34.

Miyazaki Ichisada 宮崎市定 1974. "Sōdai kansei josetsu—*Sōshi* shokkan shi o ika ni yomu beki ka? 宋代官制序説—宋史職官志をいかに讀むべきか" (A prefatory discussion of the bureaucratic system of the Song—just how must one read the *zhiguan* section of the *Songshi*?). In Saeki Tomo, ed., *Sōshi shokkan shi sakuin* 宋史職官志索引 (An index to the *zhiguan* section of the *Songshi*). Kyoto: Dōhōsha.

——— 1975 (orig. 1950). "Tōyō teki kinsei 東洋的近世" (The early modern era East Asia style). In *Ajiashi ronkō* アジア史論考 (A discussion and examination of the history of Asia). Tokyo: Asahi shinbunsha.

——— 1978. "Sōdai ni okeru satsujin saiki no shūzoku ni tsuite 宋代における殺人祭鬼の習俗について" (Concerning the custom of human sacrifice and worship of ghosts in the Song dynasty). In *Ajiashi kenkyū* アジア史研究 (Asiatica: Studies in Oriental History). Kyoto: Dōhōsha.

Miyazaki Noriko 宮崎法子 1981. "Ten Chōnen shōrai jūroku Rakkan zu kō 傳奝然将来十六羅漢圖考" (A study of sixteen Lohan paintings claimed to have been brought by Chonen to Japan). In *Suzuki Kei sensei kanreki kinen: Chūgoku kaigashi ronshū*. 鈴木敬先生還暦記念: 中国繪画史論集 (Memorial volume on the occasion of Professor Suzuki Kei's sixtieth birthday). Tokyo: Yoshikawa kōbunkan.

Miyazawa Toshi 宮澤知之 1985. "Sōdai senkin chitai no kaisō kōsei 宋代先進地帯の階層構成" (The making of the different levels of the advanced regions in the Song). *Yorei shigaku* 10:25–82.

Morita Kenji 森田憲司 1983. "Seinanro kyōjū Ri Teijitsu o megutte 済南路教授李庭実をめぐって" (A look at instructional official Li Tingshi of Jinan circuit). In Tanigawa Michio 谷川道雄, ed., *Chūgoku shidaifu kaikyū to chiiki shakai to no kankei ni tsuite no sōgoteki kenkyū* 中国士大夫階級と地域社会との関係についての総合的研究 (Comprehensive studies concerning the relationships between local society and the Chinese literati class). Kyoto: Monbushō funded report.

——— 1984. "Bunshō teikun no seiritsu—chihōshin kara kakyo no kami e 文昌帝君の成立・地方神から科舉の神へ" (The establishment of Emperor Wenchang—from local god to civil service examination god). In Umehara Kaoru 梅原郁, ed., *Chūgoku kinsei no toshi to bunka* 中国近世の

都市と文化 (Cities and culture in early modern China). Kyoto: Kyoto University Institute for Humanistic Studies.

Naitō Torajirō 内藤虎次郎 1922. "Gaikatsuteki Tō-Sō jidaikan 概括的唐宋時代觀" (A sketch of the Tang–Song period). *Rekishi to chiri* 9.5:1–11.

Nakamura Jihei 中村治兵衛 1972. "Sōdai Kōtokugun Shizanbyō no gyūsai ni tsuite—Sōdai shakai no ichijirei to shite 宋代広徳軍祠山廟の牛祭について—宋化社会の一事例として" (The Niuji or cattle festival at the Ci shan miao in Guangde Anhui during the Sung Dynasty—A study concerning the custom of sacrificing to cattle to pray for rain). *Shien* 109:1–24.

Needham, Joseph, with Wang Ling and Lu Gwei-djen 1971. *Science and Civilisation in China: Physics and Physical Technology (Volume 4), Civil Engineering and Nautics (Part 3).* Cambridge: Cambridge University Press.

Ogawa Tamaki et al. 小川環樹 1968. *Shinjigen* 新字源 (A new source of characters). Tokyo: Kadokawa shoten.

Ōtsuka Hidetaka 大塚秀高 1980. "Kō Mai to *Ikenshi*—rekishi to genjitsu no hazama nite 洪邁と夷堅志—歴史と現實の狹間にて (Hung Mai and his *I-chien-chih*—between history and actuality). *Tōdai chūtetsubun gakkaihō* 5:75–96.

Qian Daxin 錢大昕 (1728–1804) 1909. *Hong Wenmin gong nianpu* 洪文敏公年譜 (A year-by-year chronology of Hong Mai's life). In Hong Rukui 洪汝奎, ed., *Sihong nianpu* 四洪年譜 (A year-by-year chronology of the four Hongs). Hanyang: Hongshi huimuzhai.

Quan Hansheng 全漢升 1972a. "Nan Song chunian wujia de da biandong 南宋初年物價的大變動" (The great shift in prices in the beginning of the Southern Song). In *Zhongguo jingji shi luncong* 中國經濟史論叢 (Discussions in Chinese economic history). Hong Kong: Xinya yanjiu suo.

—— 1972b. "Nan Song Hangzhou de xiaofei yu waidi shangpin zhi shuru 南宋杭州的消費與外地商品之輸入" (Consumption of goods in Southern Song Hangzhou and the import of goods from outlying areas). In *Zhongguo jingji shi luncong.*

—— 1972c. "Songmo de tonghuo pengzhang ji qi duiyu wujia de yingxiang 宋末的通貨膨脹及其對於物價的影響" (Inflation at the end of the Song and its effect on prices). In *Zhongguo jingji shi luncong.*

—— 1976. "Song Mingjian baiyin goumai li de biandong ji qi yuanyin 宋明間白銀購買力的變動及其原因" (Changes in the purchasing power of silver in the Song and Ming and the reasons for them). In *Zhongguo jingji shi yanjiu* 中國經濟史研究 (Studies in Chinese economic history). Hong Kong: Xinya yanjiu suo.

Saeki Tomi 佐伯富 1978. "Shidaifu to junpitsu 士大夫と潤筆" (The literati and commissioned texts), in *Uchida Ginpu hakase shōju kinen tōyōshi ronshū* 内田吟風博士頌寿記念東洋史論集 (Studies in East Asian history in honor of Professor Uchida Ginpu). Kyoto: Dōhōsha.

Sakai Tadao 酒井忠夫 1937. "Taizan shinkō no kenkyū 太山信仰の研究" (A study of the belief in Mount Tai). *Shichō* 7:70–118.

Sangren, Paul Steven 1980. "A Chinese Marketing Community: An Historical Ethnography of Ta-ch'i, Taiwan." Ph.D. dissertation, Stanford University.

Satō Chisui 佐藤智水 1977. "Hokuchō zōzōmei kō 北朝造像銘考" (A study of votive inscriptions on Buddhist statues in the Northern dynasties). *Shigaku zasshi* 86.10:1–47.

Schafer, Edward H. 1951. "Ritual Exposure in Ancient China." *Harvard Journal of Asiatic Studies* 14.1–2:130–84.

———— 1967. *The Vermillion Bird.* Berkeley: University of California Press.

Schipper, Kristofer M. 1974. "The Written Memorial in Taoist Ceremonies." In Arthur Wolf, ed., *Religion and Ritual in Chinese Society.* Stanford: Stanford University Press.

———— 1985. "Taoist Ritual and Local Cults of the T'ang Dynasty." In Michel Strickmann, ed., *Tantric and Taoist Studies in Honour of R. A. Stein.* Volume 3. Brussels: Institut Belge des Hautes Etudes Chinoises.

Seidel, Anna 1984. "Le sutra merveilleux du Ling-pao Suprême, traitant de Lao Tseu qui convertit les barbares (le manuscrit S. 2081): contribution à l'étude du Bouddho-taoïsme des Six Dynasties." In Michel Soymié, ed., *Contributions aux études de Touen-huang.* Volume 3. Paris: Ecole Française d'Extrême-Orient.

———— 1986. "Traces of Han Religion in Funeral Texts Found in Tombs." In *Dōkyō to shūkyō bunka* 道教と宗教文化 (Taoism and religious culture: Volume in honor of Professor Akizuki Kan'ei). Tokyo: Heika shuppansha.

Shiba Yoshinobu 斯波義信 1968. *Sōdai shōgyōshi kenkyū* 宋代商業史研究 (A study of the Song economy). Tokyo: Kazama shobō.

———— 1970. *Commerce and Society in Sung China.* Translated and edited by Mark Elvin. Ann Arbor: University of Michigan Press.

———— 1972. "Sōdai Kishū no chiiki kaihatsu 宋代徽州の地域開発" (The development of Huizhou and its hinterland during the Song Dynasty). In *Yamamoto hakase kanreki kinen tōyōshi ronsō* 山本博士還暦記念東洋史論叢 (Collected works on Asian history celebrating the sixtieth birthday of Professor Yamamoto). Tokyo: Yamakawa shuppansha.

———— 1975a. "Urbanization and the Development of Markets in the Lower

Yangtse Valley." In John Haeger, ed., *Crisis and Prosperity in Sung China.* Tucson: University of Arizona Press.

———— 1975b. "Sōdai no Koshū ni okeru chinshi no hatten 宋化の湖州における鎮市の発展" (Urban development of towns in Huzhou in the Song period). In *Enoki hakase kanreki kinen tōyōshi ronsō* 榎木博士還歴記念東洋史論叢 (Collected works on Asian history celebrating the sixtieth birthday of Professor Enoki). Tokyo: Yamakawa shuppansha.

———— 1976. "Sekkō Koshū ni okeru teijū no enkaku 浙江湖州における定住の沿革" (The history of settlement in Huzhou, Zhejiang). In *Chūgoku tetsugakushi no tenbō to mosaku* 中国哲学史の展望と摸索 (The groping and view of the history of Chinese philosophy). Tokyo: Sobunsha.

———— 1984a. "Sōdai Koshū no toshi seitai 宋代杭州の都市生態" (The urban ecology of the Sung capital Hangzhou). *Toshishi o meguru sho mondai* 都市史をめぐる諸問題 (Aspects of urban history), no. 2. Faculty of Letters, Osaka University Bulletin.

———— 1984b. "Sōdai Koshū no shōgyōkaku 宋代杭州の商業核" (The commercial nucleus of the Song capital, Hangzhou). In Umehara Kaoru 梅原郁, ed., *Chūgoku kinsei no toshi to bunka* 中国近世の都市と文化 (Cities and culture in early modern China). Kyoto: Kyoto University Institute for Humanistic Studies.

———— 1986. "Agrarian and Commercial Change in the Lower Yangtse," revision of a paper prepared for the Conference on Spatial and Temporal Trends and Cycles in Chinese Economic History, August 1984, Bellagio, Italy.

Sickman, Laurence 1971. "Sculpture from the Tenth to the Fourteenth Century." In L. Sickman and A. C. Soper, eds., *The Art and Architecture of China.* New York: Penguin Books.

Siren, Osvald n.d. *A Chinese Temple and Its Plastic Decoration of the Twelfth Century* [about Xiahua yinsi, Datong]. Paris: Musée Guimet.

Sivin, Nathan 1978. "On the Word 'Taoist' as a Source of Perplexity. With Special Reference to the Relations of Science and Religion in Traditional China." *History of Religions* 17:303–30.

Soper, Alexander C. 1948. "Hsiang-kuo-ssu, an Imperial Temple of the Northern Sung." *Journal of the American Oriental Society* 61:19–45.

Stein, Rolf A. 1979. "Religious Taoism and Popular Religion from the Second to the Seventh Centuries." In Anna Seidel and Holmes Welch, eds., *Facets of Taoism.* New Haven: Yale University Press.

———— 1986. "Avalokitesvara/Kouan-yin, un exemple de transformation d'un dieu en déesse." *Cahiers d'Extrême-Asie* 2:17–80.

Strickmann, Michel 1977. "The Consecration Sutra: A Buddhist Book of Spells." Unpublished, incomplete manuscript.

—— 1978. "The Longest Taoist Scripture." *History of Religions* 17:331–54.

—— 1979. "On the Alchemy of T'ao Hung-ching." In Anna Seidel and Holmes Welch, eds., *Facets of Taoism*. New Haven: Yale University Press.

—— 1982. "The Tao Among the Yao: Taoism and the Sinification of South China." In *Rekishi ni okeru minshū to bunka—Sakai Tadao sensei koki shukuga kinen* 歴史における民衆と文化—酒井忠夫先生古稀祝賀記念 (Peoples and cultures in Asiatic history: Collected essays in honour of Professor Tadao Sakai on his seventieth birthday). Tokyo: Kokusho kankōkai.

Sudō Yoshiyuki 周藤吉之 1954. "NanSō matsu no kōdenpō 南宋末の公田法" (The public field system at the end of the Southern Song). In *Chūgoku tochi seido shi kenkyū* 中国土地制度史研究 (A study of the Chinese land tenure system). Tokyo: Tokyo University Press.

—— 1962. "NanSō inasaku no chiikisei 南宋稲作の地域性" (The regional nature of rice cultivation in the Southern Song). In *Sōdai keizaishi kenkyū* 宋代經濟史研究 (Studies in Song economic history). Tokyo: Tokyo University Press.

—— 1965a. "Sōdai no hatō no kanri kikō to suiri kiyaku—kyōsonsei to sono kanren ni oite 宋代の陂塘の管理機構と水利規約—郷村制とその關連において" (The administrative structure and irrigation agreements of Song dynasty embankments—regarding their connections to the village system). In *Tōsō shakai keizaishi kenkyū* 唐宋社會經濟史研究 (A study of the socioeconomic history of the Tang and Song). Tokyo: Tokyo University Press.

—— 1965b. "Sōdai kyōsonsei no hensen katei 宋代郷村制の變遷過程" (The process of change of the village system in the Song dynasty). In *Tōsō shakai keizaishi kenkyū* (A study of the socioeconomic history of the Tang and Song). Tokyo: Tokyo University Press.

Taiyuanshi Wenwu Guanli Weiyuanhui 太原市文物管理委員会 1981. *Jinci* 普祠 (The Jin temple). Beijing: Wenwu chubanshe.

Takao Giken 高雄義堅 1939. "Sō igo no Jōdokyō 宋以後の淨土教" (Pure Land Buddhism from the Song on). *Shina Bukkyōgaku* 3.34:57–93.

—— 1975. *Sōdai Bukkyōshi no kenkyū* 宋代佛教史の研究 (Studies in Song dynasty Buddhism). Kyoto: Hyakkaen.

Tanaka Issei 田仲一成 1970. "NanSō jidai no Fukken chihōgeki ni tsuite

南宋時代の福建地方劇について" (Concerning regional drama in Fujian during the Southern Song). *Nihon Chūgoku Gakkaihō* 22 : 102−18.

Tay, C. N. 1976. "Kuan-yin: The Cult of Half Asia." *History of Religions* 16.2 : 147−77.

Teiser, Stephen 1988. *The Ghost Festival in Medieval China*. Princeton: Princeton University Press.

ter Haar, Barend 1988. "Temples in Fu-chien." Paper delivered at Leiden University Workshop about Seventeenth and Eighteenth Century Fukien. Conference volume to be published by E. J. Brill.

Thorp, Robert L., and Virginia Bower 1982. *Spirit and Ritual: The Morse Collection of Ancient Chinese Art*. New York: Metropolitan Museum of Art.

Tillman, Hoyt 1982. *Utilitarian Confucianism: Chen Liang's Challenge to Chu Hsi*. Cambridge: Harvard University Press.

Tomoeda Ryūtaro 友枝竜太郎 1944. *Shushi no shisō keisei* 朱子の思想形成 (The formation of Zhu Xi's thought). Tokyo: Shunjūsha.

Tsien Tsuen-hsuin 1962. *Written on Bamboo and Silk: The Beginnings of Chinese Books and Inscriptions*. Chicago: University of Chicago Press.

———— 1985. *Science and Civilisation in China*. Volume 5: *Chemistry and Chemical Technology*. Part I: *Paper and Printing*. New York: Cambridge University Press.

Tsukamoto Zenryū 1985. *A History of Early Chinese Buddhism*. Translated by Leon Hurvitz. San Francisco: Kodansha International.

Twitchett, Denis 1981. *Printing and Publishing in Medieval China*. London: Wynken de Worde Society.

Umehara Kaoru 1986. "Civil and Military Officials in the Song: the *Chi-lu-kuan* system." *Acta Asiatica* 50 : 1−30.

Van der Loon, Piet 1977. "Les Origines de Theâtre Chinois." *Journal Asiatique* 265 : 141−68.

von Glahn, Richard 1983. *The Country of Streams and Grottoes: Expansion, Settlement, and the Civilizing of the Sichuan Frontier in Song times*. Cambridge: Harvard University Press.

Waley, Arthur, trans. 1938. *The Analects of Confucius*. London: George Allen and Unwin.

Wang Shih-ch'ing 1974. "Religious Organization in the History of a Chinese Town." In Arthur Wolf, ed., *Religion and Ritual in Chinese Society*. Stanford: Stanford University Press.

Ward, Barbara 1985. "Regional Operas and Their Audiences: Evidence from Hong Kong." In David Johnson et al., eds., *Popular Culture in Late Imperial China*. Berkeley: University of California Press.

Watabe Tadayo and Sakurai Yumio 渡部忠世, 桜井由躬雄 1984. *Chūgoku Kōnan no inasaku bunka to sono gakusaiteki kenkyū* 中国江南の稲作文化 とその学際的研究 (The rice-cultivating culture of the Jiangnan region in China and interdisciplinary studies of it). Tokyo: NHK.

Watson, James L. 1985. "Standardizing the Gods: The Promotion of T'ien Hou ("Empress of Heaven") Along the South China Coast 960–1960." In David Johnson et al., eds., *Popular Culture in Late Imperial China.* Berkeley: University of California Press.

Wei Meiyue 魏美月 1974. "Sōdai kinna seido ni tsuite no ichi kōsatsu 宋代 進納制度の一考察" (The purchase of office in Sung China). *Machikane-yama ronsō* (Bulletin of the Faculty of Letters, Osaka University) 7:23–42.

Weinstein, Donald, and Rudolph M. Bell 1982. *Saints and Society: The Two Worlds of Western Christendom, 1000–1700.* Chicago: University of Chicago Press.

Welch, Holmes 1967. *The Practice of Chinese Buddhism 1900–1950.* Cambridge: Harvard University Press.

Weng Tongwen 翁同文 1967. "Yinshua duiyu shuji chengben de yingxiang 印刷對於書籍成本的影響" (The decrease of the cost of books after the invention of printing). *Tsing Hua Journal of Chinese Studies* n.s. 6:35–41.

Wilkinson, Endymion 1973. *The History of Imperial China.* Cambridge: Harvard University Press.

Wolf, Arthur 1974. "Gods, Ghosts, and Ancestors." In A. Wolf, ed., *Religion and Ritual in Chinese Society.* Stanford: Stanford University Press.

Wu Han 吳晗 1961. "Song Yuan yilai laobaixing de chenghu 宋元以來老 百姓的称呼" (Appellations of the common people from the Song and Yuan dynasties on). In *Dengxia ji* 灯下集 (Collected writings under the lamp). Beijing: Sanlian shudian.

Wu Hung 1987. "The Earliest Pictorial Representations of Ape Tales: An Interdisciplinary Study of Early Chinese Narrative Art and Literature." *T'oung Pao* 73:86–112.

Xu Dishan 許地山 1941. *Fuji mixin di yanjiu* 扶箕迷信底研究 (A study of the superstition of spirit-writing). Changsha: Commercial Press.

Yang, C. K. 1961. *Religion in Chinese Society: A Study of Contemporary Social Functions of Religion and Some of Their Historical Factors.* Berkeley: University of California Press.

Yang, Lien-sheng 1961. "The Organization of Chinese Official Historiography: Principles and Methods of Standard Histories from the T'ang through the Ming Dynasty." In W. G. Beasley and E. G. Pulleyblank, eds., *Historians of China and Japan*. London: School of Oriental and African Studies.

Ye Changchi 葉昌熾 1980 (orig. 1909). *Yu shi* 語石 (Epigraphical notes). Taibei: Shangwu yinshuguan.

Yuan Ming 袁明 1954. "Shandong Tai'an faxian gudai tongqi 山東泰安發現古代銅器" (Ancient bronzes discovered at Tai'an, Shandong). *Wenwu cankao ziliao* 7:128–29.

Zbikowski, Tadeusz 1974. *Early Nan-hsi Plays of the Southern Sung Period*. Warsaw: Wydawnictwa Uniwersytetu Warsawskiego.

Zhang Guogan 張國淦 1974. *Zhongguo gufangzhi kao* 中國古方志考 (A study of old Chinese local histories). Taibei: Dingwen shuju.

Zürcher, Erik 1959. *The Buddhist Conquest of China: The Spread and Adaptation of Buddhism in Early Medieval China*. Sinica Leidensia, volume 2. Leiden: E. J. Brill.

———— 1980. "Buddhist Influence on Early Taoism: A Survey of Scriptural Evidence." *T'oung Pao* 66:84–147.

———— 1982a. "'Prince Moonlight': Messianism and Eschatology in Early Medieval Buddhism." *T'oung Pao* 68:1–75.

———— 1982b. "Perspectives in the Study of Chinese Buddhism." *Journal of the Royal Asiatic Society of Great Britain and Ireland* 2:161–76.

Zurndorfer, Harriet 1981. "The *Hsin-an ta-tsu-chih* and the Development of Chinese Gentry Society 800–1600." *T'oung Pao* 67:154–215.

INDEX TO TEMPLE INSCRIPTIONS

Year	Place	Source	Page
758	Jinyun, Zhejiang	*Liangzhe jinshi* 2:14a–15b	58
931	Wukang, Huzhou, Zhejiang	*Liangzhe jinshi* 4:34a–37b	110
1046	Huating, Jiangsu	*Jiangsu jinshi* 8:51a	63n.20
1078–85	Guangde, Anhui	*Cishan zhi* 3:14b–15a	150
1079	Yichuan, Shaanxi	*Jinshi cuibian* 138:2b–7a	90n.13
1090	Huolu, Hebei	*Changshan zhenshi* 12:13a–17a	86
1098	Shaoxing, Zhejiang	*Liangzhe jinshi* 7:4a–5b	52
1099	New Market, Huzhou, Zhejiang	*Tongzhi Huzhou* 53:8b–10a	15, 118–19
1100	Licheng, Shandong	Beijing, Gedi 1164, 1165, 4924	15–16
1101	Wukang, Huzhou, Zhejiang	*Dongtang ji* 9:15a–20a	110
1107	Liyang, Jiangsu	*Jiangsu jinshi* 10:21b–22b	16, 24
1112	Anji, Huzhou, Zhejiang	*Liangzhe jinshi* 7:24b–29a	111
1117	Wu township, Huzhou, Zhejiang	*Danyang ji* 9:2a–3a	34–35
1117	Suzhou, Jiangsu	*Qinchuan zhi* 13:44b	113n.11
1124	Jiangyin, Jiangsu	*Baqiong shi jinshi* 111:28a–30b	63–64
1127	Jinyun, Zhejiang	*Kuocang jinshi* 2:1a	58
1128	Xiaoshan, Shaoxing, Zhejiang	*Liangzhe jinshi* 8:1a–2a	90n.13
c. 1131	Linhai, Zhejiang	*Taizhou jinshi* 5:3a–7b	58, 75–76
1133	Deqing, Huzhou, Zhejiang	*Guixi ji* 11:1a	181
1134	New Market, Huzhou, Zhejiang	*Tongzhi Huzhou* 53:14a–15a	115–16
1135	New Market, Huzhou, Zhejiang	*Liangzhe jinshi* 8:36a–37a	90n.13, 91, 119

1139	New Market, Huzhou, Zhejiang	*Liangzhe jinshi* 8:39a–40a; Fu Ssu-nien 12558	91n.14, 119
1140	New Market, Huzhou, Zhejiang	*Liangzhe jinshi* 8:40b–42a	119–20
1150	Ningbo, Zhejiang	*Qiandao siming* 10:4a	148–49, 151
1157	Huzhou city, Zhejiang	*Wuxing jinshi* 8:20a–23a; *Tiaoxi ji* 22:7b–10b	22–23, 35–36, 167–70
1160	Ningbo, Zhejiang	*Liangzhe jinshi* 9:9b–11a	76
1163	New Embankment, Huzhou	*Wuxing jinshi* 9:16b–20a	91n.14, 116–17, 121–22
1176	Qingdun, Jiaxing, Zhejiang	*Qianlong Wuqing* 6:1a	132
1179	Guangde, Anhui	*Cishan zhi* 10:25a	150
1181	Linhai, Zhejiang	*Jiading Chicheng* 31:8a–9b	98
1183	Anji, Huzhou, Zhejiang	*Liangzhe jinshi* 10:6b–9a	112
1186	Yixing, Jiangsu	*Jiangsu jinshi* 11:38b–40a	68–69
1187	Wu township, Huzhou, Zhejiang	*Tongzhi Huzhou* 19:5a–6a; *Chongzhen Wucheng* 9:29b–31a	132, 187
1196	Linhai, Zhejiang	*Taizhou jinshi* 7:14b–17a	99
1196	Wugang, Hunan	*Baqiong shi jinshi* 117:4b–5b	82, 90, 90n.13
1197	Suzhou, Jiangsu	Beijing, Gu collection 925	58–59
1203	New Market, Huzhou, Zhejiang	*Tongzhi Huzhou* 53:27b–28b	120, 122
1209	Changxing, Huzhou, Zhejiang	*Jiaqing Changxing* 26:20a–21b	153
1211	Qingdun, Jiaxing, Zhejiang	*Qianlong Wuqing* 6:1b	132
1216	Qingpu, Jiangsu	*Jiangsu jinshi* 14:47a–52b	88
1223	New Market, Huzhou, Zhejiang	*Liangzhe jinshi* 11:18b–19b	121
1225	Nanjing, Jiangsu	*Jiangsu jinshi* 15:26a–28a	16
1227	Yixing, Jiangsu	*Jiangsu jinshi* 15:22b–26a; Beijing, Gu collection 946	58–59, 90n.13

1228	Hangzhou, Zhejiang	*Xianchun Lin'an* 73:16a	146
c. 1230	Gutian, Fujian	*Houcun xiansheng quanji* 88:2b–3a	155–56
1230	Wuxi, Jiangsu	Fu Ssu-nien 02288	100–102, 90n.13
1234	New Market, Huzhou, Zhejiang	*Liangzhe jinshi* 11:34a–35a	121–22
1240	Zhuji, Zhejiang	*Yuezhong jinshi* 5:45a–47a	72
1247	Anji, Huzhou, Zhejiang	*Wuxing jinshi* 12:1a–8a	91, 112–13
1251–52	Zhenjiang, Jiangsu	*Zhishun Zhenjiang* 8:13a–14a	147, 152
1256–57	Gui'an, Huzhou, Zhejiang	*Wuxing jinshi* 12:10b–14a	115
1258	Guangde, Anhui	*Cishan zhi* 8:8a	155
1260	Hangzhou, Zhejiang	*Liangzhe jinshi* 12:37a–43a	90, 90n.13, 91
1261	Jiande, Zhejiang	*Jingding Yanzhou* 4:4a	143–44
1261	Nanjing, Jiangsu	*Jingding Jiankang* 44:36a–37a	144
1262	Guangde, Anhui	*Cishan zhi* 10:28a	59
1264	Jiaxing, Zhejiang	*Liangzhe jinshi* 13:23a–27b	90n.13, 92, 102–103
1270	Suzhou, Jiangsu	Beijing, Gu collection 968–1	59
1270	South Bank, Huzhou, Zhejiang	*Wuxing jinshi* 12:20a–27a	58, 70, 103, 115, 123
1275	South Bank, Huzhou, Zhejiang	*Nanxun zhenzhi* 26:18a–19a	125–26
1346	Changshu, Suzhou, Jiangsu	*Qianlong Suzhou* 23:32b	154

INDEX

accounting for disaster, 71
administration, Song units of, 114n.13
advanced degrees, 97
Analects, 141n.8
ancestor worship, 14n.15
ancestral temple, 126
Ancheng wang, 181
Anhui: Guangde commandery, 59, 139, 148–49, 157, 165, 200; Huizhou, 200; Huizhou, Wuyuan county, 133, 140, 141, 146n.15; Longshu county, 182; Ningguo, 200; Shuzhou, 73; Xinzhou, 142
animal and nature gods, 34, 182–83, 191
assistant deity, 155
Auspicious Response temple, 123
Avalokitesvara. *See* Guanyin
Awakening Dragon monastery (appendix 1), 168

Bai miao, 190
Bai Yuchan, 43
Baihua dawang, 88
Baiyuan shen, 191
Bao'en guangxiao monastery, 168n.4
Baoning jiangjun, 119
Baoren wang, 185
baozheng. *See* guard leader
base temples, 128, 133; to Five Manifestations, 141
benmiao. *See* base temples
biji. *See* miscellaneous notes
Black Dragon Pool, 191
Board of Rites, 90n.11, 92
Bol, Peter, 160n.1
books, 4, 10, 11
Book of Poetry, The, 144
Book of Rites, The, 38, 84
branch temples, 128, 133; to King Zhang, Huoshan, 152
Broadly Efficacious King, 76

Buddha, 30–31, 54, 120, 172
Buddhism: canon, 12, 24–26; doctrine, changes in, 42; gods, 180; scriptures, use of, in ceremony, 12–13, 32; services, decline in cost of, 46. *See also* monasteries; religious practitioners
bureaucracy, organization of, during the Song, 96n.18
bureaucratization of the pantheon, 88

Cai Jing, 168n.4
Cai Qin, 189
canal-digging: by General Zhu, 119; by King Zhang, 149
Cao Qing, 184
Cao Xiaozi. *See* Filial Cao
career choices of elite, 160
caretaker. *See* temple caretaker
Celestial Heart (Tianxin) rites, 46
Celestial Masters Daoism, 43n.18
Chao Buzhi, 89
charms, Daoist, 12, 44
Chen Changyan. *See* Sheriff Chen
Chen Chun, 99, 104, 145–46, 146n.15, 163, 165
Chen Fu, 112n.9
Chen Jian, 120
Chen Nan, 43
Chen Wangsu, 173
Chen Xu erhou, 193
Cheng Dachang, 64
Cheng Hao, 146n.15
Cheng Yi, 146n.15
chenghuang. *See* city god
Chief Administrator Shen, 185
Chikusa Masaaki, 81n.2
Chongning monastery, 22, 168, 168n.4
city god, 34, 72; dragon serves as, 182n.4; history of, 181; in Huzhou, 181, 185, 189; similarities of, to Buddhist guardian deities, 182n.5

civil service examinations, 7, 65, 67, 71, 97, 131; content of, 11; god of, 133; King Zhang, 148; prayers before taking, 14; Zitong, 143–45

clergy, Buddhist and Daoist. *See* religious practitioners

Cloud Crane Immortal, 194

Collected Important Documents from the Song, 23, 79

Commander Fan, 38–39, 85, 100, 163, 164, 173

commercial economy, coexistence with barter, 108–9

commercial revolution, impact of, 7; on cities, 5; on literacy, 11; on miracles, 27, 75–78; on popular religion, 3, 10, 28

commercial tax receipts from Huzhou, 107

commoner gods. *See* deities: commoner

Confucius: temple in Huzhou, 181, 189; view of deities, 141n; worshipped as deity, 36–37

corvée labor, used to maintain temples, 39, 98, 98n

Court of Imperial Sacrifices, 83, 90n.11, 92

cows, sacrifice of, to King Zhang, 157

Culture-Propagating King, 36n

daibu jinshi. *See* self-styled advanced degrees

Daning monastery, 168

Daoism: canon, 24–26; gods, 180–81; immortals, 54; revival, 43; services, 46. *See also* religious practitioners

Dazu, 53n

Deep Response temple, 110n.6

Deep Virtue temple, 110n.6

deification, qualifications for, 37

deities: accuracy of depictions of, 54–55; assistant, 155; assumption of human form of, 56; categories of analysis of, 179–80; commoner, 37, 113n.12, 115, 180; Daoist view of, 26; jurisdiction of, 129, 130; principles governing behavior of, 13; punishment of, 12, 30, 57–58; sex with, 56; similarities of, to bureaucrats, 30, 88, 182; skepticism about, 49–52. *See also* regional cults

Dekuang temple, 184

demographic change: empire-wide, 4; Hangzhou, 5; Huzhou, 114, 178

DeWoskin, Kenneth, 21n.25

Di Renjie, 99

Ding Bogui, 145

Ding Ren, 152

divination sticks, 58n.8, 64, 68n.28, 68–69, 151

Donghai wang, 31

Donglin tudi, 190

Dongping wang, 186

Dongyue. *See* God of the Eastern Peak

door gods, 55

dragon deity, 32, 34, 71, 110, 111n.7, 130, 147, 163, 182; in Huzhou, 184, 191, 193; serving as city god, 182n.4

dreams, 27, 151; appearance of a deity in, 38, 54, 55, 62–64, 63n.20, 71

dudie. *See* ordination certificates

Dunhuang, texts from, 25, 171n.2

e. *See* temple plaques

earth god, 34, 182; of Changxing, 194; of Donglin, 190; of Five Chicken Hill, 50, 65, 161; of Green Mound, 187; in Hong household, 30–31, 172; of Hongzhou, Jiangxi, 57; of New Embankment, Huzhou, 116; of New Market, Huzhou, 119; Pichang, of Kaifeng, 131; of Poyang, Jiangxi, 51–52; of Yongfeng, Jiangxi, 129; of Yongzhou, Hunan, 94

Eastern Peak, God of the. *See* God of the Eastern Peak

Efficacious emperor Jiang, 192

efficacy, ix–x, 27, 75, 165

elders, 96

Emissary Fang, 155, 157–58

Emperor Huizong, 32, 43, 168n.4

Emperor Lizong, 154, 154n

Emperor Ming Taizu, 100n

Emperor Ningzong, 154n

Emperor Song Taizu, temple to, 186

Emperor Wen, 183

Empress Yi, 195

Enlightened King of Suodu, 187

Erlang, 55, 94, 131, 143n.10

Eternally Efficacious temple, 15, 91, 121n.24, 188

exempted advanced degree holders, 97
extra-local cults. *See* regional cults

fa. See methods
facilitated degrees, 116n.15
Fan Fosheng, 173
Fan jiangjun, 192
Fan Ru, 173, 173n.5
Fan Ruwei, 38n.11
Fan Wang. *See* Commander Fan
Fang Hui, 108
Fang La rebellion, 115, 116, 119, 123,
    125, 125n.32, 125n.33
Fangfeng family, 109, 110, 184, 191
fenmiao. See branch temples
festival for General Zhu, 122; for King
    Zhang, 151; violence at, 157
Filial Cao, 115, 184, 186, 189
Filial Righteousness monastery, 168
fiscal intendants, 91
fish pond king, 194
Five Manifestations, 93, 133, 133n.6,
    140–42, 164, 165, 183; in Huzhou, 194;
    number of temples to, 133n.5; regional
    temples, 196–200
Five Transmitters. *See* Five Manifesta-
    tions
forged documents, 125, 125n.33
Franke, Herbert, 19n.22
Fujian, 7, 11, 18, 21, 47, 147, 156, 198–
    99; Fuzhou, 5, 139, 140, 165, 198; Gu-
    tian, 93; Jianyang, 71; Ningde, 139;
    Putian, 139, 164; Quanzhou, 199;
    Shaowu, 44, 199; Shunchang county,
    38; Tingzhou, 139, 149, 199; Xinghua,
    33n.4, 145, 199; Zhangzhou, 145; Zhe-
    jiang border, 87
fulao. See elders
Fuying temple, 188

Gan Bao, 20n
gazetteers. *See* local histories
genealogies, 9
General Fan, 109, 192
General Su, 186
General Wu, 187
General Zhu, 15, 118–22, 124, 166; ap-
    pearance to lineage members, 121n.3;
    inscription about, 15; in Huzhou, 188
generic gods, general discription of, 181–
    82

Gentlemen Li and Cui, 123–26, 187
God of the Eastern Peak, 81, 82n.4, 111,
    111n.8, 113n.11, 115, 128n.2, 180, 181;
    temples in Huzhou, 184, 187, 189, 190,
    191, 193, 194
God of the Pine Stream, 40, 174
god of walls and moats, 38–39, 57, 71,
    173. *See also* city god
god who rules over mountains and
    streams, 32
Goddess Mother Hall, 53
gods. *See* deities
gods of heaven, earth, and water, 115n.14
gongtian fa, 59n.13
government funds for temple repairs, 84
government recognition of deities. *See* ti-
    tlegranting
Grand Canal, 6, 7, 107, 108, 139, 149,
    150, 165
Grand Mentor Xie, 194
granting of titles. *See* titlegranting
Great Emperor Wu, 88
Great Peace monastery, 168
Gu Duanming, 101
Guan Yu, 182n.5
Guangde Cishan Zhangwang. *See* King
    Zhang
Guangdong, 7, 147, 156; Leizhou, 87
Guanghui temple to King Zhang, 187
Guanghui temple to Song Taizu, 186
Guangling wang, 76
Guangming wang, 190
guanhu. See official households
Guanyin Sutra, 35n.8
Guanyin, 22, 34–35, 53, 54, 63–64, 68,
    73–74, 115n, 128n.2, 167–70, 180–81;
    in Crow township, Huzhou, 34–35; in
    Huzhou, 35, 184, 187; manifestations
    of, 35, 35n.8, 169, 169n.6; off Ningbo
    coast, 32
guard leader, 102
guardian deities of monasteries, 63n.20
Guo Shangshu, 184

Han Yu, 19–20
Hangzhou, 5, 7, 77, 107, 108, 131, 139,
    143, 164, 165; distribution of books in,
    11, 18; Huoshan, 152; regional temples
    in, 197; shift of capital to, 4, 5; sutra
    recitation societies in, 42; Xincheng
    county, 40

He Dedai, 101
He Wei, 129
He Zhitong, 83, 85
healers. *See also* religious practitioners
Heavenly Consort, 138, 145–48, 146n.15, 164, 165; appearance to Xu Jing of, 33, 33n; modern views of, 13n.14; number of temples to, 133n.5; regional temples to, 196–200
Heavenly Peace monastery, 23, 168
Heilong Tan, 191
hemp, 113
Henan (Kaifeng), 3, 5, 63, 85, 108, 131
Hong Gua, 171n.1
Hong Hao, 29, 171n.1
Hong Kong, 74n
Hong Mai, 17–18, 20, 29
Hu Jinsi, 186
Huang Chang, 83
Huang Liang, 173
Huang Zhen, 157–59, 165
Hubei, 67n; Hanyang, 71; Huolo county, 86; Xiangyang, 55; Xiazhou, 24, 54, 93; Xingguo commandery, 66
Huixian ren, 190
Huiying temple, 188
Huizhi, 169
Hunan: Lake Dongting, 56n, 130; Xiangtan, 89; Yongzhou, 94
Hundred Flowers Great King, 88
Huzhou, 70, 91, 92, 114–15, 143, 144, 148, 149, 152, 153, 163; Anji, 111, 112, 157; Changxing county, 149, 154; Crow (Wu) township, 34, 114, 131; Deqing county, 115; Gui'an county, 115; miracles in, 22–23, 47, 167–70; New Embankment (Xintang) canton, 116; New Market (Xinshi) township, 15, 114, 115, 118, 124; regional temples in, 197; South Bank (Nanxun) township, 103, 108, 109, 123, 125, 161; topography, 105–7; transport costs to, 5–6; Wucheng county, 108, 115, 139; Wukang county, 110
Hymes, Robert, 139n, 149n

illiteracy, effect on rites, 44, 45–46
illiterate participation in Buddhist rituals, 42, 45–46; in Daoist rituals, 43–46
images. *See* statues

Imperial Secretariat, 79, 92, 164
inner alchemy, 12, 43
Inoue Ichii, 182n.5
inscriptions: comparison with *The Record of the Listener*, 22–23; gods' purported desire for, 62–63, 161. *See also* temple inscriptions
itinerant artist, 54–55, 140

Ji Zha, 189, 194
Jiang lingdi, 192
Jiangsu, 156; Changshu, 154; Changzhou, 53, 143, 196; Danyang, 143; Jiangyin, 63; Liyang, 16, 24; Nanjing, 16, 131, 143, 200; Qingpu county, 88; Suzhou, 6, 54, 58, 59, 71, 88, 107, 108, 131, 140, 143, 153, 196; Taizhou, 42; Wuxi, 100; Yixing, 58, 68, 157; Zhenjiang, 112, 149, 196; Zhenzhou, 130
Jiangxi: Chong'an county, 61; Dexing, 93, 142; Fuliang, 36, 55, 76, 164; Fuzhou, 44, 139, 142, 143, 165, 200; Ganzhou, 49, 55, 70; Hongzhou, 57; Jianchang, 76, 164; Jiangzhou, 139, 200; Jizhou, 49; Lake Boyang, 5, 165; Leping, 73; Nanchang, 5; Ningdu, 93; Raozhou, 44, 46, 56, 139, 143, 199; Ruijin county, 62; Yongfeng county, 129; Yuzhang, 43
jiao. See purification ceremonies
Jiaying temple, 123, 187
Jin shrine (Jinci), 53
Jingzhong temple, 192
jinshi. See advanced degrees
Jiu Shen, 192
Johnson, David, 96, 181, 182n.4
Jujiu, 36, 169
Jurchen attacks, 3, 75, 115

Kaifeng. *See* Henan
Keeping-the-Peace-General, 119
King Fuchai of Wu, 194
King Ji of Western Wu, 194
King of Hell, 55
King of Opportune Aid, 62
King of Peace Wall, 181
King of the Eastern Sea, 31, 32
King Sun, 188
King Zhang, 113n.12, 139, 140, 148–59,

164, 165, 183, 191; annual festival to, 165; base temple of, 59; in Huzhou, 185, 187, 193; number of temples to, 133n.5; regional temples, 196–200; temples to, as listed in local histories, 179–80; transformation into a pig, 149n
King Zhang Xun, 186
Kleeman, Terry Frederick, 143n.9
Kong Hou, 188
Kong Yu, 188
Kongzi. *See* Confucius
Korea, 31, 145

Lake Tai, 107, 139; god of, 183, 187
land reclamation, 6n.7, 114
landholdings of monasteries, 60n.14, 60n.15; of temples, 58–61
lang ranks, 96–97, 123, 124n.9
lay Buddhists, 42, 45n
lay religion, choices in, 27, 31–34
leifa. See thunder rites
Li and Cui *chengshi* (deities), 123–26, 187
Li Choufu, 147
Li Hou, 194. *See also* Marquis Li
Li Jing, 112, 112n.10, 186, 191
Li Lu, 153
Li Mama, ix–x
Li Shun, 143
Li Xinchuan, 23n
Li Zhongyong, 36
Libu. *See* Board of Rites
licentiates, 97n
licentious cults, 84–86, 99, 142, 162
Liezi, 18
Liji. See Book of Rites, The
Lin Lingsu, 43n
Lin Xiangru, 188
lineages, 8; activities on behalf of gods, 14n.15, 121, 121n.23, 126, 161
ling. See efficacy
Lingchang temple, 186
Lingji temple, 185, 191, 193
Lingying Cai hou, 189
Lingying temple, 192
Lingyou temple, 184, 186
Lingyou zhaoying temple, 192
literacy, 10–13, 67–68, 126; in Hong Kong, 11n; of gods, 15
Liu Kezhuang, 147n.17, 155

Liu Yizhi, 22, 35, 167n, 170
local histories, 24, 105, 179, 179n.1
local officials, responsibilities of, 12
localistic tendencies, breakdown of, 132
Lohans, paintings of, 53
Long, Charles H., 13n.12
Longxing monastery, 168
lotus pods and roots, 117, 164
Lotus Sutra, 35n.8, 169n
Lower Yangzi: distribution of books in, 11; definition of, 4n.2; market network, 111, 117; theater in, 74; licentious cults in, 85
Lu Gui, 190
Lu Jiuxu, 9
Lu Jiuyuan, 9
Lu Xinyuan, 167n
Lu You, 74
Lu Zai, 116–17, 121–22, 164, 188
Lu Zao, 62
Lü Dongbin, 31, 34, 54–55, 77–78, 164, 181, 190

Ma Jin, 66
Ma Xianmin, 68
Maitreya, 181
Mao Pang, 110
Maoshan Daoism, 43n
Marquis Kong, 188
Marquis Li, 113n.12, 153–55, 153n, 194
Marquis Liu, 188
Marquis Shi Ming, 190
Marquises Chen and Xu, 193
Master of Rites, Wang, 46
Matsumoto, Kōichi, 43n
Mazu. *See* Heavenly Consort
medieval transformation, effect on popular religion, 160
Mencius, 147, 155
merchant support for cults to: Li and Cui, 123–24; Lu Zai, 117; God of the Eastern Peak, 111, 113, 115; Heavenly Consort, 145–46; King Zhang, 149, 157; regional deities, 164
methods, Daoist, 43
mianjie jinshi. See exempted advanced degree holders
migration, 131
Minister Shen, 192

miracles, 3, 13, 39, 48, 75, 127, 140; agricultural, 9, 111, 163; apprehending a criminal, 41, 117, 174; Chinese terms for, 13n.13; commercial, 10, 75–78, 117, 142–43; double-checking of, 91; false claims to, 121–22, 125; of General Zhu, 119; of King Zhang, 150; means of publicizing, 73; purportedly Buddhist, 120; relation to local topography, 113, 158; rival claims to, 72; similarity of Lu Zai's and General Zhu's, 121–22; traditional, 117, 123, 162
miscellaneous notes, 14, 16–17
monasteries, Buddhist: awards of plaques to, 81n; guardian deities of, 63n.20, 182n.5; listed in local histories, 179; temples on grounds of, 58
money supply, growth in, 6
Mongol conquest, 3, 144–45, 159
Monk Zhang, 44
monks, Buddhist and Daoist. See religious practitioners
moonblocks, 64–66, 64n.23, 64n.24, 71, 123, 145, 151
Morita Kenji, 143n.9, 144
Mou Zicai, 144
Mount Tai, 130n. See also God of the Eastern Peak
Mozi, 20
Mu Bing, 92
Mute Zhang, 143

nagas, 111n.7
naming practices, 9, 100–101, 101n
nanxi (Southern drama), 50n
neidan. See inner alchemy
Neo-Confucianism, 19–20, 37, 141, 162; shrines of, 146n
Neskar, Ellen, 146n
New Policies, 81
nifeng. See provisional title
Nine Shens, 192
Ningbo, 42, 60, 73, 139, 143, 148, 164, 198; Dinghai, 143, 149; Fenghua county, 54, 143; Yin county, 76
Notes from My Studio, 18n.20, 49
nunneries, Buddhist, as listed in local histories, 179

ocean travel, dangers of, 31–34

official households, 96, 98
officials' support for regional cults, 164
oracles, 27
oracles. See divination sticks; moonblocks; spirit-writing
ordination certificates, 42, 160
outer alchemy, 12, 43
Ouyang Dachun, 16
Ouyang Hu, 155

paper, 10
Peng Xiu, 111
Pichang, 131; god of examinations, 63
Pingshui da wang, 187
Pinnü, 65
plaques, temple. See temple plaques
plays, gods' purported desire for, 161
polder technology, 6n.7, 114
Poor Girl, 65
popular pantheon, breakdown of, in Huzhou, 195
popular religion, unstated principles of, 48
population. See demographic change
power. See efficacy
prayer, 13; for rain, 49, 72
printing. See wood-block printing
processions, popular religious, 35
provisional title, 92
public field system, 59n.13
purification ceremonies, 44, 44n, 46, 154
Purple Maiden, 41, 66–67, 76–77, 164

Qian Qing, 193
Qian Yueyou, 180n.3
Qianfu ci, 125
qilao. See elders
Qin Erniang, 172
Qingyuan Zhenjun, 55

Rapid Response Duke, 16
rebellion in Huzhou, 154
reciprocity between men and deities, 27, 28, 48, 60–61, 78, 124, 160–61
recognition, gods' purported desire for, 32, 59
Record of the Listener, The, 17–21; comparison with inscriptions, 22–23; reliability of, 21–22
regional consciousness, formation of, 132

regional cults, 28, 183; attacks on, 128–29, 146; changing distribution of, 139–40; classical citations against, 130, 144, 147, 155; classical citations in favor of, 144, 147, 155; justifications for, 165

register of sacrifices, 83–84, 124, 125, 162, 163, 179; degree of exclusivity, 86, 89–90; flexible nature of, 87, 88; petition for inclusion of gods in, 103; temples not listed in, 86–88, 103n

religious practitioners, 12–13, 26, 40, 46–47, 69–70, 72; Buddhist, 70–71, 76, 76n; Chinese terms for, 58n.9; Daoist, 36, 47; rise of uneducated, 43–46, 160

Renji temple, 191

Repeated Fortune temple, 125

returning immortal, 190

Revering Peace and Ten Thousand Longevities monastery, 168

Revering Peace monastery, 22, 167

rice, new types, 6, 6n.7

rite to give food to the hungry ghosts on land and water, 46, 46n.22, 153

Rongzhai suibi. See Notes from My Studio

Ruan Yuan, 102n

salt smugglers, 123

sanguan dadi, 115n

Scattered Talk from East of Qi, 67

Schipper, Kristofer M., 26

Secretariat Chancellery, 87

Secretary Guo, 184

self-mutilation, 35

self-styled advanced degrees, 102

shadow privilege. See yin privilege

Shandong: Licheng, 15; Tai'an, 53

shangshu sheng. See Imperial Secretariat

Shanxi (Taiyuan), 53

Shehong, 143n.10

Shen Boyi, 192

Shen Gua, 130

Shen jiangjun, 185

Shen Linshi, 188

Shen Puye, 185

Shen Qing (General), 185

Shen Shangshu, 192

Shen Yue, 184

Shen Yuqiu, 181

shenbing. See spirit soldiers

Shengmu dian, 53

shengyuan. See licentiates

shenjiang. See spirit generals

Shenzong (emperor), 42

Sheriff Chen, 40, 67, 174

Shi Jing, 172

Shi Ming hou, 190

Shi Miyuan, 154, 154n

Shiba Yoshinobu, 105

Shizong guangling hou, 190

Shuiluhui. See rite to give food to the hungry ghosts on land and water

Shuisan. See Water Three

Shun, 38

Shunji wang, 62

Shunying hou, 16

Sichuan, 7, 12, 18, 86; Chengdu, 56, 77; Fuzhou, 144; Gongzhou, 86; Langzhou, 94; Liangshan, 144; Luzhou, 143; Wanzhou, 144

sidian. See register of sacrifices

silk, 112, 112n.9, 113

Sima Qian, 19

social strata: described in The Record of the Listener, 19; in inscriptions, 95–97

Song huiyao. See Collected Important Documents of the Song

Songxi shen. See God of the Pine Stream

sources, 4, 14–26

Soushen ji, 20n

southeast China, popular pantheon in, 28

spirit generals, 26

spirit mediums, 13, 41, 61. See also religious practitioners

spirit money, 50, 51n

spirit soldiers, 26, 149

spirit-writing, 27, 41, 41n, 64, 66–68, 66n, 76–77

Spring and Autumn Annals, 130

stages, theatrical, 74n. See also theaters

state cult, 12

statues of gods, 52–57, 89, 161; clothing, 110, 123, 154; of Guanyin, 22–23, 35; texts found in, 25; transported by boat, 117, 150

Stem Nine, ghost of, 29, 171

stove god, in Hong household, 18n.20, 30–31, 172

Strickmann, Michel, 25

Su Hao, 173

Su jiangjun, 186

subdeities, to King Zhang, 152–58
Sugiyama Masaaki, 125n.31
Sun Hao, 188
Sun Wang, 188
Suodu mingwang, 187
Supervisor Zhao of Tongguan Mountain, 109, 183, 192
suppression of popular cults, 84–86
Surangama Sutra, 169n

Taibei, ix. *See also* Taiwan
Taichang si. *See* Court of Imperial Sacrifices
Taihu shen, 187
Taishi Zhang, 15, 118
Taiwan, ix, 62n.17, 64n.24, 68, 74n, 115n
Tan Yue, 181
Tang-Song transition, and popular religious change, 128n.1
Tang Zhongyou, 98
tax payments from Huzhou, 114
tax-status of temples, 59
taxes, link to god's efficacy, 110
technical innovations, 7
temple caretaker, 13, 68, 155
temple inscriptions, 14–16, 73, 179; forgery of, 125; parody of, 51; recurrent language in, 111
temple plaques, 82, 82n.3, 110, 162; denial of request for, 90; to General Zhu, 119; to Heavenly Consort, 145; to Li and Cui, 124; to Marquis Li, 153
temples, 3, 57–61, 65, 161, 179; on grounds of Buddhist monasteries, 58; twentieth-century descriptions of, 53n
textiles, 111, 113
tezou ming jinshi. See facilitated degrees
theaters, 74
threatening the gods. *See* deities
thunder rites, 43
Tianfei. *See* Heavenly Consort
Tianhou. *See* Heavenly Consort
Tianmu shan longwang, 191
Tianning monastery, 168, 168n.4
Tianning wanshou monastery, 168n.4
tianxin fa. See Celestial Heart rites
titlegranting, 3, 9, 28, 31n, 82, 142, 161, 164; annual figures, 176–77; collusion between local elites and officials, 99, 104, 163; duplication of, 83; to Emissary Fang, 155; to family members of General Zhu, 120; to Five Manifestations, 141; frequency of, 37–39, 79–80, 82–83; history of, 80–81; inspection procedure, 100, 104; to King Zhang and family members, 148, 151; as a means of enhancing status of supporters, 95, 162; reasons for, 83, 94, 157, 161; regulations concerning, 90–92
toilet-death, 70
Tongguan shan Zhao Jian, 183, 192
Tongling wang, 183
townships, 114
transgressing upon another god's territory, 129–32
transport costs, in lower Yangzi, 6
tribute scholars, 97, 102
tudi. *See* earth god

underworld bureaucracy, 89n
urbanization, 5

van der Loon, Piet, 74
village service system, 96
visions of deities. *See* dreams
von Falkenhausen, Lothar, 130n

waidan. See outer alchemy
Wang 33, 100–102, 104, 163–64, 166
Wang Anshi, 81
Wang Gu, 81
Wang Huan, 56
Wang Ke, 150
Wang Rizhen, 124n.29, 125n.32
Wang Wenqing, 43n
Wanshou monastery, 168n.4
Ward, Barbara, 74n
Water Three, 171
waterways, gods of people who trade on, 132
Watson, James, 96n.17
Wei Ba, 188
Wenchang. *See* Zitong
Weng Zaiyi, 147
Wenxuan wang. *See* Culture-Propagating King
white ape, 34n.5
white monkey god, 182, 191
wine, 76, 150, 164

wood-block printing, 4, 10, 10n, 34n.6, 73, 73n, 162. *See also* books
writing, sacred power of, 12
Wu dadi, 188
Wu Fuchai, 109, 194
Wu Han, 100n
Wu jiangjun, 187
Wu Jie, 167
Wu Kui, 173
Wu Wen huangdi, 183
Wu xi Ji wang, 194
Wu Zixu, 171n.2 ·
Wutong. *See* Five Manifestations
Wuxian lingguan, 194
Wuxian. *See* Five Manifestations

Xi wu jizi, 189
Xianchun Lin'an zhi, 180n.3
Xiang wang, 186, 189
Xiang Yu, temples in Huzhou, 183, 186, 189
xianggong jinshi. See tribute scholars
Xiangying temple, 185
Xianyou hou, 189
Xiaoyi monastery, 168
Xichu bawang, 183
Xie Taifu, 194
xiangmiao. See branch temples
Xu Jing, 31, 145n.14
Xu Ruzi, 186
Xu Tianyou, 192
Xu Wenzhi, 153, 154
Xuanjiao Liu Hou, 188
Xuanwu. *See* Zhenwu
Xue Jixuan, 114

Yan Zhenqing, 184, 186
Yang Cunzhong, 192
Yang Wei, 89, 89n
Yang, monk, 35, 36
Yanluo Tianzi, 55
Yanyu island, 33, 33n
Yao, 38
Yao shi, 195
Yao Xide, 144
Yao Yi, 116
Yellow Emperor, 38
Yellow Register purification ceremonies, 46n.23
Yellow River, 130; god of, 18n.20

Yi hou, 195
Yi Jian, 18–19
yin privilege, 8, 96–97
yinci. See licentious cults
Yongle temple, 53n.5
Yongling temple. *See* Eternally Efficacious temple
Yu Sheng, 38, 38n.11, 173, 173n.5
Yuan Cai, 8, 160
Yuande temple, 110n.6, 193
Yuanying temple, 110n.6
Yuedi, 193
yuejiang. See transgressing upon another god's territory
Yunhe xianren, 194
Yupi wang, 194

Zai Jiyuan, 189
zaoshen. *See* stove god
Zbikowski, Tadeusz, 50n
Zeitlin, Judith, 17n.18
Zeng Zhazhi, 192
Zhang Kan, 131
Zhang Xie Comes First in the Exams, 50–51, 65, 161
Zhang Xie zhuangyuan. See Zhang Xie Comes First in the Exams
Zhang Xun wang, 186
Zhang Yazi, 143
Zhao Bing, 75, 98, 164
Zhao Hong, 154n
Zhao Yun, 154n
Zhaoying hou, 189
Zhejiang, 147, 156; Chongde, 131; Chuzhou, 149, 197; Fujian border, 87; Jiaxing (Xiuzhou), 29, 41, 63n.20, 77, 102, 108, 131, 171, 174, 197; Jinhua, 47; Shaoxing, 52, 72, 87, 198; Taizhou, 75, 98, 139, 140, 164, 165, 198; Wenzhou, 139, 197; Wuzhou, 18; Yanzhou, 143, 197. *See also* Hangzhou; Huzhou; Ningbo (Mingzhou)
zhen. See townships
Zhenwu, worship of, 30–31, 30n, 44, 171–72, 171n.2, 180; in Huzhou, 190
Zhenzong, emperor, 81
Zhijiu. *See* Stem Nine
Zhong Kui demon-quelling method, 171
Zhongdao, 22, 167

Zhonglie temple, 184

zhongshu sheng. *See* Secretariat Chancellery

Zhou Bida, 83, 85

Zhou Chu, 58, 58n.7, 68, 68n.28, 166

Zhou Dunyi, 146n

Zhou Mi, 67

Zhou Rong, 68

Zhu Fei, 126

Zhu Fu, 120

Zhu Ji, 191

Zhu jiang. *See* General Zhu

Zhu Lin, 125, 125n.33

Zhu Ming Fujun, 191

Zhu Ran, 125, 125n.33

Zhu Ren, 120

Zhu Renfu, 125

Zhu Si. *See* General Zhu

Zhu Xi, 37, 98, 99, 141–42, 141n, 146, 146n

Zhu Yu, 74

Zhu Zao, 126

Zhuo she shen, 195

zhushen, 155

Zigu. *See* Purple Maiden

Zihua, 193

Zitong, 133, 143–45, 183; Huzhou, 185; landholdings of temple to, in Ningbo, 60; number of temples to, 133n.5; regional temples, 196–200

Zuo Commentary, 130, 155

Zürcher, Erik, 25